North Yorkshire County Council Library Service

17/7/19

Scotland Yard's Gangbuster

DICK KIRBY
has also written

Rough Justice
Memoirs of a Flying Squad Officer

The Real Sweeney

You're Nicked!

Villains

The Guv'nors
Ten of Scotland Yard's Greatest Detectives

The Sweeney
The First Sixty Years of Scotland Yard's Crimebusting Flying Squad 1919–1978

Scotland Yard's Ghost Squad
The Secret Weapon against Post-War Crime

The Brave Blue Line
100 Years of Metropolitan Police Gallantry

Death on the Beat
Police Officers killed in the Line of Duty

The Scourge of Soho
The Controversial Career of SAS Hero
Detective Sergeant Harry Challenor MM

Whitechapel's Sherlock Holmes
The Casebook of Fred Wensley OBE, KPM
Victorian Crimebuster

The Wrong Man
The Shooting of Steven Waldorf and
the Hunt for David Martin

Laid Bare
The Nude Murders and
the Hunt for 'Jack the Stripper'

London's Gangs at War

Operation Countryman
The Flawed Enquiry into London Police Corruption

Praise for Dick Kirby's books

'The continuing increase in violent crime will make many readers yearn for yesteryear and officers of Dick Kirby's calibre.'
Police Magazine

'His reflections on the political aspect of law enforcement will ring true for cops, everywhere.'
American Police Beat

'Thoroughly researched and enjoyable history, crammed with vivid descriptions of long-forgotten police operations . . . races along like an Invicta at full throttle.'
Daily Express

'Dick Kirby . . . knows how to bring his coppers to life on each page.'
Joseph Wambaugh, Author of the Choirboys

'Kirby writes with authority and clarity . . . highly recommended.'
Real Crime Magazine

'An experienced, natural raconteur.'
History By the Yard

'A dedicated police historian.'
Police Oracle

'Rarely, if ever, have I been so captivated by a book . . . the way in which Mr Kirby has gone about it is exceptional.'
Police Memorabilia Collectors Club

This book is dedicated to
Bert Wickstead's grandchildren: Jen, Alan, Edward,
Evie-Jean and Daisy plus the men and women – the
Gangbusters – who staffed Scotland Yard's Serious Crime Squad.

And to Ann:
Can wisdom be put in a silver rod
Or love in a golden bowl?

William Blake
The Book of Thel

SCOTLAND YARD'S GANGBUSTER

BERT WICKSTEAD'S MOST CELEBRATED CASES

DICK KIRBY

First published in Great Britain in 2018 by
Pen & Sword True Crime
An imprint of
Pen & Sword Books Ltd
Yorkshire – Philadelphia

Copyright © Dick Kirby 2018

HBK ISBN 978 1 52673 153 1
PBK ISBN 978 1 52675 173 7

The right of Dick Kirby to be identified as Author of this work has been asserted by him in accordance with the Copyright, Designs and Patents Act 1988.

A CIP catalogue record for this book is
available from the British Library.

All rights reserved. No part of this book may be reproduced or transmitted in any form or by any means, electronic or mechanical including photocopying, recording or by any information storage and retrieval system, without permission from the Publisher in writing.

Printed and bound in England by TJ International, Padstow, Cornwall

Pen & Sword Books Limited incorporates the imprints of Atlas, Archaeology, Aviation, Discovery, Family History, Fiction, History, Maritime, Military, Military Classics, Politics, Select, Transport, True Crime, Air World, Frontline Publishing, Leo Cooper, Remember When, Seaforth Publishing, The Praetorian Press, Wharncliffe Local History, Wharncliffe Transport, Wharncliffe True Crime and White Owl.

For a complete list of Pen & Sword titles please contact

PEN & SWORD BOOKS LIMITED
47 Church Street, Barnsley, South Yorkshire, S70 2AS, England
E-mail: enquiries@pen-and-sword.co.uk
Website: www.pen-and-sword.co.uk

Or
PEN AND SWORD BOOKS
1950 Lawrence Rd, Havertown, PA 19083, USA
E-mail: Uspen-and-sword@casematepublishers.com
Website: www.penandswordbooks.com

Contents

About the Author		ix
Acknowledgements		xi
Foreword		xiii
Prologue		xv
Chapter 1	A Gang Leader Named 'Killer'	1
Chapter 2	Anti-Semitism in North London	7
Chapter 3	The Synagogue Arsons	13
Chapter 4	'Britain's Biggest Post-War Bank Robbery'	35
Chapter 5	Birth of the Serious Crime Squad – The Dixons	49
Chapter 6	Mayhem in East London – the Tibbs Family	65
Chapter 7	Norma Levy – Sex in Government	87
Chapter 8	The Porn Squad and the Maltese Syndicate	101
Chapter 9	Trials – and Some Dodgy Cops	125
Chapter 10	Legal & General	149
Epilogue		179
Appendix	The Citation for Wickstead's Queen's Police Medal	185
Bibliography		187
Index		191

About the Author

Dick Kirby was born in 1943 in the East End of London and joined the Metropolitan Police in 1967. Half of his 26 years' service as a detective was spent with the Yard's Serious Crime Squad and the Flying Squad.

Married, with four children and five grandchildren, Kirby lives in a Suffolk village with his wife. He reviews books, films and music, is a consultant for a television series and writes memoirs, biographies and true crime books – this is his sixteenth.

Kirby can be visited on his website: www.dickkirby.com.

Acknowledgements

First I have to thank that splendid former Flying Squad officer and Deputy Assistant Commissioner, Mike Taylor, QPM for his very kind foreword to the book. Next, Brigadier Henry Wilson of Pen & Sword Books for his unstinting support and backing – worthy of Bert Wickstead himself. Additionally, thanks go to Matt Jones, also of Pen & Sword, plus George Chamier for his lynx-eyed editing; what I miss, he finds.

I owe a debt of thanks to the following people and organizations for their invaluable 'behind the scenes' assistance, without which I should have faltered, not once but on many occasions: David Allen of the Bow Street website; Mick Carter from the ReCIDivists' Luncheon Club; Alan Moss of *History by the Yard*; Bob Fenton QGM, Honorary Secretary of the Ex-CID Officers' Association; Louise Richards and Tobias Phillips from Equiniti Pension Solutions Operations; Susi Rogol, editor of the *London Police Pensioner*; Kathy Schuller of the Metropolitan Women Police Association; Martin Stallion of the Police History Society; Daniel Sugarman of the *Jewish Chronicle*; Barry Walsh of the Friends of the Metropolitan Police Historical Collection; Paris Sydes, Heritage Assistant at the Redbridge Museum and Heritage Centre; Terri Stone from the Parndon Wood Crematorium, Harlow; Stuart K. Fairclough PGCE, MIfL, QJM, NPM, AMIMI, IAATI and members of the DT3 Association, namely Sue McClaren, Steve Parsall, Rod Brafield, Bob Chalmers, Alan Wright, Bob Hendry, John Wilding, Derek Marrable, John Wilkin, Henry Philpot, David Lamb, Tony Osborn, Colin Elliott, Stephen Ditchburn and Derek Smith.

There are always some people who, for reasons best known to themselves, refuse to assist an author in the compilation of a non-fiction book, and it happened whilst researching this particular tome. A pity, because I sought them out since I believed their input would be invaluable, and so it might have been. Nevertheless, I have endeavoured to ensure that the content of the book is as accurate as possible and I acknowledge that any faults or imperfections are mine alone.

But those shy people were in the minority; the following, to whom I am most grateful, gave unstintingly of their time and answered my questions (some of which I'm sure were, on occasion, impertinent) fully, freely and promptly:

Assistant Commissioner Neil Basu QPM; Peter Binstead, Alan Brooks, the late Terry Brown GM, Tony Bruce, David Buchanan, Mick Carter, Gordon Cawthorne MBE, Stan Clegg, Pat Collins, Peter Condon, Peter Connor, Jack Cooper, Ian Corner, Ruth Corner, Fred Cutts LL.B, Roger Davey, Ken Dellbridge, Neil Dickens QPM, Stuart Douglas, John Farley QPM, Dr Gerry Gable DUniv, MA(Crim), Liam Gillespie, Mick Gray, John Griffiths, Michael Hall, Graham Hickson, Bill Kelleher, John Lewis, Alf Marriott, Sue Maudsley, Dave McEnhill, Dick Miles, Geoff Parratt, Colin Pridige, David Pritchard, Frank Pulley BEM, Bob Robinson, Allan Rowlands, Gerry Runham, Dave Scrivener, Betty Shimell, John Simmonds, Tony Stevens, Roger Stoodley, Mr Justice Michael Stuart-Moore QC, Bernie Tighe, Geoff Turner, the late Bill Waite BEM; Jenny Wickett; Andrew Wickstead, Ed Williams, the late Ray Wood, OBE; John Woodhouse and John Woodward.

I am most grateful to the following who provided me with the photographs: Ken Bowerman GM; Stan Clegg, Ruth Corner, John Farley, Gerry Gable, Bernie Tighe, Roger Stoodley, John Vaughan, Andrew Wickstead and Lisa Wickstead. Other photographs are from the author's collection, and whilst every effort has been made to trace copyright holders, the publishers and I apologise for any inadvertent omissions.

My thanks also go to my daughter, Sue Cowper, and her husband, Steve, for rescuing me from the most mundane of computer-generated cock-ups. To them, and the rest of my family, go my thanks for their unfailing help, love and assistance: my sons, Mark and Robert, my youngest daughter, Barbara Jerreat, and her husband, Rich, and my grandchildren, Emma Cowper B. Mus, Jessica Cowper B. Mus and Harry Cowper, plus Samuel and Annie Grace Jerreat.

Most of all my thanks go to my dear wife Ann, who for in excess of 50 years has stood by me, during the good and the not-so-good times.

Dick Kirby
Suffolk, 2018

Foreword

Michael B. Taylor QPM, former Deputy Assistant Commissioner, New Scotland Yard

Dick Kirby has produced a frank and entertaining insight into the work of one of Scotland Yard's more enigmatic detectives. I believe it to be a well established fact that those occupations which attract recruits with a sense of vocation tend to dull their enthusiasm with experience and the passage of time. The police service certainly contains a proportion of members who have lost their bright-eyed and bushy-tailed attitudes somewhere along the way. Though they may well continue to give good, honest and reliable service, the words 'keen' and 'initiative' are likely to be absent from their annual appraisals.

As in so many ways during his well publicised career, Bert Wickstead did not conform to this example. In fact, he seems to have done exactly the opposite. Indeed, his early reputation, as accurately described in these pages by my good friend and former colleague, John Simmonds, is not such that you would have been overjoyed to work with Bert, particularly in a junior position. I am personally aware that early in his CID career, Bert upset a senior CID officer and was moved across London at short notice. Bert regarded this, with some justification, as totally undeserved, and I believe the incident had a lasting and dispiriting effect on him.

So how did somebody whose reputation for slow work output and poor management skills was well known become known as the Gangbuster – the Old Grey Fox – and a leader of highly professional specialist detectives who continually appeared in the national press as yet another high-profile case hit the headlines to the credit of Scotland Yard in general and Commander Albert Wickstead in particular? Dick Kirby has produced a very plausible explanation, involving (as it does) Bert's contempt for the rules, his love of West Ham Football Club and the ability of a certain CID officer to induce fear and trembling – or at least, some honest self-appraisal – in somebody of Bert Wickstead's attitude. For the details you will have to read the book and make up your own mind, but it was certainly at around the time of this incident that Bert decided some upward pressure on his hosiery would be beneficial.

The rapid rise of the Gangbuster is well documented in more than one publication, but Dick Kirby has tackled the task with more thoroughness and less hero-worship than most. Bert and his team went from one major coup to the next. One enquiry began to uncover possible elements of police corruption, and I joined Bert's team as an A10 (Complaints against Police) officer to investigate those aspects. Shortly afterwards, that enquiry was put on hold as the Charles Taylor investigation surfaced, and I became involved in that. On the night before we were due to make the bulk of the arrests and search a good number of places across London, Uncle Bert (his office name, provided he was nowhere around) gave me the good news that he would not be there as he was going to give the eulogy at the funeral of a former member of his team who had died very young. He at least outwardly gave the indication that he was confident this was something I could handle, and he went home. It was a display of confidence that made me appreciate how Bert could engender such a high degree of loyalty and trust in his colleagues.

In the same case I saw another aspect of Bert's ability. At the end of a lengthy trial, Commander Wickstead entered the witness box for a brief appearance. There were ten defendants, with some of the most eminent leading counsel defending them. When Bert was offered for cross-examination, nine Queen's Counsel had the good sense to ask him no questions. One defendant, however, had employed a junior barrister, who was anxious to shine in front of his senior colleagues.

'Mr Wickstead', he said with heavy emphasis, 'Or should I call, you "The Old Grey Fox"?'

'I'd much rather you didn't. I can't stand it', came Bert's snappy reply.

'Why ever not?' the barrister ploughed on.

''Cos I'm not old', said Bert.

Amidst the laughter the young counsel sat down, a sadder but a wiser man. The measure of Bert Wickstead is that once the court rose, he sought out the barrister, and whatever was said, it was clear they parted amicably. I thought all the more of Bert for that, though some would have said that Bert denying his appreciation of his nickname under oath was sailing a tad close to the wind for perjury!

Working with the Old Grey Fox was all-consuming and, at times, frenetic, but it was never dull.

Campbeltown
Argyll
December 2017

Prologue

John Farley (who features large in this book) was unequivocal in his opinion of Bert Wickstead. He told me, 'He was the finest police officer I ever met.'

It was a view shared by former Deputy Assistant Commissioner Michael Taylor QPM, who also liked and admired Wickstead and who said of him, 'He was one of just three men I know whom the troops would follow blindly.'

'Bert was fantastic in command', Gerry Runham told me. 'He made a plan and stuck to it.'

Others had different perceptions of Wickstead. The late Ray Wood first met him in 1969 and admitted that he felt 'terrified' in his presence, although he managed to recover his resolution thereafter and become one of Scotland Yard's bravest undercover officers and the only detective constable ever to be awarded the OBE. When Wickstead chaired a selection board for temporary detective constables during the same year, Dick Miles was one of the applicants.

'During the board, he didn't say one word', recalled Miles. 'He just sat there, staring at me . . . it was obviously done to try to unnerve me.'

In Miles' case this attempt at demoralization failed to work, since he successfully passed this baptism of fire and went on to become an assistant chief constable.

Undeniably, Wickstead was capable of astonishing rudeness. He seldom walked; rather he barged through life, as he did on one occasion along the 4th floor corridor at the Yard which housed C11 (Criminal Intelligence) on one side and C8 (The Flying Squad) on the other. A senior officer stuck his head out of his office door.

'How's it going, Bert?' he called.

'Fuck off, you bent cunt!' was the reply.

It's not clear from which side of the corridor the officer had emerged, not that it mattered. At that time, Wickstead's epithet would have suited the head of both those departments.

But there was no doubt that Wickstead was charismatic. Since he was one quarter of an inch under five feet ten he could not be considered tall, but he had a commanding presence. Stocky and smartly dressed, usually in a grey suit and Paisley foulard tie which was fashionable in the 1970s, with a silk handkerchief protruding from his breast pocket, when Wickstead entered a police briefing room or No. 1 Court at the Old Bailey, spectators fell silent. Nobody was in any doubt that they were in the presence of a superstar.

Within the Metropolitan Police, the personnel had mixed feelings about Wickstead. Officers with corrupt propositions on offer only made them once; thereafter they avoided him like the plague. Senior officers – straight ones – either liked or tolerated him because of his successes. Junior officers – especially members of his team – adored him, because he would back them one hundred per cent. This was demonstrated during a meeting, chaired by a deputy assistant commissioner, of the other detective chief superintendents from C1 Department at the Yard.

When the matter of budgetary restraints was aired, one of Wickstead's contemporaries took the opportunity to remark contemptuously, 'Well, we all know Mr Wickstead's views on that, with his men putting in expenses of £20 per week.'

Over 40 years ago that kind of disbursement was indeed a lot of money, but the remark was sufficient for Wickstead to leap to his feet, slam his fist down on the table and roar, 'Yes – and it's all wrong!'

Before the astonished officer could reply, Wickstead, still at full volume, continued, 'Because with the sort of work they're doing, they ought to get *ten times* as fucking much!'

To police officers Wickstead was truly a Marmite character – either loved or loathed. But those views did not extend to the criminal classes. Wickstead did not disguise the fact that he hated criminals. Their presence on his 'manor', whether it was North London, the East End or anywhere under the aegis of the Serious Crime Squad, would not – could not – be tolerated. Most were terrified of him, with good reason; he was certainly not to be trifled with.

When a young uniform officer arrested a low-life for quite a serious offence, the offender sneered, 'You can't nick me – I'm Bert Wickstead's snout!'

Lodging the prisoner in a detention room, the worried officer spoke to one of Wickstead's detective sergeants, who forwarded the message 'upstairs'. Back came the unequivocal message: 'Yes, 'e's my snout – now fucking charge 'im!'

Snouts were only as good as their ability to know when to keep their traps shut. Liberties – especially the unauthorized use of Wickstead's name – were not to be tolerated.

Prologue

It was a time when detectives were often accused of using physical force when questioning suspects. However, it appears that in this respect Wickstead was the odd man out; I could find nobody who ever worked with him who gave the slightest suggestion that he was ever violent towards prisoners; and indeed, I found no record of anyone in the criminal classes who alleged that he resorted to those methods. But in the same way that the Greek god Pan's shout was sufficient to inspire panic, Wickstead subdued and terrorized prisoners by virtue of his forceful manner and personality. What was alleged was that Wickstead 'verballed' his prisoners – in other words, attributed untrue and incriminating statements to them; but then again, those allegations have been made against all detectives by the criminal classes and their lawyers ever since the CID was formed in 1878. When criminals are confronted in court with an impressive array of evidence by the prosecution, it is a simple (and sometimes effective) expedient to discredit the police officers by making them out to be liars. Why not? The criminals have everything to gain if their accusations are accepted by the jury and little to lose if they're not.

*

Albert Sidney Wickstead was born on 26 April 1923 in Plaistow, East London. He had a brother, Peter, and their father was Sydney Arthur Wickstead, a former Royal Marine, born in 1897, who after demobilization became a foreman at the docks in the East End. Wickstead's mother, Winifred Alexandra Wickstead née Port, died when he was five years old. His father later remarried Jesse Chalkhorn; she gave birth to Wickstead's half-brother Ian, later to join the Metropolitan Police and serve as a uniformed officer in West London – 'A useful thief-taker' according to one of his contemporaries.

Bert Wickstead attended Burke Senior School, left at the age of fourteen and after working as a clerk and a factory hand, at the age of seventeen and a half saw wartime service when he enlisted in the Royal Corps of Signals. Later, he was beguiled by a notice set outside a senior officer's tent which read:

ARE YOU TOUGH?
IF SO, GET OUT!
I NEED BUGGERS WITH BRAINS!

Feeling that he fitted the criteria, Wickstead volunteered and was selected for the Special Boat Service (SBS). As part of 'Z' Group he was among the first to be posted to Ceylon, followed by 'A', 'B' and 'C' Groups, each comprised of twenty all ranks with a major in charge. There Wickstead – who possessed brains, toughness and tenacity – worked with the Secret Intelligence Service, Force 136 of the Special Operations Executive and Special Operations Australia, who carried out 174 operations involving assassination, sabotage and reconnaissance. It's a tribute to that unit's professionalism that in all of those operations it sustained only 27 casualties. Later, Wickstead's duties with the SBS took him to India and Burma. After over seven years' service, on 13 December 1947 he was demobilized with the rank of sergeant and, at a loose end, contemplated returning to the army.

Instead, there was a chance meeting with an uncle, John 'Jack' William Wickstead, a detective sergeant (second-class) in the Metropolitan Police now rapidly approaching the end of his service. Like his nephew, he had seen wartime service, over 30 years earlier, and he too had stayed on in the army after hostilities ceased. Jack Wickstead was a plodder and one not over-burdened with brains; he had failed his 1st class civil servant's examination on no fewer than six occasions, and his rather dreary postings were from 'T' to 'F' division and then back again.

But he suggested that the Metropolitan Police might well be a good career, and for an ex-serviceman such as Wickstead with fairly limited educational qualifications, especially since he had married while he was in the army, to a certain extent it was.

However, only to a certain extent. Having joined on 15 March 1948, twenty-five-year-old Wickstead was posted to 'S' Division, where he patrolled as Police Constable 233'S'. Following the war, Britain was still in the grip of austerity; practically all foods and every saleable commodity were still on ration, wages and prices were frozen and at the beginning of 1948 the railways were nationalized. At the time of Wickstead joining the police, the electricity companies would also be taken into public ownership. One year after joining, his weekly wage was £6 6s 6d; following the wholly inadequate Oaksey Committee's findings, a token annual weighting allowance of £10 to compensate for the higher cost of living in the capital was granted, and consequently by 20 March 1950 his weekly stipend had rocketed to £6 10s 4d. In a bombed-out, starved-out country that was practically bankrupt, perhaps Wickstead regretted leaving the Far East, where the sun always shone, food was certainly more plentiful and, as an army sergeant, much of his work could be delegated. That might have been the case had that vision been achieved via the medium of rose-tinted spectacles. However, following the dissolution of the British Raj in India, bloody partition had ensued; Ceylon (now Sri Lanka), having gained independence from Britain, saw riots sweep through the island; and Burma (now Myanmar), which had similarly been granted independence, was rewarded with ethnic conflicts and chaos.

Taking all that into consideration, at least Hampstead was not in the grip of civil insurrection; but nor was it exactly a hotbed of crime where an embryo detective might make his bones. Nevertheless, Wickstead walked those rather uninteresting streets, both as a uniform officer and an aid to CID, for 5½ years. Finally, there was a breakthrough; he was awarded his first commissioner's commendation in a case of larceny and receiving, just prior to being appointed on 18 January 1954 as a detective constable, thereby becoming one of the Met's 1,400 CID officers.

It was the age of some of the great detectives; true, in four short years, the legendary Detective Chief Superintendent Jack 'Charlie Artful' Capstick would retire, and the following year, Detective Chief Superintendent Ted Greeno MBE – he was known as 'The Underworld's Public Enemy No. 1' – would follow him into retirement, both men immensely tough, extremely well-informed veterans of the Flying Squad and Murder Squad. But as Wickstead's twelve-month probationary period as a detective constable commenced, other detectives were active and soon to become household names. Ernie 'Hooter' Millen was just about to join the Fraud Squad; he would soon play a decisive part in the Brighton police corruption enquiry, as would Tommy Butler. Both men would go on to head the Flying Squad, and with his investigation into the Great Train Robbery, Butler's fame was assured. At one stage, Butler had served at Paddington police station with Ian 'Jock' Forbes and Leonard 'Nipper' Read, the former to become an astute investigator who solved the Cannock Chase Murder and the latter to achieve world-wide fame as the man who smashed up the Kray brothers' empire.

This was just a tiny cross-section of the inspirational detectives of that era. They were expected to wear trilby hats (they made the officers look 'distinguished'), whilst bowler hats were the prerogative of more senior detectives who would become Wickstead's contemporaries.

Following a short-lived posting to Harrow Road, Wickstead was posted to 'N' Division's Caledonian Road, which would be his home for the next 4½ years. Freddie Andrews, a local villain, had just had a memory lapse after failing to identify gang boss Billy Hill as the person responsible for slashing his face open and was now wanted for officebreaking; Wickstead recognized Andrews, arrested him and was again commended, as he was, two years later for his initiative in a case of housebreaking. Wickstead's next, year-long, posting was at the Yard's C1 Department in one of the eight rather unexciting squads in that unit, where he did as little work as was humanly possible.

His successor, David Pritchard, told me, 'Bert never completed any enquiry he was given.'

Promotion to detective sergeant (second class) took Wickstead away from the Yard and to 'G' Division for just nine short months. It was back to 'N' Division on 7 June 1960 where he was commended for his role as office manager in the Pen Club murder case. It also acted as an eye-opener to the world of organized crime, which featured such luminaries as the Nash brothers and the Kray twins.[1]

On 11 February 1963 Wickstead was promoted to detective sergeant (first class) and sent to Barnet police station, back on a rather lethargic 'S' Division; in his memoirs, Wickstead claimed that this posting to inactivity did not suit him at all. It's difficult to see why; in all fairness, up to now he had hardly been a ball of fire. He had 15 years' service under his belt and a total of five commissioner's commendations; good, but not earth-shaking. (By comparison, at the same stage of his career, Alf Dance of the Flying Squad had been commended by the commissioner on no fewer than 69 occasions; in the following 12 years, he would collect 23 more.) Perhaps it's more likely that Wickstead objected to cycling the 20-mile round trip across London from his home in Caledonian Road, but after five months he managed a transfer back to 'G' Division and Dalston police station.

'I remember Bert as a DC and a second-class and he was as lazy as arseholes,' recalled a contemporary, 'and then he went to 'G' as a first class and that's when his career really took off.'

Another officer at that time told me, '"Nipper" Read [then a detective inspector on 'G' Division] wasn't impressed with him.'

But then Wickstead's circumstances suddenly changed. He had been in the habit of sliding away from the office on Saturday afternoons to follow the fortunes of West Ham United and then telephoning his subordinates to 'book 'im off duty'. This came to an abrupt halt when it was Fred Gerrard, the area detective chief superintendent who answered the telephone; in response to Wickstead's peremptory message, and in a distinctly frosty voice,

---

1 For full details of this investigation, see *London's Gangs at War*, Pen & Sword True Crime, 2017

he told him to report to his office at City Road police station the following Monday morning at 9 o'clock – sharp. Gerrard had worked on 'G' Division during the post-war years as a detective sergeant (occasionally with the Ghost Squad), certainly more industriously than Wickstead. What passed between the two on that eventful Monday morning was never disclosed, but there is little doubt that Gerrard, who was a stickler for discipline, told Wickstead to pull his socks up – or else.

It was make or break time; maybe Gerrard had provided the spark which lit Wickstead's fuse – either that, or perhaps salvation arrived in the shape of a local tearaway who rejoiced in the nickname of 'Killer' and who suddenly got far too big for his boots.

Chapter 1

A Gang Leader Named 'Killer'

Nicknames tend to reflect the appearance of the person upon whom they've been conferred. Therefore, if someone is dubbed 'The Vicar' it would be reasonable to assume that his physiognomy exudes a saintly or at the very least a benevolent expression. Similarly, the sobriquet 'Knuckles' would suggest that its owner possesses a distinctly pugilistic countenance.

But seventeen-year-old John Brian McElligott was, as Wickstead described him, '5 foot 4 inches and weighed seven stones, dripping wet'. It was only after he had acquired a semi-automatic Beretta pistol and ammunition that the epithet 'Killer' was bestowed upon him.

McElligott was the dangerous leader of a gang of young thugs and on 30 November 1964, in the Balls Pond Road, he had shot and wounded fourteen-year-old Rodney John Brown. There had been a spate of armed robberies in which fashionable leather coats were stolen from their owners at gunpoint, including one from a Peter Coulthurst in Kingsland Road, Hackney on 1 December 1964. By now Wickstead had formed a squad made up of eight feral aids to CID, taken from the rightly feared 32-strong 'G' Division Aids' Squad based at City Road police station; they knew the perpetrator's nickname was 'Killer' but had no clue as to his real identity. Groups of the then fashionable Mods and Rockers were stopped and questioned, but although several of them admitted to having heard of someone nicknamed 'Killer', if any knew his true identity they were not disclosing it. But then the team received a tip-off that one of 'Killer's' gang was working on a building site opposite Dalston police station; the entire workforce was brought into the police station, the worker was identified and he started naming names and providing addresses.

It seemed not a moment too soon, because on 29 December Police Sergeant Michael Rose, in charge of a nondescript 'Q'-Car, call sign 'Golf one-one', responded to a call at a premises in Hilborough Road, Dalston, where two youths had been seen breaking into a house. One of the youngsters ran off, and when Rose gave chase, he produced a pistol, pointed it at Rose from a distance of 15 yards and threatened to shoot him. Undeterred, Rose continued to advance and the youth took aim and fired; fortunately, the bullet went over Rose's head. The gunman then turned and ran; chased by Rose, he disappeared into a block of flats and vanished. The culprit was McElligott; and although Rose was unaware of it, McElligott was no more than three quarters of a mile from his home address in Baring Street. Later, a .22 cartridge case was found close to where Rose had been shot at.

But by New Year's Day McElligott was in custody at Dalston, charged with robbery and shooting at Rose with intent to murder; he had also been positively identified by Peter Coulthurst and his companion, Margaret Johnson, as being responsible for the robbery of the leather jacket. That jacket and several others were subsequently recovered.

The next day, McElligott appeared at Old Street Magistrates' Court and was remanded in custody; but following the court appearance, a group of youths confronted Coulthurst and Miss Johnson in Kingsland High Street, shouting and threatening that they would be 'cut up and scarred' if they gave evidence against McElligott. As the couple hurried away, the youths followed them, still uttering threats.

By 9 January 1965 McElligott's associate, seventeen-year-old John Peter Barratt, appeared in the dock at Old Street Magistrates' Court charged with shooting at Rodney Brown and with armed robbery; he was remanded until the following day, when he and McElligott were both further remanded in custody. However, their places in the dock were then taken by seven youths aged between fifteen and seventeen who had been charged with conspiracy to defeat justice by uttering threats to Coulthurst and Miss Johnson.

'This is a prosecution which will be undertaken by the Director of Public Prosecutions because of the whole picture of all the circumstances surrounding the case of McElligott and Barratt', Wickstead told the magistrate, Harold Sturge.

One of the sixteen-year-olds told the magistrate, 'Sergeant Wickstead said we know McElligott, but we don't.'

'I think the case has been exaggerated a lot', said a seventeen-year-old trainee draughtsman, and a sixteen-year-old trainee salesman told the bench, 'In the statements, they say I was with them. I've got proof I wasn't with them. I have statements from other people that I was seen.'

Mr Sturge was unimpressed. 'The nature of the charge is a very, very grave one indeed', he said. 'On the face of the evidence, it seems a proper case for custody.'

The following week, matters were hardly any better. Wickstead repeated that the witnesses had been 'put in very great fear', but Mr Henry Charles Pownall acting for one of the sixteen-year-olds put in a spirited attempt at bail, saying that a statement had already been taken from the person who was alleged to have been frightened and from anyone who was with him and that evidence could no longer be tampered with.

'You may think it an important point that everyone of these boys was at large for a week after this alleged incident when this person was threatened', he told Mr Sturge. 'But apparently not a word has been said, not an action done to that person or anyone connected with him during that week.'

However, Mr Pownall – later His Honour Judge Pownall, whose sense of fairness 'made him popular with juries' – was out of luck.

'The mere fact that nothing else has been done or nothing was done may only be evidence of the fact that they thought they had done enough', said Mr Sturge, adding, 'The police do fear – and I think rightly fear – that there is the possibility and indeed, the grave possibility if not probability that witnesses who are to appear to give evidence against the accused may feel afraid to tell the truth when they come before this court.'

On 4 February 1965 a further charge was added, alleging that the seven youths 'by threats attempted to dissuade Peter Coulthurst and Margaret Johnson from giving evidence in the case against John Brian McElligott at Old Street Metropolitan Magistrates' Court'.

Outlining the facts to the bench, Mr Peter Palmes for the Director of Public Prosecutions stated, 'They did not touch them but made it obvious that they thought Coulthurst had "grassed" on this man, "Killer"', and the seven were committed in custody to the Old Bailey to stand their separate trial.

In the meantime, others of McElligott's gang had been rounded up and stood trial at the Old Bailey. On 2 April 1965 His Honour Judge Carl Aarvold OBE, TD in passing sentence declared:

> There seems to have been a poisonous growth affecting the youth of Hoxton, the core being John McElligott. The spread of infection caught on with all whom he came into contact. The influence he wielded depended on his willingness to carry a gun and to use it. One of the symptoms of the disease he spread was the failure of other youths to recognize the craven coward that he actually was. Responsibility for this state of affairs is, of course a social problem which I hope will cause much heart-searching in parents, schools, churches and every decent person in the Hoxton area.

McElligott had been found guilty of wounding Rodney Brown with intent to cause grievous bodily harm, shooting at Police Sergeant Rose with intent to cause grievous bodily harm or resist arrest, unlawful possession of a firearm, robbery of a leather coat and breaking and entering. He was sentenced to 5 years' imprisonment.

Peter Barratt was convicted of possessing an offensive weapon and wounding Rodney Brown with intent to cause grievous bodily harm. He and eighteen-year-old Michael Patrick Sullivan, who pleaded guilty to breaking and entering with intent to steal, were both sentenced to six months in a detention centre.

William John Adams, aged seventeen, pleaded guilty to robbery and possessing an offensive weapon and was sentenced to four months in a detention centre.

George Frederick Roberts aged fifteen and sixteen-year-old Daniel Michael Price were both convicted of possession of an offensive weapon and assault with intent to rob, and they, together with Dennis Raymond Blackhall, aged eighteen, who pleaded guilty to possessing a gun and assault with intent to rob, had their sentences postponed pending the result of probation reports.

Wickstead was one of a number of officers commended by the Trial Judge, the Director of Public Prosecutions and, on 5 October 1965, by the commissioner of police. As an additional bonus, Wickstead was promoted to detective inspector and although retained on 'G' Division was moved to fill a vacancy at Stoke Newington police station. Sergeant Rose was highly commended and six weeks later was handed £20 from the Bow Street Metropolitan Magistrates' Reward Fund; the following April, he was awarded the George Medal.

And that should have been that – except that it wasn't.

On the night of 15 February 1966, McElligott, together with twenty-year-old Colin Michael Duggan, who was serving a 3-year sentence for larceny, used basketball stands to climb over the wall of Aylesbury gaol and vanished – for a week.

'He was very elusive to find', the late Terry Brown told me, but early on the morning of 22 February, he, with other officers plus Detective Inspector 'Nipper' Read, acting on a tip-off from a local constable, went to a house in Shoreditch. In Alfred Hitchcock's 1935 film *The Thirty-Nine Steps* the hero, Richard Hannay, pursued by foreign spies, makes an escape from his flat by disguising himself in a milkman's cap and coat. Nipper simply reversed Hannay's role; borrowing a passing milkman's cap and coat, rattling a cradle of milk bottles and calling out, 'Milk-O!', he persuaded the occupier of the ground-floor premises to open the door. With that, the officers were in and up to the first floor, where a highly surprised pair of gaolbirds were handcuffed and soon on the way back to their natural habitat.

As Terry Brown told me, 'He was a little kid, pasty-faced, and without his gun he was nothing.'

Stan Clegg was one of the aids who had been commended. 'We went to an address in Green Lanes in the early hours and nicked one of the suspects,' he told me. 'On leaving his address, surprise, surprise, out of the undergrowth sprang a press photographer; needless to say, Bert denied all knowledge that he arranged it!'

It was clear that Wickstead revelled in the limelight. The *Evening News* described him and his officers as 'The Magnificent Seven', rather inaccurately since there were ten of them, but it was still a nice piece of hyperbole.

'I think that kicked off Bert's career!' Clegg told me, and it could well be that he was right.

'Bert was going to make a name for himself', said one of Wickstead's contemporaries to me. 'He took on anybody and anything. Was he a gangbuster? He was certainly a one-off.'

No, Wickstead was not yet a gangbuster; that sobriquet would take a little longer to arrive. But he had learnt a valuable lesson: the aids to CID that he had used in this investigation had been under the command of Detective Superintendent Ian 'Jock' Forbes (later Deputy Assistant Commissioner Forbes QPM) and they clearly worshipped their senior officer, a very tough veteran of the Flying Squad. 'Nipper' Read drily told me, 'Ian gave his aids rather more latitude than was strictly desirable!'

Wickstead wanted that same adulation – and he got it. He never forgot those aids, and in years to come many of them would become members of his Serious Crime Squad.

Wickstead was certainly a headline-grabber as his next case, involving savage attacks on Orthodox Jews by a violent young gang of thugs, would prove.

CHAPTER 2

Anti-Semitism in North London

Once upon a time, in the 1960s, there were two gangs in North London; one was called 'The Little Highburys' and the other was known as 'The Big Highburys'. As far as who 'The Big Highburys' were or what they did, I can't help you; they and their activities don't feature in this book. However, it is safe to say that the 'The Little Highburys', although their average age was fifteen and 75 per cent of them were still at school, ought by virtue of their disgusting, cowardly behaviour to have been elevated to 'Big'. Thankfully, that category would be cruelly denied to them.

The area of London where the gangs operated was in and around Stoke Newington, the home of approximately 20,000 Orthodox Jews. Jews have, of course, experienced a long history of persecution; the pogroms which followed the demise of the Russian Tsar Alexander II in 1881 resulted in the death of 5 million, and with Hitler's holocaust, 60 years later, accounting for 6 million more, they were all but wiped out. Little has changed for Orthodox Jews since they lived in nineteenth century Eastern Europe; they are insular, deeply conservative, speak Yiddish and worship in any of the seventy-four synagogues in that area. The men's appearance is distinctive: they wear high-crown black hats and frock coats, and have long sidelocks of hair. To many Gentiles their garb looks rather strange, but to 'The Little Highburys' it provided justification for unparalleled viciousness.

This was demonstrated on the evening of 3 December 1965. The elderly Ralph Lewis Black was returning home from the synagogue along Fairholt Road, Stoke Newington, when he was confronted by five or six youths, one of whom shouted, 'A fucking Jew!' and another, 'Get out of my way, you fucking Jew!' He was then punched in the ribs and stomach and his hat was knocked off. He told the youths to leave his hat alone and as he bent down to retrieve it, several bottles were thrown at him. Although none of them hit him, Black shouted out after the retreating youths. It was, as he later admitted, 'A mistake'. Two of them returned and attacked him again. Black fell to the ground and felt what he thought were several punches in the back, but managed to get home, where he found he was bleeding. He then went to hospital, where it was discovered that he had been stabbed six times.

Later the same night, in nearby Green Lanes, seventeen-year-old Joseph Springer and his friend David Lieberman were returning home from Yeshiva – an institute for Torah and Talmudic study. They saw two groups of youths observing them from opposite sides of the road. One called out, 'Are you two Jews?' and another shouted, 'There's a couple of Jews coming along!' The two young men turned and ran, but something hit Springer on the back of his head and he fell to the ground, losing consciousness, whereupon some of the group kicked him in the face, damaging his left eye. This assault was witnessed by Lieberman, who was pushed over and then was himself kicked by four or five of the gang. Meanwhile, Springer was being repeatedly stabbed. It was a frenzied attack; there were fourteen cuts to his clothing, and he was stabbed a total of twelve times. The depth of the wounds varied from one-eighth of an inch to two inches, but the additionally horrific aspect of the attack was this: the blade of the knife was just one-eighth of an inch long. It was clear that the whole blade *and the handle as well* must have been ferociously plunged through three layers of clothing and the skin to make the wounds, the deepest of which was close to his left kidney.

The person responsible for the stabbing of both Black and Springer was Kenneth Leonard Skinner. He was a schoolboy and just fourteen years of age.

*

John Farley (later Detective Superintendent Farley QPM) was then an aid to CID at Stoke Newington and in the years which followed he would be dubbed 'The Ferret' by Michael Corkery QC because of his clever way of digging out information. Farley's unearthing of intelligence began early in his career. The attacks on the three men were very high-profile, and Wickstead was under a lot of pressure to identify and catch the assailants.

Aids to CID were not permitted to investigate reported crimes themselves, but as Farley told me, 'I got interested in the case and put myself about in the Stamford Hill, Seven Sisters Road area. As I recall, a considerable amount of walking the area in plain clothes – no radio or transport. I struck lucky and came up with the names of one or more possible suspects, one of whom was the youth who did the stabbing; his surname was Skinner. Bert acted on my information and officers from the old 'G' Division Aids' Squad were brought in to assist with the subsequent raids.'

Farley had worked quickly; within a week of the attacks most of the miscreants had been arrested, and in just under two weeks Wickstead's team had arrested a total of twelve youths.

'I remember their parents coming in', Farley recalled, and it's true to say that the boys' parents were absolutely shocked at their offspring's behaviour, having no idea of what they'd been up to.

As well as Skinner, there was John William Slack, a sixteen-year-old apprentice electrician, and John Stephen Hoy, Stephen John Lake, Leonard Compton, Peter O'Carroll, John Hill and Ronald Charles Wilkinson, all fifteen-year-old schoolboys. There were two more schoolboys, Ramsey Ahmed and Charles Peter Douglas, aged fourteen and sixteen respectively, plus fifteen-year-old Alan Henry Jeffryes, an instrument maker, and John Henry Taylor, a fifteen-year-old warehouseman.

When Wickstead initially interviewed Wilkinson and suggested he was involved in the attacks, he replied, 'No, I was not. I was nowhere near there.'

Two days later, he was again interviewed and said, 'You obviously know. I'm sorry I was telling lies on Friday. I was frightened.'

Asked what part he played, he replied, 'Not much, really'.

Slack said, 'I've been wondering when I would have to come in. I was there with Taylor, Skinner, Douglas and Jeffryes. I ran across the road with them when they hit the Jew but I couldn't get in to have my little go.' He then made a written statement.

So, too, did Douglas, who when he was first asked if he was present during the attack replied disingenuously, 'I might have been.'

In later agreeing to make a statement, he said, 'Yes, I might as well. If I don't tell you my side, they will put it on me.'

Hill told Wickstead, 'I ran over with the others. I couldn't get in very much and I went over the hedge.'

Hoy said, 'I only kicked him but only because the others were doing it.'

Skinner admitted stabbing Black and then, dealing with the attacks on Springer and Lieberman, he said:

> I did it. I think I was the only one who had a knife that night. It was a pencil sharpener knife that I use at school.
> Someone said, 'Are you two Jews?' They did not answer. I knelt down beside him. I took a knife out of my pocket and stabbed him in the back, several times, fairly hard. He

was making funny noises. Later I heard the Jew was dead, so I hid the knife. We set out that night looking for a fight. We did not attack them because they were Jews. We don't like fighting Jews because they will not fight back.

Having read the details of these confrontations – the perpetrators demanding to know whether or not their victims were Jews, and the savagery of the attacks – the reader might find the last two sentences in Skinner's statement somewhat difficult to accept. I know I did.

There were more whining confessions from others of the group, comprised of the Little Highburys who aspired to be big ones: 'I only kicked him, once. Skinner stabbed him with a knife. I only put the boot in, once. The boy was screaming' and 'I think it was Skinner who done the Yid. I had a little go with the boot.'

They appeared at Highbury Juvenile Court on 18 January 1966. All of them were charged with causing an affray, to which Skinner, Lake, Jeffryes, Compton, O'Carroll, Ahmed and Taylor pleaded guilty. Two boys were acquitted and two of the group were charged with possessing offensive weapons, bottles and a hypodermic syringe. All of them were committed to the Old Bailey.

There, Lieberman told the jury that when he got to his feet he saw the face of his friend Springer 'covered in blood'; and when Springer gave evidence about the attack he said, 'The next thing I remember is lying in an ambulance.'

A doctor admitted, 'It was touch and go whether he would live.'

Seven of the gang were sentenced to varying periods of detention and others were made the subject of probation orders, but Skinner had already pleaded guilty to two cases of inflicting grievous bodily harm with intent to do so on 1 April, and it was on 19 April 1966 that His Honour Judge Rogers pronounced sentence. He said:

> You stabbed a young man many times and after he had fallen down, you stabbed him again. I have given a great deal of anxious thought to the best way to deal with you, both from the public interest point of view and in your own interests.

He then sentenced Skinner to 3 years' detention, 'in such a place as the Home Secretary may direct'.

The Judge also commended Wickstead and his team, and five weeks later, so did the commissioner. John Farley was, quite rightly, one of the ten officers commended, as was Detective Sergeant Ron Brown, who was then at the end of his service. It was he who conducted the interviews with Wickstead and he brought a little amusement to the otherwise sombre court proceedings when asked in cross-examination, 'Why weren't solicitors invited to be at the interviews?'

Brown's response was a masterpiece of deadpan: 'I don't think there were enough chairs.'

CHAPTER 3

The Synagogue Arsons

It was not only Stoke Newington that suffered from anti-Semitic violence in the 1960s; it was occurring all over London, wherever there were Jewish communities. And as well as groups of Neo-Nazis venting their hatred on members of those neighbourhoods, their venom was often directed against the Jews' places of divine worship, their synagogues.

Tony Bruce, then a police constable at Edgware, recalls pigs' ears being nailed to the front door of a synagogue in Edgware Way in 1963; he and another officer were detailed to patrol all the local synagogues in an effort to prevent a repeat of this offensive behaviour, but by the spring of 1965 arson attacks had started to occur.

On 14 March 1965 the Brondesbury Synagogue at Chevening Road, Kilburn, NW2 was completely destroyed by fire, with damage estimated at £120,000. The blaze started on the ground floor and quickly spread through the building. More than forty fire-fighters tackled the blaze.

Although the Rabbi, Dr A. Melinek, said, 'We have no idea how it started. I have heard there has been a lot of Anti-Semitism but we cannot as yet link this with the fire', five weeks later it was the turn of the Spanish and Portuguese Synagogue, Heneage Lane, EC3.

On 4 June there were two separate arson attacks: one at the Edmonton and Tottenham affiliated synagogues, where incendiary bombs were used, and another at the Herbert Samuel Hall – New West End Synagogue, in Bayswater, where an incendiary device was thrown through the window.

Over three weeks later, the Borehamwood & Elstree Synagogue in Croxdale Road had a petrol bomb thrown at the door – those responsible were seen running away – and three days after that, on 30 June, the Bayswater Synagogue at Chichester Place, Paddington was attacked.

One week went by; then the Spanish and Portuguese Synagogue, this one situated at 2 Ashworth Road, Maida Vale, was torched, and two days later, on 10 July, the branch of the same synagogue at Launderdale Road, W9 was attacked, as was the synagogue at 843 Finchley Road, NW11. Four days after that, the Stanmore and

Canons Park Synagogue in London Road, Harrow was subject to the attentions of arsonists.

This prompted Quintin McGarel Hogg, MP for St Marylebone (later Baron Hailsham of St Marylebone KG, CH, PC, QC, FRS) to ask the Home Secretary, Sir Frank Soskice (later Baron Stow Hill PC, QC) how many cases of the recent attacks on synagogues had resulted in police action and whether he was satisfied that adequate measures were being taken for their protection. On 21 July, in the House of Commons, Sir Frank replied:

> Since last September 1st there have been five incidents of arson and four of attempted arson at synagogues, one case of arson at the home of a Jewish family as well as fifty-eight cases of 'lesser offences such as slogan daubing and fly posting'.

The second part of his answer to Hogg's question was not quite as inspiring as one might have hoped: 'Last March, a youth was fined £3 for possessing an offensive weapon and another man has been arrested in connection with an arson attempt on a synagogue.' Sir Frank's answer closed with a platitude typical of a politician on the back foot: 'The police are in close touch with the religious authorities and are paying special attention to synagogues throughout the London police district.'

Two matters arose out of the Home Secretary's reply. Firstly, the arson arrest referred to was that of one Aubrey Desmond Cadogan, who had set fire to Palmer's Green and Southgate Synagogue at Brownlow Road, New Southgate on 9 July. On 23 November 1965 Cadogan, who claimed he was nowhere near the scene of the arson, that he and his mother were Jewish and that the mound of Fascist and anti-Jewish literature found in his flat must have been planted, was sentenced to 5 years' imprisonment at the Old Bailey. However, quite apart from the fact that he appeared to be rather unstable mentally, there was little or no evidence to connect him with the other arsonists who will shortly appear in this chapter.

The second matter was that the police were indeed paying special attention to synagogues; although since these offences were spread over such a wide area of the capital, it begged the question why a special squad had not been set up – perhaps from the Regional Crime Squad which had been formed the previous year – to deal with them. However, that was about to change. On 31 July 1965 the arsonists made a ground-breaking mistake when, first, they torched the Ilford District Synagogue in Beehive Lane,

Ilford, causing damage to the tune of £139. Then the Sha'are Shomayim synagogue, built in 1932 and situated at 47 Lea Bridge Road, Clapton, E5, was subjected to an arson attack the same night. In fact, there was not a great deal of damage, assessed at just £1,000; petrol had been used as an accelerant and the flames were doused. Sprayed on the walls were anti-Semitic slogans: 'Heil Hitler', 'Werewolf' and 'We shall free Britain from Jewish Rule', watchwords such as the National Socialist Movement might have used.

Unfortunately for the gang, Bert Wickstead, who had arrived at Stoke Newington police station on 21 June 1965 as the newly promoted detective inspector, covered the area where the second arson had occurred; and he was not best pleased.

★

It's time to break off to introduce the National Socialist Movement (NSM). This was a right-wing group which had been formed on 20 April 1962 to commemorate what would have been Adolf Hitler's 73rd birthday, by John Colin Campbell Jordan with John Hutchyns Tyndall as his deputy; it had risen phoenix-like from the ashes of both the British National Party and the paramilitary Spearhead Group, both of which had been as unpleasant in their aims as was this newly-formed unit.

There had been training camps where cries of '*Sieg Heil!*' and the Horst Wessel marching song had been heard and uniforms resembling those of Hitler's *Sturmabteilung* (Brown Shirts) were seen, as was weedkiller which, with the addition of sugar, could be converted into explosive. The word 'weedkiller' on the canisters was altered to read 'Jew-Killer', and an instruction on them read, 'Place a few crystals in a sealed room full of Jews'.

On 1 July 1962 there had been a meeting at Trafalgar Square where, within the space of two hours, the number of attendees rose from 2,000 to 5,000. With banners proclaiming 'Free Britain from Jewish Control' and comparing a Jew to 'a poisonous maggot', the meeting swiftly degenerated into a riot; the police had the utmost difficulty in restoring order, twenty people were arrested and prison sentences were passed on the organizers: nine months for Jordan, six for Tyndall.

Within a month there was more trouble in Ridley Road, Dalston, where ten mounted officers and 200 foot police struggled unsuccessfully to keep order against several thousand demonstrators. Fifty-four people were charged, it took an hour for the police to clear Kingsland High Road and amongst the injured were the

Mayor of Hackney and his wife, who required medical treatment after being struck with an iron bar.

Cars drove down Ridley Road late on Saturday 1 September with the occupants shouting, 'Heil Hitler!', 'Keep Britain White!' and 'Down with the Jews!' The Revd W. Sargeant, vicar of Holy Trinity, Dalston, said that he had received a telephone call that evening telling him, 'We dynamited the Jewish synagogue last night and if you don't keep your mouth shut, we'll do the same to you.'

The following day, almost 1,100 police officers were on duty at Victoria Park Square, Bethnal Green when violent disorder broke out; over forty people were arrested. One of the prisoners later appeared at Tower Bridge Magistrates' Court and was fined £4 for using insulting behaviour; he asked for leave to appeal.

Two weeks later, once more in Ridley Road, fighting broke out following a meeting, two police officers were thrown to the ground and fourteen people (two of them juveniles) were arrested. The following day, at North London Magistrates Court, ten of the prisoners pleaded guilty to using insulting behaviour and were collectively fined a total of £79. Peter John Bishop aged eighteen told the magistrate, Mr Evelyn Russell, that he had lost his father during the war 'and I considered it my duty to go and make a protest.' He had previous convictions for similar offences and the magistrate told him he was lucky not to be going to prison. Fining him £15, Mr Russell said, 'If these meeting rouse feelings you cannot keep under control, stay away.'

Following his release from prison, Tyndall was in trouble again in August 1964 when Jomo Kenyatta, Kenya's Prime Minister, arrived in London on a state visit. An associate was sentenced to two months' imprisonment for assaulting Kenyatta outside the Park Lane Hilton; Tyndall, who shouted through a loudhailer, 'This is the man who murdered our white brethren in Africa', was convicted of using insulting words and notched up his fourth conviction with a £25 fine.

Into the lives of both Tyndall and Jordan now came an extraordinary woman. She was an utterly fanatical Jew-hater and the press, who love nicknames, dubbed her, with complete justification, 'The Queen of Britain's Nazis'.

★

Françoise Suzanne Marie Dior was born on 7 April 1932 in Île-de-France, the region which includes the city of Paris; she was the niece of the couturier Christian Dior. Tall, slim and blonde, she became a lifelong admirer of Adolf Hitler and his doctrines.

Referring to Hitler as 'my eternal leader', she would later say, 'I started to admire the German army during the occupation in France, but I was a little girl. I remember the feeling of beauty I had when they were marching through the streets and their songs and the feeling of order and discipline you could get from it', adding, 'and, of course, from their nice behaviour towards me.'

Rather less enthusiastic about her niece's sentiments was her aunt, Catherine Dior, who was lucky to have survived her time in the notorious Ravensbrück concentration camp, where she had been sent for carrying out intelligence work for the Allies.

Just after her twenty-third birthday, Françoise married Robert-Henri Aynard François Nompar, Comte de Caumont La Force, but it was a short-lived liaison – they divorced in 1960 following her dalliance with the former Cuban ambassador – although the marriage produced one daughter, Anne-Marie Christiane de Caumont La Force. She committed suicide at the age of twenty, as a result, it was said at Françoise's incitement, following a lesbian affair with her own mother.

Extremely wealthy, Françoise travelled between France and England in the 1960s, using her money to finance the French chapter of the World Union of National Socialists. She also became exceptionally interested in the activities of the British NSM. A zealous anti-Semite, who said she wanted to see synagogues burned by Act of Parliament, she became engaged to Tyndall prior to his imprisonment; but when a move was made to expel her from the country, *The Times* announced her engagement to Colin Jordan on 30 September 1963. Five days later, they were married in a civil ceremony at Caxton Hall; demonstrators hurled eggs at them as they gave the Nazi salute, and the wedding was followed by a second ceremony at 74 Princedale Road, W11.

This had been the home of the near-lunatic Arnold Spencer Leese, who had died seven years previously. He had served several terms of imprisonment and had been interned for four years during the Second World War for his pro-Nazi and virulently anti-Semitic views. An extremely unpleasant and odd personality, he had clashed with the Fascist leader, Sir Oswald Moseley who, Leese claimed, had failed to deal with 'The Jewish Question'. A veterinary surgeon, acclaimed for his exciting 1927 publication *A Treatise on the One-Humped Camel in Health and in Disease*, Leese bequeathed his house to Jordan, who used it for his base of operations.

Several hundred protestors were waiting for the newly married couple and after cries of 'Dirty Fascists!' and 'Let's get at them!' were heard, arrests were made when eggs and bottles were thrown and wreaths bearing the inscription 'In memory of thousands of British men, women and children, killed by the Nazis' were flung at the door; sections of Princedale Road had to be cordoned off and traffic diverted.

One month later, at Marylebone Magistrates' Court, a chief inspector told the magistrate, Nigel Robertson, 'The whole atmosphere was pregnant with the chances of grave breaches of the peace.'

Telling two Irish teenage brothers, 'Mob indignation is a dangerous thing and mob law can never be condoned by any magistrate', Mr Robertson ensured that the full fury of the law was unleashed against the brothers when he fined them £2 each.

Not that the threat of mob violence had interrupted the solemnity of the proceedings, because safely inside Princedale Road the happy couple mingled blood from the cuts on their ring fingers over a copy of *Mein Kampf*, and the newly-wed Mrs Jordan told reporters, 'All I want is little Nazi children.' Their honeymoon in the Scottish Highlands was slightly marred by Jordan's insisting upon taking his mother with them, but although cracks started to appear very early on in their relationship, Françoise nevertheless immediately applied for (and was granted) British citizenship, which she kept for the rest of her life.

'I well remember Colin Jordan and his wife, having covered quite a few of their public meetings, many held near the public baths off Porchester Road in Bayswater', Gordon Cawthorne, then a junior Special Branch officer (and later Detective Superintendent Cawthorne MBE) told me. 'Mrs Jordan . . . loved to dress in black leather – something which must have attracted Jordan, who like many fascists tended to be turned on by anything kinky. I don't think their marriage lasted long.'

Cawthorne was quite right; one month after exchanging marriage vows the unhappy couple separated, with Mrs Jordan rather dismissively stating that Tyndall and Jordan, 'Weren't worth a night in bed between them.'

She was seldom out of the headlines; on 8 January 1965 a Jewish taxi driver named Busell appeared in court after a contretemps between him and Mrs Jordan, who had flagged down his taxi. Recognizing her – possibly because of the swastika which she was wearing on a necklace – he exclaimed, 'I don't want you. I'm a Jew – you stinking Nazi!'

Not easily fazed, Mrs Jordan replied, 'Well, if you're a Jew, what are you doing out of the ovens?'

Unsurprisingly, Mr Busell took umbrage at this remark and tore off her swastika. This resulted in a £3 fine for Busell, compensation of 20 shillings and a £10 bind-over to be of more reasonable behaviour for the next twelve months.

Thereafter, Françoise Jordan busied herself with the workings of the NSM together with some of its members, of which more later . . .

*

In the meantime, the investigation was not progressing as smoothly as Wickstead would have liked, as demonstrated by John Simmonds' recollections:

> In the late '50s/early '60s I heard of Bert Wickstead from various officers. His reputation was that of being a hard man both with the villains and subordinate officers.
>
> At Stoke Newington his nickname was 'Bullwhip Bert' and he lived up to that reputation. He did not endear himself to his subordinates; basically he was a bully.
>
> In September 1965 I was posted to Hackney as a second-class DS. Hackney and Stoke Newington shared Night Duty CID and sometime in October I was on night duty CID with two TDCs.
>
> I was in the CID Office about 9.30 pm with my two TDCs when the Stoke Newington Station Officer rang. He was someone I knew; he was not necessarily looking for the Night Duty CID but any CID Officer who could assist him with a potential abduction of a young Jamaican boy about four years of age. He told me there were no CID Officers on duty at Stoke as they had all booked off.
>
> We went to Stoke Newington, spoke to the parents and became concerned when we discovered that a known child molester lived in the same road and that this four-year-old child had apparently left his parents a note in perfect handwriting saying, 'Dear Mummy and Daddy I am going to stop the night with my friend.' For a child who could not read or write, this note gave us all great concerns for his welfare.
>
> I checked the CID duty book and saw that the DI, Bert Wickstead had shown 'engaged in office until 10.00 pm and off duty'. I was reading this at 9.55 and in light of the potential seriousness of the case and with a known suspect who we were going to 'visit' I considered that I ought to notify the DI. I rang him at home and after explaining the case to him, he started ranting down the phone at me

calling me all the fucking incompetent bastards and that if I couldn't deal with the abduction of a fucking child, then I shouldn't be in the fucking CID, and slammed the phone down on me.

The fact that this was a serious crime reported during his watch clearly escaped him and had I not been available at Hackney when I was, I know the Station Sergeant would have taken it further because he loathed Bert.

After visiting the suspect and not finding the child, we eventually found him about 3.00 am at a house where he had fallen asleep while playing with another Jamaican child. The parents, who were not the brightest in the bunch but nevertheless honest, caring people, had put him to bed and left a note at his home address, forgetting to say who they were and where they lived.

I have gone into detail on this to explain the next dealings I had with Bert.

At this time there had been a series of anti-Semitic activities in North London, there was a lot of publicity and the Jewish community were calling for police action. Various articles had appeared in the press and a number of public meetings were held. As Stoke Newington was the centre of these activities, DI Bert Wickstead was appointed as the focal point of police activities and he was seen to be liaising with the local Rabbi and other prominent Jewish leaders. All events were to be notified to the Assistant Commissioner.

It followed that a detailed instruction went out to all and sundry that in the event of any ant-Semitic offences, it must be thoroughly investigated, Scenes of Crimes offices must attend, the scene must be photographed and the ACC notified, etc.

About two days after the 'abduction' I got a call about midnight, again from Stoke Newington, that somebody had nailed a bacon rasher on to the door of the Lea Bridge Road Synagogue. I attended the scene, met the Rabbi, called out SOCO and the Photographer, made local enquiries, sent the required messages, wrote up the Night Duty OB and left it on Bert's desk with all relevant copies of the paper work. I then went home at 6.00 am.

I was asleep in bed when my phone went at about 8.50, I woke up and heard my wife answer the phone, saying I was asleep in bed, there was some other conversation and I suddenly woke up fully when I heard my wife say, 'Don't you speak to me like that!' She came running up the stairs, clearly very angry and said, 'There's a DI who has told me to fucking get you out of bed.' She said, 'I am not going to be spoken to like that, whether he is a DI or not!'

I went to the phone and said, 'Hello', then he said, 'Wickstead here, get yourself down to Stoke Newington immediately, I'm going to stick you on.'[1] He was incandescent, so I said, 'What for?' He told me I fucking knew. I asked him what I had done wrong; he said I should have called him out. I asked why, what could he have done more than me (I had covered every aspect and knew there was nothing left out). He shouted he should have been called out so I reminded him that two days earlier he had questioned my ability to deal with a potential child abduction which was far more serious. By now he was beside himself, telling me to get down to Stoke Newington now and he was going to 'stick me on'. I calmly said 'Mr Wickstead, I am going back to bed. If you want to come to my house do so, or see me at Hackney Police Station tonight, but I must warn you that any 'sticking on' will be me punching you on the nose for using offensive language to my wife', and I hung up on him.

When bullies are given some of their own medicine they generally cannot take it. He did not come to my house nor did he go to Hackney that night, and I never spoke to Wickstead from that day until some seventeen years later when as DCS on 'X' Division, Bert rang me and asked me if I was interested in taking over the Serious Crimes Squad at Limehouse which he had created and was his baby. I was happy to accept the offer and agreed.

Of course, Wickstead's behaviour was completely illogical. Everything that should have been done had been done, and Simmonds believes that not being called out robbed Wickstead of a self-publicizing photo opportunity. Given his fondness for self-aggrandisement, this is a very likely explanation; that, plus frustration that almost three months had passed since the offence in Lea Bridge Road and he was no closer to solving it.

It did look like members of the NSM were involved, and this was an organization which the Metropolitan Police Special Branch

---

1 This was police parlance, meaning to report an officer for acting contrary to the disciplinary code

was keeping under close observation. At that time, they (and the Security Service, MI5) had access to twenty telephone intercepts for which the Home Secretary had signed warrants, and undeniably one (or more of them) would have been devoted to the activities of the NSM. However, that organization was too shrewd to discuss on the telephone where and when their next target would be. But within a few days of thoroughly upsetting Mrs Barbara Simmonds, Wickstead got the breakthrough he needed and it came neither from Special Branch, nor MI5, nor any run-of-the-mill police informant. Special Branch routinely used deep-penetration undercover officers to infiltrate subversive groups, and if they had any such officers within the ranks of the NSM, and if any pertinent information was forthcoming, it was not being disseminated in Wickstead's direction. But the NSM had indeed been penetrated, and the agents came from a shadowy unit who were known as 'The 62 Group'.

*

This organization was made up of the remnants of the 43 Group, which had been set up after the Second World War by returning Jewish servicemen (although it included a number of Gentiles as well); they broke up far-right movements and fought with Fascists; their youngest member was the hair stylist, the late Vidal Sassoon CBE. Believing the threat of Fascism to have been curtailed, the group was later disbanded.

But when the National Socialist Movement was formed in 1962, so was the 62 Group. Gordon Cawthorne described this organization to me as being 'An outfit made up chiefly of tough and aggressive Jews, dedicated to disrupting any extreme right-wing activity or person they came across'.

Harry Bidney (who had also served with the 43 Group) was one of the members and he lost no time in establishing his credentials when, spotting Colin Jordan on his way to court, he and Harry Kaufman booed and Bidney shouted, 'Dirty Nazi Bastard!' They were promptly arrested for using insulting behaviour.

'I'm an ex-serviceman and was infuriated when I saw people wearing swastikas', Bidney told the magistrate, Mr Herbert Beaumont, when he and Kaufman appeared at Bow Street on 21 August 1962. Perhaps Mr Beaumont felt some sympathy for the two defendants because he soothingly remarked, 'You must not be so demonstrative about it in future' and fined the pair of them a modest five shillings each.

The same clemency appeared to be extended to Gerry Gable, who in 1964 with another man, was convicted of entering the flat of David John Cawdell Irving, author and holocaust denier, in the guise of GPO engineers. The Chairman at Middlesex Sessions fined the men £28 each, with an additional £5 fine for Gable, for the theft by finding of a GPO pass.

Gerry Gable had gained a seat on the board of The 62 Group, created the anti-Fascist magazine, *Searchlight* and organized intelligence for the group, including the use of infiltrators into the NSM.

★

On 25 October 1965, following a Fascist meeting in Ridley Road, Dalston, nineteen-year-old Paul William Dukes was one of seventeen youths and girls arrested; he was convicted of possessing an offensive weapon and fined. Dukes was a member of the NSM and he was in line for promotion to the rank of *Obersturmbannführer* – Lieutenant Colonel to you.

It appears that Dukes had had a change of heart regarding his beliefs. He had several Jewish friends, including a Jewish girlfriend who unsurprisingly 'did not agree with his politics', and as he left the Magistrates' Court, Harry Bidney saw that he looked very unhappy. He followed him, engaged him in conversation and bought him a cup of tea in the Lyons tea shop at Dalston Junction.

Dukes – who had apparently provided fuses for some of the incendiary devices – suddenly burst into tears and made a number of incriminating admissions. He agreed to meet Bidney later and when he did, Gable was also present; Dukes was persuaded to accompany them to Stoke Newington police station, where Gable told Wickstead that he had promised Dukes that he would be fairly treated.

Dukes was asked, 'Would you like to make a written statement?' and he replied, 'Yes. That's why I'm here. I want to clear my conscience and finish with that mob for good.' He then made a lengthy statement in which he admitted his involvement in the arsons at the Lea Bridge Road and Ilford synagogues, and he also named names, before appearing at North London Magistrates' Court on 27 October. Amongst those named were Colin and Françoise Jordan. A report was submitted to the Director of Public Prosecutions, who decided that there was insufficient evidence to launch proceedings against Colin Jordan. However, the matter of his wife was put in abeyance, at least for the time being . . .

Within a matter of days Dukes was joined in the dock by five of his associates. Malcolm Sparks, aged nineteen, already possessed previous convictions for storebreaking and arson. Like

Dukes, and despite being so young, Sparks had received accelerated promotion to the rank of *Obersturmbannführer*; he was also charged with two offences of arson. When he was arrested he had a Dutch Waffen SS badge in his lapel, and following a search at his home at Malmesbury Road, South Woodford, Essex, the police discovered a rich haul of Nazi paraphernalia: two German army tunics, a Nazi pennant, a drawing of a stormtrooper throwing a hand grenade, a large quantity of Wehrmacht and Nazi badges and a slightly singed swastika armband which, Sparks solemnly stated, had been retrieved from the 1933 fire at the Reichstag.

Hugh Llewellyn Hughes, aged twenty-six, a driver from Battersea who had previously served in the British army and had a conviction for assaulting a police officer, and Alex Gordon, a cinematographer, were charged with the two arsons, as were Graham Chant aged eighteen, a hospital porter with convictions for larceny and shopbreaking and Colin William Rainbird, aged twenty, unemployed, of Edmonton. All of them were committed for trial to the Old Bailey.

On 8 February 1966 workmen industriously scrubbed the outside walls of the Old Bailey where swastikas had been daubed, and Dukes, Chant and Rainbird pleaded guilty; the other three denied the offences.

Two days later, there appeared a surprise witness for the defence: her name was Mrs Françoise Jordan.

A word of explanation: witnesses for the defence do not simply turn up at court, step into the witness box and start spouting; they are interviewed beforehand by the defence solicitors and a statement obtained, so that (a) they are satisfied that the witness can provide testimony helpful to the defence and (b) the statement will be of assistance to the defence counsel in leading them through their evidence. However, no matter how diligent the preparation may be, some of these witnesses' testimony can be catastrophic, as in the case of Francis Davidson 'Mad Frankie' Fraser. He interrupted his 15-year prison sentence, courtesy of the Mr Smith's Club affray and the Richardson Torture trial, to arrive at the Old Bailey and inform the jury that somebody other than Ronnie Kray (who was 'a good bloke') had fatally shot George Cornell in The Blind Beggar. Fraser also provided an eloquent character reference for Ronnie's brother Charlie, who later stood trial on charges of conspiracy to import cocaine with a street value of £39 million; not that it did either brother any good at all, since the outcome was 30 years' imprisonment in Ronnie's case, and 12 years in Charlie's.

Quite often it's a case self-aggrandisement for the witness concerned, as it was with Fraser ('It's a larf, innit?') and as it certainly was in the case of Mrs Jordan, who strutted into No 1 Court at the Old Bailey clad in a black leather coat and boots and wearing two swastikas, one around her neck, the other on an armband. The defence team must have shaken their heads in stunned disbelief, because her appearance earned her a judicial bollocking from Mr Justice (later Lord Justice) Phillimore, who made her remove the offensive insignia.

It had been aired in court that Colin Jordan was implicated in the arson campaign, and his wife told the court, 'My husband is dead against any kind of criminal activity. It is the worst kind of propaganda for the movement.'

That evidence might have been compelling, but not all of it, because at the conclusion of her testimony, Sparks changed his pleas to guilty.

On 15 February Hughes was found guilty on both charges and Gordon was found not guilty of the offence at Ilford but guilty of the Lea Bridge Road synagogue arson. In passing sentence, Mr Justice Phillimore said:

> Some of you no doubt believe in the doctrines of the National Socialist Movement which, as I understand them, are those of Hitler and the Nazi Party of many years ago. I do not punish you for your beliefs. Anybody in this country can believe anything they like. I do not punish you for being members of this movement. But you have chosen to interfere with the freedom of worship of respectable Jewish citizens of this country and destroy their property. You defaced the walls of their synagogues and then set them on fire. I have no doubt that in doing these acts you have been led into this by the indoctrination you have received in this pernicious movement. I am quite satisfied that the people in charge of this movement inculcated not only hatred of the Jews and coloured people but encouraged active strikes against them. These are grave crimes and it is my duty to make an example of you in the hope that those who share in your beliefs will think twice before following your example.

Dukes was sentenced to six months' imprisonment, and given the amount of time he had already spent in custody, it would pretty well have coincided with his release.

Chant, Rainbird and Gordon were each sentenced to 3 years' imprisonment, Sparks received 4 years and Hughes, 5 years on each charge, to run concurrently.

At the conclusion of the case, the 62 Group's actions were recognized when Harry Bidney received the judge's congratulations. Wickstead was awarded another commissioner's commendation but although he was convinced that Françoise Jordan was deeply involved in the synagogue arsons, he had insufficient evidence to arrest and charge her. However, a further series of arrests would dramatically change that situation.

★

In fact, some of the arrests had been carried out whilst Hughes & Co were standing trial. Wickstead had received even more assistance from the 62 Group when twenty-four-year-old John William Evans was arrested; not only did he admit arson at seven synagogues, he also implicated Françoise Jordan.

'Evans was nicknamed "The Undertaker",' Gerry Gable told me. 'For a young person, he looked really gaunt, really sinister.'

He appeared to be an extremely odd young man who, according to Wickstead, 'insisted on driving an old hearse around the streets'. Evans' detailed written statement of admissions also named others who he said were involved: seventeen-year-old Raymond Francis Hemsworth, twenty-three-year-old Michael Trowbridge, twenty-year-old David Thorne and Gordon Parker, aged nineteen; on 4 March 1966 they were all remanded in custody. But by now, information from the disclosures in court were receiving considerable publicity, and on 16 March, now separated from her husband, thirty-three-year-old Françoise Jordan fled to France with her nineteen-year-old secretary, Terence Robert Cooper.

Meanwhile, the five men appeared at the Old Bailey on Tuesday, 5 April 1966, and while Gordon Parker was acquitted of two cases of arson and was discharged, the other four all pleaded guilty to a variety of charges. All of them admitted setting fire to the Brondesbury Synagogue on 13 March 1965, and Evans and Hemsworth also admitted arson at the Bayswater Synagogue on 30 June; Evans and Hemsworth also asked for other offences to be taken into consideration – five in Evans' case, three in Hemsworth's.

The total amount of the damage caused came to £130,000. But there was no need for the defence barristers to speak in mitigation for their clients, because Wickstead did it for them. Telling the court that the four defendants had come under the influence of persons in the National Socialist Movement, he stated, 'They are now penitent and want nothing more to do with anti-Semitic activities.' He added that although attempts had been made on synagogues at Elstree, Finchley, Stoke Newington, Ilford, Bayswater, Brondesbury, Stanmore and Maida Vale, these defendants were not responsible for all of them, and since their arrest no other arsons had occurred.

In passing sentence, His Honour Judge Carl Aarvold OBE, TD said:

> Your minds seem to have been ensnared by a philosophy that permits, and may even encourage, the burning down of places which are holy and venerated by others. You were used by unscrupulous people to further their own evil designs and one does not know whether to pity or blame you. I hope I may be forgiven if I allow Inspector Wickstead's words to carry more weight with me than do the dreadful facts of this case. In those circumstances I propose passing a sentence of imprisonment which will allow you all to be released on Thursday. I hope you will take advantage of the festival of Easter to come under an influence very different from that which caused you to commit these offences.

The Judge then commended Wickstead, as did the commissioner two months later.

So with his helpful comments to this penitent band of arsonists, had Wickstead gone soft? Not a bit of it. He now had a number of arrows in his quiver with which to shoot down a very impenitent lady.

*

On 4 June 1965 Françoise Jordan had been sentenced in France, *in absentia*, to four months' imprisonment for defacing the British Embassy in Paris by posting stickers which stated 'Hitler was right' on the walls. Now, however, justice caught up with her and in October 1966 she was made to serve her sentence in Nice. She must have been a recalcitrant prisoner, because she served every day of her imprisonment, being released on 3 February 1967. She and Cooper then travelled to Munich before returning to Britain in April 1967. One of the 62 Group agents discovered that they were living at the home of Cooper's parents, 13 Joan Gardens, Dagenham.

Gable passed this information on to Wickstead, who still needed time to gather sufficient information and asked if there was a way to keep them from moving on from that address. There was.

As Gable told me, 'I worked out an approach as a journalist from Birmingham who was a NSM supporter and I had documentation to back it.' Gable knew that Jordan had an interest in paganism and the occult, and he had a very rare edition of *The British Edda*, a book on English, Sumerian and Egyptian mythology written in 1930 by Laurence Waddell, with a gold swastika on the spine.

In his guise as a journalist Gable mentioned this to Jordan and she asked if she might borrow it. He agreed, telling her, 'This is a National Socialist bond between us and I'll rely on you to return it when you've read it.' This gave Gable a second chance to establish that she was still living at the Dagenham address; but to be sure, members of the 62 Group carried out 24-hour surveillance on the house for a week.

Finally, Gable told me, 'Bert said, "Pull your people back"', and Jordan was arrested. Taken to Stoke Newington, she was questioned by Wickstead, who asked what her position was at the NSM.

'Not very important, office manager', she replied, adding, 'I became the secretary later.'

'Is it a fact that you hate the Jewish race?' asked Wickstead and received the reply, 'Yes. I make no secret of this.'

When Wickstead asked her about the plan to set fire to the Stanmore synagogue, she replied, 'I wanted it done. I would like to make an Act of Parliament to burn down all synagogues by law.'

She was then asked if she was responsible for the series of synagogue arsons. This was her reply: 'I did not start them. If I say I want something done which should be done and it is done, I am not responsible if I am not there.'

Wickstead asked if it was correct that whilst she was at a meeting at Malcolm Sparks' house in Woodford she had suggested blowing up the 8ft 6in bronze statue of Sir Winston Churchill which was situated at Salway Hill, on the edge of Epping Forest.

She replied, 'Sparks was a madman. He liked violence. Who needs to make suggestions to such a man?'

And so the questioning and answers continued, including her oft-repeated quote from the unsavoury *Obersturmbannführer* Julius Streicher, Hitler's propagandist – 'The Jews are our misfortune' – as well as her own view that 'Everybody talks about what they would like to do with the Jews. The gas chambers were too humanitarian for them.'

When Wickstead asked her about the Brondesbury Synagogue arson, she replied, eyes gleaming, 'It was like *Kristallnacht!*'[2]

But still Wickstead could not charge her; the offences with which she should have been charged were incitement and conspiracy to commit arson and these required the *fiat* (consent) of the Director of Public Prosecutions; only after he had studied all of the evidence and decided that there was a sufficiency of it could arrest warrants be obtained.

However, those warrants were eventually forthcoming, and on 7 August 1967 Françoise was charged with inciting members of the National Socialist Movement to set fire to synagogues and conspiring with John William Evans and David Thorn to set fire to the Stanmore Synagogue between 1 May and 31 July 1965.

When Jordan swaggered into North London Magistrates' Court, Gable and Wickstead were seated together.

'She shouted at me, "You Jewish bastards!"' Gable recalled, 'And I turned to Bert and in a stage whisper, I said, "100 per cent right, madam!"'

Entering the witness box, Wickstead told the court, 'This matter is being dealt with by the office of the Director of Public Prosecutions. I am applying for a remand in custody. It will take four weeks before the case has been prepared and I have strong objections to bail.'

Indeed he had; now that he had finally got her, Wickstead was not going to let her go. He mentioned the serious nature of the charges, that there had already been threats to witnesses and his belief that if 'this woman' was released, that fear would be increased; also that although she had surrendered her passport, he believed that she would flee the country again.

'I think the inspector is completely ridiculous', said Mrs Jordan dismissively, adding that she had given her passport to Wickstead 'as a favour'.

When the question of sureties was raised, Wickstead stated that he was not prepared to accept any surety named by Mrs Jordan. 'She has mentioned some names to me and they are mixed up with this movement', he told the Magistrate, Mr W.

---

2 She was referring to 'The Night of Broken Glass', when all over Nazi Germany on the night of 9/10 November 1938, Hitler's Brown Shirts smashed the windows of Jewish shops and synagogues and set fire to them. It was estimated that 91 Jews died during that atrocity; it was known as *Kristallnacht* because the shards of broken window glass were illuminated in the flames.

Hughes, who refused bail, telling her that she could apply to a high court judge.

And after a further appearance on 16 August at North London Magistrates' Court, she did just that. The hearing in chambers by Mr Justice Geoffrey Lane on 22 August lasted just five minutes and was conspicuously unsuccessful; her next appearance at North London Magistrates' Court on 25 August was even swifter – one minute – and when she left, bound for Holloway prison in a red Cortina police car, she obliged sightseers with a number of Nazi salutes.

At the committal proceedings on 7 September Mr John Wood for the DPP opened the case and three of the four witnesses called for the prosecution were allowed to write down their addresses; there was no such concern for the fourth witness, whose name was Colin William Rainbird, since he was still serving his 3-year sentence at Maidstone prison. Now Wickstead's mitigation for the defendants in the second trial became clear – those convicted young men (plus Rainbird) would form the basis of Mrs Jordan's prosecution.

Jordan's solicitor told the Magistrate, Mr W. E. Denby, that the evidence against his client was 'pitifully weak'; but having heard the evidence, plus Wickstead's warning that if granted bail, 'prosecution witnesses might be prevailed upon not to give evidence at her trial', Mr Denby disagreed and committed her in custody to the Old Bailey.

A week later, Françoise Jordan made one more determined effort for bail, this time in front of Mr Justice Lawton; it was just as unsuccessful as the others.

The trial commenced on 12 January 1968 before Mr Justice Cusack. There were now three charges: conspiring with David Thorne, John Evans and Raymond Hemsworth to set fire to synagogues between 1 March and 1 August 1965; unlawfully inciting members of the National Socialist Party to commit similar offences; and between 1 May and 14 July 1965, conspiring with David Thorne and John Evans to set fire to the Stanmore Synagogue. To these offences, Mrs Jordan pleaded not guilty.

The case was outlined by Mr E. J. P. Cussen, and when Evans gave evidence and was asked by the judge why they were burning synagogues, he replied, simply, 'Because we didn't like Jewish people.'

Colin Rainbird gave evidence that on two occasions when he attended meetings at the Woodford branch of the movement Mrs Jordan had presided. General policy had been discussed and also the possibility of destroying Churchill's statute by using explosives, towards the cost of which Mrs Jordan had contributed £10.

David Thorne, who had already pleaded guilty to the Brondesbury Synagogue arson, gave evidence that after he had committed that offence Mrs Jordan had asked him if he was responsible. When he told her he was, she warned him, 'Take care not to involve the movement.'

Following an NSM meeting at Woodford, he suggested while in a car – John Evans was a fellow passenger – that they should burn the Stanmore Synagogue. He told the court, 'Mrs Jordan had always wanted to come with us on an escapade of synagogue burning.'

However, that offence never took place. When they arrived there, the lights were on and a dance was in progress. Either the risk was considered too great or the prospect of murder was unacceptable, but in any event the plan was abandoned.

Raymond Hemsworth also gave evidence and said that when they discussed the idea of burning synagogues, 'It seemed a good idea to Mrs Jordan.'

When Françoise Jordan herself came to give evidence – she affirmed, rather than taking the oath on the Bible – she was on a bit of a sticky wicket because her anti-Semitic views were very well known. Consequently, her strident views had to be dampened down a little, whereas accusations could be met with outright denials.

Therefore, she admitted that when she had heard of the Brondesbury fire she had said, 'Jolly good', but only because she thought it had burned down by accident. In the light of what she had told Wickstead (plus anybody else who cared to listen) she had to admit that she did not think it was a crime to burn down synagogues; but it was a crime when it harmed the movement. She informed the jury that she had told the arsonists that one day all synagogues would be burned by an Act of Parliament, all Jews would be deported and no synagogues would then be needed.

She was pretty well obliged to admit that she hated the Jews as a race, saying, 'I have never made any secret about my attitude to Jewish people. I despise them. I think they are evil', but then swiftly adding the codicil, 'but not as individuals.'

Now came the denials. When asked if she had conspired to set fire to synagogues she replied, 'Of course not, because Hitler was dead against it.' She denied donating £10 for the acquisition of explosives, stating that at that meeting she had tried to interest the other members of the group in the works of Nietzsche and Wagner, 'but my words fell on stony ground; they were not interested. They were only interested in burning this statue.' She rebuffed the suggestion that she had wanted to go on a burning expedition, and although she admitted that the burning of Stanmore Synagogue had been discussed in the car, she claimed she had piously told Thorne and Evans, 'You are mad. If you intend to do it, I will get out of the car immediately and report you to my husband.'

It appeared to work. On 17 January, after over five hours' deliberation, the jury could not agree on the Stanmore conspiracy charge; it was ordered to be left on the file, not to be proceeded with without leave of the court or the Court of Appeal (Criminal Division). The charge of incitement was withdrawn, but despite the Trial Judge telling the jury, 'not to find her guilty because you dislike her opinions', she was nevertheless found guilty on the first conspiracy charge.

Telling her, 'I am well aware of your views on racial matters, particularly in relation to the Jews. That might be an explanation for what you did, but not a justification', Mr Justice Cusack sentenced her to eighteen months' imprisonment. Predictably, she turned to the jury, executed a Teutonic heel-click and shrieked, '*Heil Hitler!*' before being hustled off to prison.

Wickstead was extremely grateful to Gerry Gable, whom he held in high esteem, as well as to members of the 62 Group, whom he rather coyly referred to as 'My League of Shadows'. They had made a massive input into the synagogue arsons' investigation as well as interceding when Wickstead and a colleague were intimidated by a bunch of right-wing thugs as they left the Old Bailey.

Gable's opinion of Wickstead? 'Bert could be a very difficult man, because he would come up with a clear vision of what he was tackling and not let anything get in his way in bringing bad people to book.'

And as for the NSM – who, it was said, organized 34 arson attacks on Jewish owned buildings during the 1960s – at its height, it had 187 full members. But by 1966 there were just 35 paid-up and active members. Their numbers had been depleted through imprisonment, perhaps fear of prosecution and maybe just general lack of interest.

*

After that, it was all downhill for Mrs Jordan. On 27 October 1967 she divorced Colin Jordan, and following her imprisonment, Cooper was arrested and appeared at the Old Bailey on charges of conspiracy to steal papers, the property of the diplomatic mission of the Democratic Republic of the Congo, forging three Metropolitan Police warrant cards and possessing an offensive weapon, a truncheon; also found in his possession was a sketch plan of a plot to kidnap the Congolese Ambassador. He was found guilty, but the judge regarded him as 'a fantasist' and suspended his custodial sentence. After Françoise Jordan's release from prison in 1969, she and Cooper – both of them having been expelled from the NSM – left first for Jersey, then France. They lived together in a former presbytery in Ducey, a small Normandy village, from August 1970 until July 1980, before separating. Later, in France, Cooper was accused of bank robbery, firearms offences and manufacturing explosives for the Breton Liberationists; he died in a microlight aircraft accident in April 2006.

Françoise Jordan's former paramour, John Tyndall, is also dead. In 1966 he was imprisoned after being found driving around Notting Hill in a covered lorry containing six other men, one woman and thirty wooden coshes, six metal bars, two metal pins and two saw blades. He joined (or formed) various other right-wing parties, ending with the British National Party, and in 1986 he was sentenced to twelve months' imprisonment for inciting racial hatred. He was charged with a similar offence in 2005, and his death, on 19 July 2005, came two days before his appearance at Leeds Magistrates' Court.

Colin Jordan was sentenced to eighteen months' imprisonment in 1967 for circulating material likely to incite racial hatred, and in 2001 he was charged with a similar offence, although the judge ruled that he was unfit to stand trial due to his serious heart condition. Perhaps it was just as well; had he been found guilty and his previous convictions been read out, since he had been fined £50 in June 1975 for shoplifting three pairs of women's knickers from the Leamington Spa branch of Tesco, this would not have enhanced his reputation. He died on 9 April 2009.

★

Now back to the wretched Françoise, who would not be Mrs Jordan for very much longer and who was living in rather reduced circumstances. A number of financial investments which had looked promising were not as remunerative as she might have hoped; she mortgaged the presbytery for some ready cash but was unable to keep up the repayments, and it was sold in 1982. She joined the Rally for the Republic movement and married writer and former diplomat Comte Hubert de Mirleau, from one of France's oldest noble (although not particularly wealthy) families. She kept up her contacts in the extreme Neo-Nazi movement, *Parti Nationaliste Français et Européen*, but her health and wealth went rapidly downhill.

La Comptesse Françoise Dior-de Mirleau, who never returned to Britain, died of lung cancer at the American Hospital, Neuilly-sur-Seine, aged sixty, on 20 January 1993.

The Jews are a compassionate race, but when 'The Queen of British Nazis' departed this world, it is not thought that there was anyone available to say Kaddish for her.

CHAPTER 4

'Britain's Biggest Post-War Bank Robbery'

Following the Jordan case (for which Wickstead was again commended by the commissioner) and his successfully solving nineteen murders in two years, promotion came fast. With just over two years in the rank of detective inspector, he was transferred as a detective chief inspector to East Ham, where he was obliged to investigate reports of thefts from single officers' rooms at East Ham section house. His meticulous investigation had two results: first, the culprit was caught red-handed; it was a bus inspector; second, the occupier of one of the section house rooms and owner of a pet alligator had to be admonished – after its morning 'run' the reptile had not been restored to its aquarium and had unnerved a cleaner, whose mop it had savagely attacked.

So the section house officers were guiltless; not so two officers who, hand in glove with thieves, would wait until their associates had prepared to sell shopkeepers stolen goods before stepping in and blackmailing them in return for their silence. Wickstead took swift action there, and a uniform sergeant and an aid to CID were each sentenced to 8 years' imprisonment.

This may have been a contributory factor in a further promotion only seventeen months later, but Wickstead's advancement to detective superintendent lasted just three weeks. The reason for this was because the rank was temporarily withdrawn, so that on 1 June 1969 Wickstead became the detective chief superintendent, in charge of all the detectives on 'J' Division at Leyton police station. From detective inspector to detective chief superintendent in under four years was not bad going by any stretch of the imagination, and now that he had his own division Wickstead was going to put his stamp on it.

It was a large area to cover: 'J' Division ranged from Ilford in the south to Walthamstow in the west, Waltham Abbey in the north (which bordered Hertfordshire Constabulary) and Chigwell to the east (which abutted Essex Constabulary); a total of thirteen police stations spread over approximately 90 square miles in all.

One of the Special Patrol Group units was based at Leytonstone; they had excellent crime-fighting capability, which within a few years Wickstead would utilize to the full. Another crime-busting initiative was connected with the divisional 'Q' Cars, which proved their worth during their 50-year reign. When Wickstead had served on 'K' Division, that area was so large that it was split into two – known as Inner and Outer 'K' – with one detective chief superintendent at East Ham, the other at Romford. Accordingly, they had two 'Q' Cars, 'Kilo one-one' for Inner 'K' (which Wickstead would often accompany on patrol) and 'Kilo one-two' for Outer. 'J' Division was not split into two, but Wickstead decided the resident 'Q'-Car, 'Juliet one-one', could do with a companion. Therefore he created 'Juliet one-three' with a crew made up of one officer from 'K' Division and another from 'J' Division with the roving commission to go anywhere – not only 'J' and 'K' Divisions but Essex, Hertfordshire or anywhere else they fancied. Precisely how Wickstead obtained permission for a Met vehicle to enter two (or more) different constabularies willy-nilly and carry out arrests appears to be shrouded in mystery – perhaps the truth of the matter is that he didn't. But with or without permission, the fact remains that 'Juliet one-three' brought in an impressive record of work.

As ever, Wickstead was a martinet. He growled, he roared and his subordinates trembled – but they knew exactly where they stood with him and they got things done.

Former Detective Constable Dave Scrivener told me, 'I liked him. He was hard and strict, but he was fair. He wasn't liked by the hierarchy but he was admired by the troops.'

Not, however, by all of them. When twenty-three-year-old aid to CID Roger Davey was minding the otherwise deserted shop at Barkingside's CID office, someone he described as 'an elderly man, wearing a mac and hat' arrived and demanded to know, 'Who the bloody hell are you?'

Somewhat aggrieved, Davey responded by saying, 'And who the bloody hell are *you*?' – that was his introduction to the Division's new detective chief superintendent.

'I didn't like him', Davey told me.

Wickstead needed hard-working, resolute officers behind him, because within eight months of his arrival his division would be confronted with Britain's biggest bank robbery of the post-war years. What was more, it took just 90 seconds to carry out.

*

On the morning of Monday, 9 February 1970 a Security Express van had collected £237,736 9s 10d from a chain of supermarkets in the London area and delivered the cash to Barclays Bank, 144

High Road, Ilford. At 9.45 am six bags containing the money were taken from the van to the bank's lift for transfer to the vault. As one of the guards, Robert Blaber, brought in the sixth bag he was confronted by a man wearing a black wig and carrying a shotgun, and Blaber threw the bag at him. A second man wearing a ginger wig pressed what appeared to be a gun into Blaber's back and told him, 'Down on the floor or you're a dead man'.

The first robber then pointed his gun along the counter and similarly advised the staff to lie down on the floor, and four more of the gang, wearing stocking masks topped with white crash helmets, grabbed the money bags and loaded them into a white Ford Transit van which was double-parked outside the bank. The gang then escaped; but not before the raider wearing the ginger wig had squirted ammonia in Robert Blaber's face to mark his insolence for daring to resist.

Within seconds the police had been alerted; Wickstead was informed at his Leyton office and was on his way to Ilford, and the whole cast-list of characters who make up a major crime enquiry – photographers, fingerprint officers, scenes of crime officers – descended on the bank, together with officers taking statements from the traumatized staff.

For this was a major incident, no error there, and as such, should the Flying Squad have been called in to deal with it? Undeniably, they had the best information on armed robbers – 10 Squad was known as 'The East End Team' – but although neither Wickstead nor anybody else was aware of it at the time, the robbers all came from different parts of London. However, the enquiry would not be handed over to the Squad; Wickstead had such a poor opinion of their trustworthiness that he had written on his Divisional Record Sheet 'NOT C8' in red ink, in case anyone might think that they were doing him a favour by posting him to the Flying Squad.

No, this was Wickstead's baby and he was going to keep it; he had his own private list of possibles as to who might have carried out the raid. Now he told his detectives to add their own suspects to the list; when the same names cropped up, they were to be traced, their premises searched and they were to be unceremoniously brought in for questioning. In fact, it was not really a requirement for the names to be duplicated; anyone who Wickstead thought might possibly possess even a modicum of information or involvement was brought in. It was a scattergun approach; and although it's a ploy that would never be sanctioned nowadays, it worked then.

Villains were brought in and spoken to in a no-nonsense manner, until one admitted that one of the robbers was now using the name of Alfred Prill, although his real name was Ronald Dark.

Dark had been born in 1935 and after a term in approved school he went to Borstal after stealing £50 from his brother. He would develop into a violent criminal, a burglar and robber who had good connections. When he was on remand at Brixton Prison in 1959, his wife was one of two people killed in a car crash; Dark's four-year-old son was also seriously injured. The driver of the car gave his name to police as Albert Cox, but further enquiries revealed that his real name was Robert McCandless, aged twenty-nine, who was sought by police after breaking out of Lincoln prison six weeks previously, where he had been serving a 10-year sentence for robbery.

The reason why Dark had been on remand was because for eighteen months he had been on the run following his involvement in breaking into the London Cooperative Society in Clapton and stealing a safe containing £2,051, also breaking into a firm of wholesale grocers, blowing the safe and stealing £2,470. In January 1960 he pleaded guilty to these offences, asked for two more to be taken into consideration and was sentenced to 5 years' imprisonment.

Released from prison on 7 June 1963, he next came to notice when he gave evidence at the Great Train Robbery trial; on 19 February 1964 he told Aylesbury Assizes that on 10 August 1963 (two days after the robbery) he had delivered groceries in a lorry (together with Bob Welch and Tommy Wisbey) to what he now knew to be Leatherslade Farm. However, before they set off from Jimmy Hussey's address – he was unable to accompany them, due to looking after his ailing mother – Hussey had helped himself to an apple from the consignment and *that* was how his prints were on the tailboard of the lorry. Whilst Dark and Wisbey were at the farm, Wisbey slipped in the bathroom, and that was how *his* fingerprints came to be on the bath rail. The reason for Welch's fingerprints being found on a can of Pipkin's Ale? Well, as a publican, he had picked it up at the farm because 'he was interested in these new cans'. Oh, and Dark also stated that Jimmy Hussey could not have been on the robbery which took place at 3.00 am on 8 August 1963 because on 7 August Hussey had attended Dark's birthday party and had not left until 2.00 am the following morning. It didn't sound particularly convincing – certainly not to the trial judge, who said so rather forcefully – or to the jury, who found Wisbey, Hussey, Welch and a number of their associates guilty of the train robbery.

It was not too long before Dark was in trouble again; on 31 December that year he was sentenced to 4 years' imprisonment for wounding with intent and causing grievous bodily harm. Exactly one month later, Dark granted himself a little unofficial parole when he and another prisoner used a grappling hook and an improvised rope-ladder to scale the 20ft wall at Wandsworth prison. Dark was on the run for three months before being recaptured at Mill Hill.

*

Four days after the raid at Ilford, Dark and his girlfriend, Barbara Mary Hepburn, had gone to Southend, where he had purchased her a £65 sheepskin coat from a furrier's. They then moved around the country, using several aliases, including Mr and Mrs Prill and Mr and Mrs Davis, before arriving at the Beaford House Hotel, Winkleigh, Devon, where Dark took the opportunity to grow long sideburns and a moustache. In addition, through an intermediary, James William Love (later to be sentenced to 4 years' imprisonment), he instructed an accountant to purchase Edgerley House, Lapford, Crediton, Devon, a beautiful country house in 12½ acres of land, complete with paddocks – in the names of Mr and Mrs Prill. The price, at £10,500, may seem modest today, but the property in 2018 is worth £1m. From that moment on, Dark lived the life of a country squire, rode to hounds (having purchased two horses for £600) and bought a Mini Cooper 'S' for £950. For these, plus any other purchases, he paid in what was later referred to as 'fistfuls of notes' from a large sum of money kept in a toilet bag, which he asked the hotel's owners to look after for him.

The owners of the hotel, Lew and Phyl Wickett, were completely unaware of the money's provenance; in fact, their daughter Jenny told me, they regarded 'Mr and Mrs Prill' as being 'one of the family' – so much so that the couple were seated at a kitchen table in the hotel at 3.00 pm on 15 July when armed police burst in.

Liam Gillespie was a detective sergeant with the Regional Crime Squad and he and several others had gone to the West Country, sleeping under canvas ('It was pouring with rain', he recalled) and waiting until 'Dark picked up some horses'. The raid was carried out following consultations between Devon Constabulary, the Regional Crime Squad and the Flying Squad, and with a service revolver pointed directly at his head Ronnie Dark's days of freedom came to an end. It seemed everybody had an interest in Dark. Deputy Assistant Commissioner Ian Forbes, National Co-ordinator of the Regional Crime Squad, telephoned Gillespie to say, 'Well done – good arrest', although Frank 'Jeepers' Davies MBE, the Commander of the Flying Squad, was less than complimentary. 'Why the hell wasn't he handed over to the Squad?' he demanded to know, and Gillespie swiftly referred him to the

Regional Crime Squad's Commander, Roy Yorke, to provide an explanation.

But Wickstead was the deciding factor. 'Don't interview him', he told Gillespie. 'Just bring him here'. Wickstead (of whom Gillespie told me, 'I got on very well with him') was responsible for recommending Gillespie for a commissioner's commendation for the arrest.

Miss Hepburn was also arrested and the reason was this: since October 1968 she and Dark had been 'an item', and this date more or less coincided with (a) Dark being committed to the Inner London Sessions on a charge of larceny, for which he failed to surrender to bail and (b) the escape from Durham Prison of John Roger McVicar, an extremely violent individual then serving a 23-year sentence for robbery with violence, conspiracy to rob, assault on police and using firearms with intent to resist arrest. It was known that Dark and McVicar had been on the run together, and when Dark and Miss Hepburn were brought to Ilford police station, both were charged with harbouring McVicar between 26 January and 8 February 1969 and both were said to have admitted the offence. In addition, Dark was charged with the Ilford robbery and conspiracy to rob.

Prior to Dark's and McVicar's arrests, in a confidential report sent to the Under Secretary of State, Home Office, dated 30 June 1970, it was stated unequivocally, 'Both these men will strongly resist capture.'

In fact, this was not the case. No resistance was shown by Dark (nor was any displayed by McVicar during his subsequent arrest on 11 November 1970); but when violent criminals without immediate access to firearms are confronted by determined police officers who are pointing revolvers at the centre of their foreheads and who, the criminals believe, would like nothing better than to blow the living shit out of them, they do tend to come along peacefully.

*

Meanwhile, the suspects for the bank job had been pulled in, and now is as good a time as any to comment on Wickstead's interview techniques. Every male suspect was formally addressed as 'Mister'. This was not a courtesy; it was done to put up a fence between Wickstead and the suspect, each keeping to their own side of the boundary. There were no first name terms, no familiarity, no wheedling, none of the 'Look, Jimmy, why don't you tell us your side of the story?' used by many detectives. No, Wickstead's approach was unequivocal: 'Tell me what I want to know!' Hard and ruthless criminals were terrified of him. During this investigation, a well-known East End hard man was brought into Ilford police station. His fortitude deserted him when he was told that Wickstead was going to interview him; sobbing loudly, he had to be bodily carried up the stairs to the detective inspector's office, where his nemesis waited.

One of the suspects was Michael John Paul Green, identified by a Mr Baker, a messenger/cleaner employed by the bank, who saw him loitering outside prior to the raid. 'I thought he was watching the girls as they arrived', said Mr Baker, but since it appeared that the raid had been planned at Green's flat at Burnt Oak Broadway, Edgware, Baker was obviously mistaken as to Green's intentions. Moreover, £226 was found behind a clock in Green's living room, and when questioned he stated, 'If I go down for this, I'll get a lot of bird, won't I?' He then added, 'I'm in the first division now' – as indeed he was.

Wickstead rightly believed there was an inside man; fifty-three-year-old security guard Edward William McCarthy was pulled in, and £500 was found in a plastic bag at his home at Wilmot Street, Bethnal Green.

Tony Stevens and John Corner were both attached to the Flying Squad, and although Wickstead had grave reservations regarding the Squad, he knew Stevens to be trustworthy from their time at East Ham; he was therefore given the Wickstead seal of approval, and the two Squad officers were dispatched to arrest Arthur John Frederick Saunders. This was some three months after the robbery. Saunders had disappeared, although he had taken the precaution (as many innocent people do) of lodging a statement with his solicitor to the effect that if he was arrested he would not assist the police unless a solicitor was present. Because of information they had received, the officers went to Hendon police station, where Stevens asked the station officer to issue him with a firearm. He told me what happened next:

> He opened the safe and gave me a gun with five bullets. I asked him for six, with a spare clip but he insisted on five. When I asked him why, he said the empty chamber was in case of a mistake. He was quite insistent, and having resisted the impulse to call him a raving idiot I went upstairs and saw the superintendent, who rang down and instructed the station officer what the regulations were. When we got to Saunders' flat about lunchtime, he wasn't in, although I think his wife/girlfriend was. She said he would be back soon, so we plotted up in the corridor.

Eventually, he arrived slightly drunk and eating a bag of chips. I jumped out at him and lunch went up in the air. Of course, he said, 'I guess you can say I've had my chips', and at court the famous 'ripple ran round the court' when I gave evidence of this.

When we searched his flat, I found a Ford ignition key on the mantelpiece. I seized it because the getaway vehicle was a Ford van. Incredibly, the key fitted the ignition. When I gave evidence of this at the Bailey, much to my surprise, it wasn't disputed. I was sure it was going to be alleged that I planted it.

In addition, £1,000 was found in a cupboard (at the time, that represented a newly sworn-in police constable's annual salary), £103 in a bedroom and a further £141 in Saunders' pocket – and a black wig was also discovered at the house. And when Wickstead asked if he was on the robbery, Saunder's reply was, 'There's no point in saying "no", is there?' Later he added, 'Whatever I was doing, I didn't have a shooter.'

An open and shut case? It looked like it.

★

The prisoners appeared weekly at Barking Magistrates' Court to be remanded in custody until such time as they could be committed to the Old Bailey for trial. A prison van with motorcycle outriders, sirens wailing, would roar down East Street's one-way system, slow down to turn left into Clockhouse Avenue, then pull up opposite the municipal swimming baths at the rear of the court. On one such bumpy journey one of the prisoners was heard to remark, 'I should have brought my crash helmet with me!' Since crash helmets had figured prominently in the bank raid and had been recovered in the abandoned getaway van, this remark was recorded to be later recounted (and vociferously denied) in court.

Wickstead would arrive simultaneously, to be ambushed by a phalanx of press photographers. 'He was very self-centred; he wanted everybody to look at him all the time', I was told by John Woodhouse, who was then an aid to CID co-opted on to the enquiry. 'He was domineering; he liked that.'

At this time, I was a uniformed police constable stationed at Dagenham, and this media circus was thrilling stuff for me, as well as being unprecedented. Wickstead was treated by the court staff, the magistrates and the photographers as though he was a visiting film star. He took precedence over everybody in court; his case was dealt with first. Solicitors and barristers made hopeless attempts at bail.

'Why do you think my client would abscond, if he were to be granted bail?' asked one barrister.

"'Cos I know 'im', replied Wickstead shortly. He quite obviously felt that this answer was more than sufficient to satisfy the provisions of Section 105, Magistrates' Courts Act, 1952. Dorothy Revington JP ('The policeman's friend') certainly thought so, and in no time at all the prisoners were out of the dock and into the prison van. As Wickstead posed, smoke curling up from his cigarette, the photographers' flashbulbs popped once more, capturing the natty grey suiting, the paisley foulard tie, the silk breast pocket handkerchief and the physiognomy which depicted determination and dependability – then they were gone, sirens wailing, leaving the scent of diesel fumes and the expensive smell of detectives' aftershave lotion lingering in the air, permitting us lesser mortals to come back down to earth and carry on with our mundane task of prosecuting drunks and shoplifters.

*

The trial commenced at No. 2 Court at the Old Bailey on 12 October 1970 before Mr Justice Shaw, with John Matthew prosecuting eight defendants in the dock. To various charges of robbery, conspiracy to rob and receiving stolen money, five of the prisoners pleaded not guilty.

The trial had its moments. Ten days in, Lionel Thomas Herbert Jeffrey, aged twenty-five and unemployed, who had been identified as one of those who visited Green at his flat and who refused to tell police his movements on the morning of the robbery, was discharged when the judge stated that there was no evidence on which he could be convicted on charges of robbery and conspiracy. And Saunders' three alibi witnesses (two of whom came forward in an attempt to back up his assertion that on the morning of 9 February he was somewhere other than outside 144 High Street, Ilford) were later described as 'highly unsatisfactory' and unfortunately failed to convince the jury.

However, there were lighter moments as well, as when a defence witness of villainous aspect, who described himself as 'an accountant', admitted that he was, in fact, a turf accountant. And Sue Maudsley, a very attractive member of the 'J' Division Crime Squad co-opted on to the enquiry team, noticed that a couple of male members of the jury were smiling at her. It was not too long before this news reached Wickstead's ears.

'Sit in the front row, facing the jury', he growled and added, 'and wear your shortest skirt!'

Too apprehensive of Wickstead to do anything else, Miss Maudsley obeyed. 'I was terrified of Bert', she told me. 'He had pale green eyes; you never knew what he was thinking.'

It was difficult to know what the jury was thinking, given the vision of Miss Maudsley's shapely knees, but whatever the case, on 5 November 1970 Dark, Green and Saunders were among those convicted of the robbery and also conspiracy to rob Barclays Bank at Wanstead. Dark and Green (described by Mr Justice Shaw as being 'dangerous criminals') each received concurrent sentences of 18 and 10 years, with Saunders receiving 15 and 10 years.

Edward McCarthy who had been employed by Security Express, was sentenced to 6 years, his driver, twenty-seven-year-old Charles Bowman, received 3 years and Albert Walker, 4 years; all of them had pleaded guilty to conspiracy to rob.

George Gladwin, a thirty-seven-year-old scrap metal dealer from Hermitage Road, Upper Norwood, had asked members of the investigating team, 'Superintendent Wickstead doesn't think I did the blagging, did he?' He then enquired anxiously, 'Has someone's bottle gone?' He need not have worried; he was found not guilty of both robbery and conspiracy to rob and was discharged.

It was the conclusion of a case which was reported as having 'almost the tightest security the Old Bailey had known.'

★

Three months later, the trial commenced of Barbara Hepburn and two others, on charges of conspiracy to obstruct the course of justice by assisting Ronnie Dark to evade arrest. By now she had moved from the opulence of Edgerley House to the more modest surroundings of Clapton. She was acquitted of dishonestly handling money, the proceeds of the robbery, but was found guilty on the conspiracy charge and sentenced to 2 years' imprisonment. No action was taken against her (or Ronnie Dark) on a charge of harbouring John McVicar, and then nine months into her sentence, the Court of Appeal substituted her 2-year sentence with one which would facilitate her immediate release. Mind you, with the amount of time she had spent in custody on remand, plus the actual time served, she would probably have been due for release on parole in any event.

So with some of the robbers locked up, although only some £3,000 had been recovered, that would appear to have been that

– except for two matters. First, Wickstead was seven robbers short. Second, a very curious matter would soon start to unravel.

*

Many of the top-line armed robbers of the 1970s kept themselves in peak physical condition; Ronnie Dark certainly did. (In fact, when detectives visited him in the cells following his conviction they found him doing punishing press-ups.) It made sense, because robbers' demeanour had to change suddenly from inactivity, as a result of several hours watching and waiting, into barely controlled aggression. Within seconds they had to be ready to shoot, cosh or in any other way neutralize their victims, and in order to do so they had to move very quickly and aggressively indeed. An exception was one prolific bank robber who was short and fat, balding, with lank hair and a droopy moustache; he also drank and smoked too much, suffered from a boil on his nose and easily got out of breath. His name was Derek Creighton Smalls and he was known to his fast diminishing number of friends as 'Bertie'.

Smalls had been a member of 'The Wembley Mob', who had been responsible for twenty-one armed robberies which had netted them £1,288,031. But following their last successful raid in July 1972 some of the gang were arrested, and the evidence was starting to stack up against them. Smalls had kept a low profile but he was arrested just prior to Christmas 1972. Within a month he was talking to detectives of 'doing a deal' – and the deal finally agreed on was that he would implicate everybody who had ever been involved in 'a bit of business' with him, commit his accusations to paper and then stand up in court and give evidence against them. The price for his cooperation was simple: he wanted his freedom. For the first and what would be the only – time in the British criminal justice system, he got it.

Appearing at Harrow Magistrates' Court on 3 April 1973, it became clear that Smalls was going to be the prime prosecution witness against 'The Wembley Mob'; and although several of that gang made a spirited but short-lived escape from Brixton Prison, this only resulted in their receiving an additional twelve months' imprisonment on top of their very impressive sentences of up to 22 years – in all, they got 308 years' imprisonment. So Smalls walked free, although he had participated in the armed raids, one of which had been at the Ilford branch of Barclays Bank on 9 February 1970.

Smalls would later say that in January 1970 he and others discussed carrying out a robbery at Barclays Bank, Wanstead. He said that present at the meeting had been Anthony Edlin, James

William Jeffrey and Bruce Brown (all of whom were later acquitted of the conspiracy), plus Michael Green, Ronnie Dark and Albert Walker. According to Walker, two Security Express guards were lined up to supply the information necessary to carry out a successful robbery. However, the robbery was called off at the last moment because the security van had pulled up too close to the door of the bank. There followed a further meeting with the two guards at which the possibility of robbing Barclays Bank at Ilford was debated. Smalls said that he and eight others participated in the raid; he was right. The first three to go into the bank were Bruce Brown (21 years' imprisonment), who wore a ginger wig and glasses and carried ammonia, Bryan James Turner (21 years' imprisonment), wearing a dark wig and glasses, also armed with ammonia, and Michael Henry Salmon (22 years' imprisonment), who had a stick-on moustache and who, Smalls said, 'looked like a city gent and was armed with a sawn-off shotgun'. Describing the raid, Smalls stated:

> Five of us remained in the van, not far from the bank. A man named Short was to block the road, in case there was any trouble in the getaway. I had a shotgun and in the van was a sledgehammer. I also carried a 12ft ladder to get over the counter but by the time we got to the bank, it was all over and the guards were on the floor. It was not yet necessary to use the sledgehammer. We just picked up the sacks of money. One shot was fired outside the bank and the shotgun went off accidentally in the van, narrowly missing my foot.

In addition, Donald Walter Barrett would later be convicted of the robbery, as would Robert Alles King; they were sentenced to 17 years and 16 years' imprisonment respectively. Following the raid, most of the gang (including the man Short, referred to above, who never stood trial with the others) disappeared to Spain – their approximate share-out was £20,000 each – until the next recorded robbery, which did not occur until September 1970.

There was one matter arising out of this: in naming names, Smalls had neglected to identify Arthur John Frederick Saunders as attending the conspiracy to rob Barclays Bank, Wanstead or the actual robbery at Barclays Bank, Ilford. The reason was simple; Saunders, Smalls stated categorically, had not been present at either event.

★

'Britain's Biggest Post-War Bank Robbery'

It was not sufficient for Smalls to make a statement to police exonerating Saunders. In a matter as highly charged as this the statement had to be obtained by commission on oath before Lord Justice James on 10 October 1973; and the following day, at the Court of Appeal before the Lord Chief Justice, Lord Widgery, Lord Justice James and Mr Justice Geoffrey Lane, Saunders' conviction was quashed. It was held that although he had not positively admitted his involvement with the robbery, 'there was a notable absence of any positive denial', and this, thought their Lordships, was due to the fact – as Tony Stevens mentioned to me, over 40 years later – that at the time of his arrest and interview, he had been drinking.

As the Lord Chief Justice stated, 'Many of his answers were equivocal and were such as would not lie readily in the mouth of an innocent man who might have been expected to assert his innocence much more positively.'

John Mathew for the Crown said, 'There was a distinct possibility that the appellant was convicted not so much because the prosecution had a strong case but because the appellant's own witnesses had let him down in some degree and the case against him got stronger, all the time until the evidence was concluded.'

So Saunders tottered from court a free man and one who had, of course, been totally innocent from the outset. No trace of blame was attached to Wickstead; in fact, the Court of Appeal inferred that Saunders' incarceration had been his own silly fault.

John Short, referred to above, did not resurface in the United Kingdom until 1978, when he was charged with a number of robberies, including the one at Barclays Bank, Ilford. By now Smalls was forty-two years of age, settled into his 'retirement', living under a false name and steadily upping his consumption of vodka. Could he – would he - give evidence about Short's alleged involvement? Happily, it was never put to the test; Short pleaded guilty to other robbery charges and was sentenced to 21 years' imprisonment; the Ilford robbery charge was allowed to 'remain on the file', and justice, once more, was satisfied. Smalls managed to live on for another thirty years before dying 'of natural causes' in January 2008.

Micky Green was released in 1980 and remained a thorn in the side of the authorities in Britain, Poland, France, Morocco, Holland and Eire. His name has been linked to gold bullion and drug-smuggling plots. The French sentenced him to 17 years' imprisonment in his absence, he is said to be worth £50m and is currently believed to be in Spain. Of course, he might not be.

Ronnie Dark was paroled in 1979 but within a few years he was involved in a VAT tax fraud with a gang of gold swindlers who made £6m. When it came to sentencing, there was an adjournment so that Customs & Excise might determine where the proceeds of the fraud were. Some money was recovered, but £2m had mysteriously disappeared from a branch of Switzerland's Credit Suisse bank.

In 1983 six people were jailed and massively fined, and all but two of them had bankruptcy orders made. Dark, now living in Preston Road, Wembley, was one of the two and the only one of the six to plead guilty. He also received the lightest sentence: twelve months' imprisonment and a fine of £3,000 with six months to pay. Upon his release, it's thought he moved to Spain.

*

Five years after Saunders' successful appeal, the Flying Squad was mainly devolved from the Yard, split into four geographically defined offices within the Metropolitan Police area and tasked to deal with all offences of armed robbery, to the exclusion of any other crimes. No longer were outsiders such as Wickstead permitted to investigate allegations of robbery within their own patch.

However, fifty is not a good age to start in armed robbery as a profession. That was Arthur John Frederick Saunders' age in 1986 when he and several other gentlemen in the autumn of their years were being kept under observation by the Flying Squad and were arrested for an attempted armed robbery in London's Baker Street. Caught in the act, this time their convictions stood. It was probably a coincidence that Saunders was sentenced, once again, to 15 years' imprisonment.

CHAPTER 5

Birth of the Serious Crime Squad – The Dixons

Even before Wickstead's appointment as detective chief superintendent of 'J' Division, events occurred which would shape his future – and that of the world of organized criminality – to an unprecedented extent.

On 8 June 1966 the Richardson Torture Gang had received swingeing sentences to mark their depredations, including 25 years' imprisonment for elder brother Charlie, who liked to gloatingly preside at mock courts where those who had incurred his displeasure 'stood trial'. Those who – in his opinion – had transgressed would be beaten, have their toes broken and their teeth pulled out with pliers. Younger brother Eddie received consecutive sentences (including being convicted of the Mr Smith's Club affray) amounting to 15 years; Roy Hall, who enthusiastically cranked a generator to provide violent electric shocks to the victims' genitals, was sentenced to 10 years; and 'Mad Frankie' Fraser, who gleefully did anything that Charlie directed (plus providing some inventive ideas of his own), went down for a total of 15 years. A potpourri of lesser fry, for a miscellany of blackmail, robbery, conspiracy to pervert the course of justice and inflicting grievous bodily harm with intent, received sentences varying from 8 years' to eighteen months' imprisonment.

That was followed on 5 March 1969 by Ronnie Kray being found guilty of two gangland murders and brother Reggie, of one murder. Telling them, 'Society has earned a rest from your activities', the trial judge sentenced them to life imprisonment with a recommendation that they serve 30 years. Four of their accomplices to murder also received life sentences, and their brother Charlie and Freddie Foreman were both sentenced to 10 years after being convicted of being accessories to murder, as was Cornelius Whitehead, who went down for 7 years. Like the Richardson gang, some of 'The Kray Firm' went down for lesser offences which merited eighteen months' imprisonment.

In less than three years the Richardsons and the Krays, who practically ran villainy in South and East London respectively, had been smashed up. That this had been achieved was due to dedicated bands of detectives run by Assistant Chief Constable

Gerald McArthur MBE, QPM in the case of the Richardsons, and Detective Superintendent Leonard 'Nipper' Read (later Assistant Chief Constable Read QPM) in respect of the Krays.

But as can be imagined, the removal of these two families left a vacuum of criminality just waiting to be filled by up-and-coming gangs. Some of their members had known, worked with or clashed with the Richardsons and the Krays. They had their own bits and pieces of criminality which they had carried out under the shadow of the Richardsons' combination of smart business acumen and ferocity or the Krays' psychotic use of terror, but now, of course, those they once saw as the frightening opposition were out of the way, languishing in high-security jails.

It was time to fill that gap. Who was there to stop them? Not McArthur; he had retired. Not Read; he had been royally shafted by the jealous senior officers on the 5th floor at Scotland Yard, and when unsuitable officers were promoted before him, he left the Met and joined Nottinghamshire Constabulary – but not before submitting a report to the Home Office suggesting, in the strongest possible terms, that a permanent squad be set up to confront, smash up and prosecute to conviction the criminals who sought to fill the void left by those two major gangs.

Those at the Home Office who decide these matters are not police officers; in many cases these civil servants are frightened souls, wondering if the decisions which they make might rebound on them and foil any future advancement. It happened in 1945 when what became known as 'The Ghost Squad' was formed; the officials grudgingly permitted just four officers to form this highly secretive squad to battle post-war crime but added the corollary that the increase in manpower was 'provisional only and will be subject to review at the end of next year when a further report should be submitted'. Worse was the newly appointed Metropolitan Police Commissioner, Sir Harold Scott, fresh from the ranks of the Civil Service, who nervously stated that the scheme was 'worth a trial' but added, 'its value should be kept under close review'. He need not have worried; in its four year existence, the Ghost Squad was a resounding success and the faceless men of Whitehall, plus the equally colourless Sir Harold, breathed a sigh of relief; he was soon able to add a GCVO and a KCB to his KBE.[1]

So it was in the case of the birth of the Serious Crime Squad (SCS). It was formed on 29 March 1971 as part of C1 Department

---

1 For more details of this secret unit, see *Scotland Yard's Ghost Squad*, Wharncliffe Books, 2011.

Birth of the Serious Crime Squad – The Dixons

at the Yard. Its brief was 'to combat organized crime carried out by known, professional criminals'. Wickstead was offered the job and naturally seized this opportunity with both hands.

The Commissioner, Sir John Lovegrove Waldron KCVO, had become a stop-gap leader following the unexpected death of Sir Joseph Simpson KBE in 1968 – at the time of the formation of the SCS, the Force was reeling from the revelations of police corruption as a result of *The Times* enquiry, and by the time he retired the following year, what with even more (and just as damaging) allegations about police misconduct, Sir John was glad to go. How much assistance he provided to Wickstead is debatable – certainly, not very much. Because having appointed the best man for the job to smash up the gangs of London, the commissioner and the civil servants must have felt they had nobly discharged their responsibilities.

By comparison, the Ghost Squad were well off; they had been given an office and a car. Wickstead had nothing; no office, no transport and no staff.

*

Nevertheless, there was one man Wickstead wanted immediately. This was Detective Sergeant Bill Waite, a much commended veteran of the Regional Crime Squad but more importantly, someone who had worked on both the Richardson and Kray enquiries; moreover, his card index with a cross referencing of all the major players, their associates and girlfriends, was immaculate. Nowadays, such information can be retrieved from a computer in seconds, but believe me, Bill Waite could have given any computer a run for its money.

He would be absolutely indispensable to the smooth running of the SCS. Grey of hair and ruddy of cheek, Waite drove an immaculate and ancient pale green Rover 90 and lived quietly with his invalid wife in a police flat in Richmond, Surrey; his gangbusting abilities would later be rewarded with a British Empire Medal.

Wickstead sat down with 'Mr Memory' (as Waite was known) to sort out suitable targets for the SCS, but really there was only one. They had mixed with the Krays and were known to be hardmen enforcers. They were the Dixon brothers.

Following his demobilization from the army in 1947, Sergeant 5835081 Wickstead had been put on reserve in the event of hostilities until 10 September 1952, but that time had long passed. He was now going to start his own private war

*

Members of a family of eight children, the oldest was George Kitchener Dixon, born in 1941 in Limehouse's East End Chinatown. Alan John Derek arrived the following year, and in 1944 brother Brian Thomas was born. They gained a well-deserved reputation as street-fighters; and if there were no other contenders available, George and Alan would fight each other.

When George Dixon was sixteen he became a member of the Regal Snooker Club in Mile End and met the owners of the club, Reg and Ron Kray. He was described by Reg Kray as being 'a very tall kid with very powerful shoulders, and a very good looking kid', and Reg went on to praise his abilities as a fighter.

During the early 1960s John Griffith was a probationary police constable at Limehouse and recalled the Dixon family living in a prefab, practically opposite the police station. He remembered the brothers hanging out with other youths of the same age, occasionally getting into minor trouble. A surprising recollection was arresting George one night for being drunk and disorderly.

'He didn't cause me any trouble,' Griffith told me, 'and when he was sitting in the charge room, "Big Jim" Carrol was the station officer and when he (George) saw him he started to cry!'

Perhaps this was a case of alcoholic remorse. In and out of trouble with the law, the Dixons ran protection rackets in the area and, for a percentage, collected money from bad debtors. Sometimes a harsh word was sufficient; at other times more punitive methods were necessary. George and Cornelius Whitehead were acquitted of grievous bodily harm on a club owner who, it was said, resisted efforts to have his club 'looked after'.

There was another confrontation with the law in 1963, during the investigation into the murder of prostitute Gwynneth Rees, aka Tina Smart. She was the lover of armed robber Micky Calvey, and whilst he was on remand, Rees was threatened and assaulted by a gang who thought she would be better employed accruing money for his defence rather than providing for her baby. From the description given, it was thought that the leader of the gang who had been wielding a chopper was George Dixon, but this he denied when he was interviewed by police.

He admitted he knew her but told the police, 'I was always on friendly terms with Tina and at no time have I ever threatened or slapped her.'[2]

---

2 For further details of this case, see *Laid Bare: The Nude Murders and the Hunt for Jack the Stripper*, The History Press, 2016.

Someone whom George did 'slap' was Ronnie Kray in the twins' 'Double R' club where, according to the East End hard man Micky Fawcett, 'Ronnie was punching him like mad.'

The confrontation ended when George was thrown out into the street; but interestingly, although Ronnie Kray had launched the unprovoked attack, it appeared that George Dixon was perfectly happy to engage in a one-to-one fight with Ronnie, although he may well have been put off by the number of Kray supporters in the club. Again according to Fawcett, when Reggie Kray got in a fight with an associate of George Dixon's, Fawcett took the opportunity to cut George in the face; that accounted for one of his ferocious looking scars.

Painful though that encounter certainly was, a far more frightening meeting occurred at the twins' Regency Club after George asked Ronnie to sort out a disagreement with a rival gang; George was told to stay out of the way and the matter would be resolved. But according to Fawcett, George didn't stay out of the way; he arrived at the club with a companion. It was clear that this piece of *lèse-majesté* would have to be addressed, and Ronnie casually strolled out of the room and into the toilets, where he had secreted an automatic pistol. He emerged running, put the pistol to George's head and pulled the trigger; there was a misfire and, as members of the entourage held the raving Ronnie down, George fled. According to Kray folklore, Ronnie later presented him with the dud cartridge, saying, 'That bullet saved your life' and suggesting he put it on a chain around his neck. It might be true.

Teddy Berry had fought nineteen professional bouts as a lightweight and won them all, seven by knockouts. The son of Harry 'Kid' Berry, who as a featherweight had won forty of his sixty-eight bouts, Teddy was highly respected and had coached the Kray twins during their brief professional boxing careers. His brother Henry (known as 'Checker'), who was a boyhood friend of Ronnie Kray, had also boxed, although Checker's career in the ring amounted to just one professional fight that lasted six rounds and which he lost. The brothers teamed up with George and Alan Dixon and, as Fawcett recalled, 'started to throw their weight about' at a drinking club named the Senate Rooms. There had been a fight and the amalgamation between the two sets of brothers ended when someone arrived with a shotgun – possibly Ronnie Kray during one of his more deranged periods – and blew off one of Teddy's legs.

Next, according to Reggie Kray, it was George Dixon's turn to be peppered in the legs with a shotgun, and then Alan Dixon was warned off by the twins' lieutenant, Albert Donoghue. Dixon had been terrorizing customers at the Regency Club, although just prior to Donoghue's death in a Dagenham care home in 2016 he was visited by Alan Dixon, who stated in a newspaper interview, 'He was always a nice man to me, he was always a gentleman. We all knew where we stood with him.'

It appeared that the brothers also knew where they stood with a certain Phil Snooks, who had a vehicle workshop in Coburn Road, Bow. Alan Brooks, then a police constable in plain clothes, was talking to Snooks outside his workshop when from the direction of the Morgan Arms came the Dixon brothers.

'They saw Phil and immediately crossed the road so as not to walk past him', Brooks told me. '"I'm not frightened of them", Phil said, "and they know it".'

But the Dixon brothers' fortunes changed when they joined forces with the diminutive Philly Jacobs, known as 'Little Caesar'. As a wedding present in 1965, Jacobs' in-laws bought him the Ship public house in Aylward Street, Stepney, and he prospered; he acquired three more pubs and it was the Plough and Harrow at Leytonstone which George Dixon minded. This was because the Kray twins had tried to 'nip' Jacobs for a share of the pub's profits. One can only speculate about the outcome, had there been a direct confrontation between the twins, the Dixons and their associates; but before the Dixons could go on Ronnie Kray's 'hit-list', the twins were arrested. It was under Jacobs' tutelage that the Dixon brothers expanded their interests, not only in protection but also in long-firm fraud.

For those unaware of the term, a long-firm fraud was a scam very popular in the 1960s and '70s. A premises would be rented and then domestic goods, televisions, refrigerators and washing machines, would be ordered from the distributors; as soon as the goods arrived, they would be paid for instantly. The orders would then get bigger and bigger, with payment still being made immediately, thereby establishing confidence, until finally one huge order would be given to all the distributors. The items would then be sold to the public at rock-bottom prices and those fronting the business would disappear. The distributors would not care to immediately press the 'company' for the money owed because they had been such good customers in the past, and to send sternly worded final demands might jeopardise future business. So months would often pass before the distributors realized they had been conned, and investigation by the police might take considerably longer. It was a con much favoured by both the Richardsons and the Krays when they diversified from impaling their adversaries' feet to the floor or branding them with red-hot pokers.

Birth of the Serious Crime Squad – The Dixons

On 28 May 1971 two of the Dixons' associates, Michael Bailey and Michael John Young, had staged a fight in the bar of the Greyhound pub at 32 Old Ford Road, Bethnal Green; it was a classic set-up to let the licensee know that protection was needed in order to stop customers vanishing – 130 departed that night. When two off-duty police sergeants tried to intervene they were arrogantly told it was no concern of theirs and that, in any event, their detective inspector would be informed of their reprehensible conduct.

This 'softening-up' of publicans became commonplace. Fights were arranged and then the gang would move in, saying, 'Would you like us to make sure you don't have any more bulls[3] in your pub? We'll look after you for 50 quid a week.'

With Philly Jacobs driving around in his Rolls-Royce with a personalized number plate, George Dixon was heard to say, 'We are the Dixon brothers', and one of the hangers-on added, 'We've taken over from the Krays.' It looked as though they had.

It appeared that Wickstead might be up against the same wall of silence that 'Nipper' Read had found when he had gone after the Krays, but all investigators need a breakthrough to open up their cans of worms. For Read it was Leslie Payne, the twins' financial advisor. In Wickstead's case it took the form of the very large and menacing Michael Patrick Flynn, the Dixons' fellow enforcer – and also their brother-in-law.

Flynn came to see Wickstead; he had been married to the Dixons' youngest sister, Lynne, but their separation had caused a rift with the brothers. According to Flynn, the Dixons had retaliated by threatening one of Flynn's sisters and breaking the arm of another, although the Dixons' version was that Flynn had given Lynne a beating and that they were going to take revenge on him. Whatever the circumstances, Flynn was now willing to give evidence against his in-laws, which suited Wickstead down to the ground.

What he had to tell Wickstead was this: the manager of the popular Bee Gees pop group was experiencing trouble with someone who was trying to muscle in on the act; the Dixons were called in and took Flynn along with them. George and Alan Dixon were big, but Flynn was even bigger – a character full of menace. Tony Stevens told me:

> I recall Micky Flynn, he was a deep sea diver on the oil rigs. He was a big lad and very fit but a bit of a gentle

---

3 Cockney rhyming slang: bull and cow = row

giant. George Dixon used him to intimidate people. He told us that he went with George to see the manager of the Bee Gees who wanted someone warned off who was trying to move in on him. Flynn's role was to sit there and say nothing until George gave him the nod and then to say, 'What d'you want – an arm off, a leg off or both?' When we interviewed the Bee Gees manager later, he said he didn't know what it did to the other man but Flynn frightened him to death. The manager had no further trouble so it apparently worked.

Having seen off the opposition, the Dixons then decided to launch a takeover bid themselves.

Wickstead now had a blueprint for the Dixons' arrest; what he did not have was accommodation or manpower. The first he solved by moving into vacant offices in Tintagel House, a Metropolitan Police establishment but one quite separate from Scotland Yard since it was situated on the south bank of the Thames; it had previously been used by both McArthur and Read during their investigations.

Next, Wickstead visited the office of the one-time detective, Deputy Assistant Commissioner Harold William Hudson OBE, only to find him hog-tied by red tape and the rules of the establishment; he turned Wickstead down flat when he asked for officers to staff the newly-formed SCS. Wickstead therefore asked if he could borrow some, and Hudson agreed to two from the Flying Squad. In fact, this was a case of history repeating itself; it was how the Sweeney had its first twelve officers when it was formed in 1919, and it would continue to 'borrow' officers for the next ten years.

Wickstead, as we know, was not enamoured of the Flying Squad, but he knew who he wanted: Tony Stevens and John Corner, who had been so useful to him during the Ilford bank robbery investigation; they were the first to arrive.

Next was John Farley, who had broken the back of the Skinner investigation six years previously. He had been posted to C1 Department at the Yard and was having a difficult time in the Arts & Antiques section with one of the senior officers.

'I just happened to meet Bert who was with John Corner at King's Cross', he told me. 'I told him of my troubles and he said, "Leave it to me". Within a week, I was posted on to Bert's squad.'

Gerry Runham was another officer who was part of the C1 network. 'I was on immigration with Derek Robinson', he recalled. 'Bert came along and said, "I need a couple of blokes to help me out" so we went for a couple of weeks and stayed for three years.'

Birth of the Serious Crime Squad – The Dixons

Runham had a high opinion of Wickstead's abilities: 'He had a fantastic memory; he could speed-read a book in a couple of days and retain it.'

'I was a second-hand DS (i.e. a detective sergeant, second-class) on the Company Fraud Squad when I was selected to join the SCS when it was inaugurated', Bernie Tighe told me. 'It comprised Bert W., one Detective Superintendent 'Taff' Williams, DI Ken Tolbart and eight sergeants, including myself. I was there to deal with any bogus companies, Long Firm frauds, et al'. He also recalled Micky Flynn: 'He was a tall, good-looking chap, always polite and would have made a good snout, if developed.'

Gerry Wiltshire, perhaps rather surprisingly, came to the squad. Bob Robinson explains this anomaly:

> Bert came to Dalston as a first-class. Gerry and I were DCs there and we used to have lunch in a café at Islington Green but because discipline was strict, we had to make sure we were back in time. On one occasion, we got back to the office in good time, but a uniform skipper came up and said there was a prisoner in the cells. Gerry said, 'I'll deal with him' and went downstairs without booking back on the duty slate. When he got back to the CID office, Bert had written in the duty book, 'WHERE ARE YOU?' Gerry, who was a bit fiery, grabbed hold of Bert by his tie, had him up against the wall and told him, 'Get off my fucking back!' I was one of those who pulled Gerry off him.

Perhaps Gerry Wiltshire had earned Wickstead's respect by standing up to him, but being one of his men was not without its pitfalls. Clearly no respecter of persons of whatever rank, Wickstead strode down the Yard's 5th floor corridor, which contained some of the most senior officers of the Metropolitan Police.

'Where are you off to, in such a hurry, Bert?' called out Deputy Assistant Commissioner Bernard 'Doc' Halliday OBE, genially.

'Mind yer own fucking business!' growled Wickstead, and Detective Sergeant Gerry Wiltshire, trailing along in Wickstead's wake, shamefacedly muttered, 'Morning, Guv!' to the outraged DAC.

Worse, Wiltshire attended a selection board that afternoon for the rank of first-class detective sergeant; unfortunately, one of the board members was DAC Halliday, and neither Wiltshire (nor anybody else who had heard of Wickstead's jaw-dropping rudeness during that morning's encounter) was particularly surprised when he failed to be selected.

Now the investigations got underway. Bernard Stringer, a dubious character with a long criminal record, complained that Michael Bailey had attacked him. He had once been an associate of Philly Jacobs, but the two men had fallen out and now the Dixons were after him; they found him at the Rebellion nightclub in Ilford. He was badly beaten, and it was possibly only the presence of his eight-year-old daughter which precluded more serious consequences.

'Bernie Stringer was a little rat of a man, lived in Harold Hill and did car repair work', Tony Stevens told me. 'Johnny Nicholson lived at that time in a block of flats overlooking West Ham Stadium. He later moved to Harold Hill. He had worked as a Long Firm fraudsman a bit in his youth. One of my jobs was to look after Stringer, Nicholson and Flynn, keep them happy and make sure they weren't threatened. John Corner was with me on this, for part of the time.'

In fact, Nicholson had run a fraudulent business in Wimbledon and it was his partner, a man named Brennan, from whom Leon Carleton – the owner of the Rebellion Club – had tried to extort £4,000 as the price of his silence, telling him, 'I have so many friends in the police that I'm called "Mr Scotland Yard".'

It was Bernie Tighe who dealt with the investigation into Wimbledon. 'I think Brennan lived in the Medway area', he recalled, adding, 'Bernie Stringer was as slippery as a barrelful of eels.'

When information was received that Stringer was going to be attacked again at the Rebellion, Wickstead and his men put in an appearance at the club, where he first met Leon Carleton. The Dixon brothers did not appear on that occasion, and although Carleton would later say that Stringer had threatened him (this could well have been true) he had warned Stringer, 'If you ever laid a finger on me, you would be nicked. Don't you understand? I *am* Scotland Yard.'

Bribes were surreptitiously offered to the officers and veiled threats were made, but over a period of just a few months witnesses were seen, assurances given and statements obtained; and then something happened which I assure you wasn't my fault. Somebody should have been manning the telephone at the Tintagel office; but they weren't.

★

BW on duty outside Loughton police station.

Army Days

In Ceylon

Boxing in Coco, Ceylon

Ceylon – BW seated, far right

Police Career

Peel House, Hendon, June 1948. BW 2nd row, 2nd right as Police Constable 793 'TS'.

Attending the Senior Course, Detective Training School, 7 March 1964. BW, a D/S on 'G' Division, 2nd row, 2nd left.

Interior of Fasanenstrasse Synagogue, Berlin, following Kristallnacht

Two members of The 62 Group

(*Above left*) Gerry Gable

(*Above right*) Harry Bidney

Members of the National Socialist Movement

(*Above left*) John Tyndall

(*Above right*) Françoise Dior marries Colin Jordan.

Françoise Jordan leaves court.

BW and Stan Clegg (right) make an arrest.

BW, Terry Brown (centre) and Stan Clegg (right) leave court having been commended.

Tintagel House

Limehouse police station

The Ilford Bank Robbery

(*Above*) Edgerley House, purchased by Ronnie Dark, following the robbery.

(*Left*) Bertie Smalls (centre) who provided evidence.

From mid-June to mid-July 1971 I was posted on the 'Kilo one-two' 'Q'-car with Detective Sergeant Bob Henderson and the driver, Police Constable Johnny Gray. During that one-month period, during which we achieved a creditable number of arrests – thirty-seven – one evening, we were called into Romford police station. Information had been received that there was going to be a confrontation between a scrap metal dealer and the Dixon brothers in the car park of the Moby Dick public house, situated at the junction of Whalebone Lane North, Dagenham and the Eastern Avenue. The dealer had been warned to stay away, and since it was known that Wickstead had a keen interest in the brothers, his office had been telephoned – but alas, it was unmanned.

Therefore action had to be taken – fast. We drove down to the pub and parked up, lights off, and it was not too long before a large American-style limousine arrived. The vehicle was blocked in, the doors opened and the occupants removed. They were Brian Challenger, an overweight fraudsman who suffered from claustrophobia, Robert Lazarus, related to a boxing family – and Alan Dixon. 'You're 'aving a larf, ain't yer?' he exclaimed, but with the finding of an offensive weapon in the car we assured him that was not the case and, protesting loudly, they were conveyed to Dagenham police station. They were later joined by George, scowling and looking extremely menacing, complete with solicitor, but although there was no evidence to connect him with the other three, they were charged with possessing an offensive weapon and conspiracy to assault.

The three prisoners were pretty unhappy, as was Wickstead; after all, we had stolen his thunder, and our arrival at Barking Magistrates' Court the following morning in no way replicated Wickstead's orchestrated appearances at the same court one year previously with the Ilford bank robbers. But we had been presented with a fait accompli, we had done our best to alert him the previous evening, without success. Nevertheless, the trio was granted bail, I went on to a fresh 'Q'-Car tour and Wickstead made his arrangements for his grand round-up early on the morning of 25 August 1971.

*

The briefing took place at 4.00 am; Wickstead had utilized twenty-nine Flying Squad officers, plus sixty more from the Fraud Squad, Criminal Intelligence, Divisional CID and the uniform branch. After the briefing was concluded, the officers dispersed to their targets for synchronized arrests at 5.30 am.

It has been inaccurately recorded that the briefing took place at 4.00 pm the previous day, that only twenty-nine Flying Squad officers were involved and that, by inference, it was the Squad who leaked details of the raid to both the *Evening Standard* and the criminals. This is nonsense.

Firstly, it transcends belief that Wickstead (or indeed anybody else) would have divulged his plans to arrest a large gang of criminals to a group of strangers, 13½ hours before implementation. Next, Wickstead was obsessively secretive, as confirmed by Betty Shimell, the widow of Detective Chief Superintendent Bill Shimell, who told me, 'I do remember Bill was laughing to himself and said he had a new Guv'nor called Wickstead who insisted on keeping his office door locked. As Bill said, "Such a waste of time, locking and unlocking an office door".' It's true, this practice was practically unheard of.

Thirdly, it's far more likely that it was Wickstead, with his love of self-aggrandisement, who had personally leaked the story to the press, and when those arrested sarcastically commented that the officers were 'late in arriving' there are two explanations for that. First, this is a very common ploy used by criminals to suggest that they knew they were going to be arrested since (a) the detectives were not as clever as they thought and (b) that by inference they were tipped off by a bent cop.

In fact, the explanation is far simpler; it was an open secret that Wickstead was after the Dixons. As I've already explained, as a very junior aid to CID I knew about the enquiry at least one month prior to the arrests, and nobody from the investigation team had told me. When the round-up took place, one or two escaped the net – and believe me, that's often the case. Therefore it suited Wickstead to blame 'a rogue cop' for spilling the beans.

Ten people were arrested (two of them were later released) and interviewed at City Road police station. When George Dixon was questioned about the bogus fight which had occurred at the Greyhound pub, he replied, 'It was only a joke; we never got anything' and when Wickstead interviewed him, he said, 'When the twins went away, I knew others would get nicked. I will only get fifteen months for all you can prove.' He added, 'Nobody is going to stand against me; I don't think anybody will give evidence against me.'

It sounded suspiciously like bravado; Gerry Runham told me, 'I think George was terrified of Bert.'

Alan, ever the comedian, told Wickstead, 'Alright, Guv'nor, I'll admit it – we've been naughty boys. But surely you don't have to grind us down, just because we knew the twins?'

The questioning did not take long; they were charged that evening and appeared at Old Street Magistrates' Court the following day; there were charges of conspiracies to cause grievous bodily harm, to blackmail and to cheat and defraud, and they were remanded in custody.

The committal to the Old Bailey took place some 2½ months later, and by now, the eight prisoners had increased to twelve. Gerry Runham took charge; he was responsible for dealing with the smooth running of the exhibits, documents and witnesses. Charges against Michael Bailey of making an unwarranted demand with menaces against Stanley William Davies and against George Dixon of stealing an air rifle and oil were dismissed. Three men – John Thomas Tuffen, Ronald Schwartz and Brian Benjamin Dove – accused of conspiracy to cheat and defraud were given bail, in the sums of £2,000, £6,000 and £15,000 respectively. Everybody else was committed for trial, in custody.

The trial commenced on 12 April 1972 before Mr Justice O'Connor – a hard-line judge, who six years previously had presided over the Richardson conspiracy to pervert trial. Opening for the Crown, Michael Corkery QC told the court:

> This is a story about an area of East London where the infamous Kray brothers and their associates once held sway, where violence and extortion marched hand in hand. Although the Krays and most of their associates have been removed from circulation, violence and threats of violence have continued in the area, albeit on a smaller scale. The victims in the present case are mainly people who have been in trouble with the police and who do not readily complain about the treatment they receive. They do not want the limelight of giving evidence in a trial because of the risk to themselves and their families.

It was a no-holds-barred trial, with allegations of police verbals and in which some of the prisoners, in exchange for no evidence being offered against them, crossed over from the dock to the witness box. Micky Flynn, Johnny Nicholson and Bernie Stringer all gave evidence for the prosecution. Leon Carleton had stated that he had tape recordings which related to Bernie Stringer; these were played in court. However, he also claimed that he had recordings of Wickstead which proved conclusively that he had taken bribes; but he didn't, and Wickstead hadn't. Asked about the assault on Bernie Stringer, Philly Jacobs told the officers, 'He was taking a liberty and had to be seen to.' Others were acquitted; Brian Dixon who had been charged with conspiracy to blackmail and Lambert 'Lammy' Jacobs, the brother of Philly Jacobs, both walked free from court.

Alan Dixon's sense of humour was put to the test (and was not found wanting) when Michael Corkery QC for the prosecution asked him why he had gone up to the office of the Bee Gees manager.

'It was a wind-up, Guv'nor', replied Dixon. Asked to explain the expression, Dixon replied, 'Well, put it this way. If I told you there were four birds outside this court who'd go through the card for you – and you went outside and there wasn't four birds or, if there was, they didn't go through the card for you – well, that'd be a wind-up!'

Unsurprisingly, this caused a great deal of merriment in court, although it was jollity in which the judge did not participate. The same sense of humour failure applied to seven members of the gang when they were found guilty of a number of serious offences on 4 July 1972.

Taking the witness box for the last time, Wickstead told the court that George Dixon had numerous convictions dating back to 1958 and that he talked about the Kray twins and used that as a weapon to instil fear in others. Philip Jacobs, he said, was 'an organizer and leader', but Wickstead reserved his bile for his *bête-noir*, Leon Carleton. He was shrewd and dangerous, said Wickstead, and he traded on the reputation that he was a 'fixer' of police officers; then he added, just for good measure, that Carleton was a police informant.

Passing sentence, Mr Justice O'Connor said:

> It has been established without any room for doubt whatever that you men, all with criminal records, operated as a gang engaged in serious criminal activities in the East End of London. When you were finally apprehended, you mounted a campaign of vilification against the police who had done their duty, in the hope of saving your skins. I cannot look at sorrowful pleas from wives, or past good deeds in the face of what you have chosen to do yourselves. The attack mounted on the police has been firmly negated by the jury. That you engaged in blackmail and protection, I have no doubt whatever.

George and Alan Dixon were found guilty of blackmail and conspiracy to inflict grievous bodily harm; they were sentenced to 12 and 9 years' imprisonment respectively.

Birth of the Serious Crime Squad – The Dixons

Michael Bailey and Michael Young, guilty of conspiracy to blackmail, were each jailed for 5 years. For a similar charge, Brian Taylor of Globe Road, Stepney – described by Wickstead as being 'the odd-job man of the team; he was the chauffeur who ran errands for the gang' – was sentenced to 6 years' imprisonment.

Sentencing Philly Jacobs to 12 years' imprisonment and ordering him to pay £10,000 costs, the judge told him, 'I am quite satisfied that you were at the heart of this matter. You were rich, with flourishing public houses. You have been convicted of a serious conspiracy to cause grievous bodily harm to another member of the gang.'

When it came to Leon Carleton ('I recall him as being detestable', Tony Stevens told me. 'Even the villains disliked him.'), before jailing him for 12 years, Mr Justice O'Connor told him, 'You have been found guilty of a most serious piece of blackmail. The manner of the attack you made on Brennan was as crooked a piece of work as it has been my lot to meet in the courts.'

The judge then commended Wickstead, saying:

> You and your men deserve the full commendation of the public for bringing a gang of dangerous men to justice. It was a difficult task, thoroughly, honestly, efficiently and fairly discharged.

It's difficult to say whether it was the sentences or the judge's fulsome praise which lit the fuse in the dock and the public gallery; perhaps it was a combination of both. Pandemonium broke out; there were shouts of, 'We'll get you, Wickstead – the end of the reign of Wickstead is just beginning!' Ladies in the public gallery screeched, 'You're a dirty liar, Wickstead!' and when police and ushers came to eject them from the court, scuffles broke out.

And that was that. Charges of conspiracy to cheat and defraud – these were long firm frauds – operating from Leonhouse, Charles Dean Ltd. and the John Tuffen Trading Company were the subject of a separate indictment. So was my case; it was felt that Alan Dixon would not receive any further punishment if he was found guilty, so that charge was allowed to 'remain on the file'. Challenger and Lazarus both pleaded guilty to conspiracy to assault and received non-custodial sentences.

On 21 May 1974 the Dixon brothers, Jacobs and Carleton appealed against their sentences and convictions, without success. Upon their release (although Alan in a 2016 interview claimed he had served 22 years in prison), the brothers confined themselves to legitimate business enterprises. In fact, Ed Williams, who as a detective inspector later went to Plaistow, told his team that he was going to take them for a drink in a certain pub, only to be told that they couldn't go in that particular pub, since it was run by the Dixons.

As Williams recalled, 'I told them, "That's exactly why we're going!" and when we went in, there was George behind the bar. "Hello, Captain, how's it going?" he called out to me.' Perhaps, over a period of years, the leopards had lost their spots.

The end of the trial coincided with an odd incident that had nothing whatsoever to do with the Dixon brothers.

The murder of gangland figure 'Ginger' Marks (it was probably a case of mistaken identity) which occurred on 2 January 1965 gave rise to a great deal of speculation because (a) no one has ever been convicted for it, and (b) the body has never been found.

Wickstead received some information as to where the body might be buried, since a military helicopter containing specialist equipment had identified an area on a farm in Kent which revealed a disturbance in the field. Bernie Tighe and Tony Stevens were two of the four SCS officers who accompanied Wickstead to the farm, together with two serials of the Special Patrol Group, plus local Kent officers. The tale is now taken up by Bernie Tighe:

> After some time, various bones were discovered and we thought that we were on to something. By this time, the SPG had set up a drinks area and were dispensing tea. Approaching us was a local baker's van doing local deliveries. I stepped forward to stop the van to see if he had any cakes or other eats that we could purchase. I had forgotten I had a .38 in a shoulder holster which was exposed when I put up my arm. The driver was in a state of shock and said, 'Take the whole fucking lot, mate – I'm getting out of here!' You can imagine the SPG needed no second invite!

Tragically, the bones which had been discovered belonged to a donkey which had expired some months earlier.

There were no newspaper headlines or commendations arising out of the finding of the late donkey; just a few chuckles which were immediately stifled when Wickstead was around.

There was, however, no need to keep quiet about his next coup – which due to unforeseen circumstances had been launched slap-bang in the middle of the Dixon case.

CHAPTER 6

Mayhem in East London – the Tibbs Family

Villainy – to a lesser or greater extent – often surfaces in families; witness the Richardsons, the Krays and the Dixons. But it's fair to say that for sheer concentrated violence, the Tibbs family came close to the top of the pile.

The 6ft 3ins father, 'Big Jim' Tibbs, was born in 1928 and had been in and out of trouble with the law; in 1952 he, Teddy Machin (at one time Billy Hill's right-hand man and one of four who escaped capture following the 1948 London Airport robbery), plus four others, were accused of making a disturbance at the Madeleine members' club in Mayfair.

Eight years later, on Christmas Eve 1960, a young man named Ronald Thomas Coomber was so badly kicked and punched outside the Ranch House Club, Ilford, Essex that he died in hospital from his injuries. Four men were arrested and charged with the murder; they included George Wood (one of those who *had* been caught for the London Airport robbery and sentenced to 8 years' penal servitude for it) – and 'Big Jim' Tibbs. Even though four witnesses had failed to pick out Tibbs on an identification parade and he had willingly surrendered some of his clothing to police, it was still considered that there was sufficient evidence to charge him and furthermore to commit him and the others to the Old Bailey for trial. However, the evidence revealed some disturbing features.

Two young women in their twenties who were at the club had been taken home by the four men. Later, before they could be seen by police, they were taken to the home of the men's solicitor where they made statements; one would later say her statement was made voluntarily, the other did not.

When the latter asked if she had to make a statement, the solicitor allegedly told her, 'I will give you some advice. If I was you, I would, because the boys could get nasty.' By that she understood that 'they could come round to my house'. The first witness agreed that those words had been used.

Shortly after the murder, the proprietor of the club, Bob Patience (whose wife would be brutally murdered twelve years later during the course of a robbery at the Barn Restaurant, Braintree), had left his house, was collected by men in a car and was driven to the office of an engineering firm in the High Road, Chadwell Heath. There he was told that several members of the club were potential witnesses to the murder and reminded him that as the owner of the club he would be in possession of their addresses. Therefore he should tell them that to forget what they had seen would be 'advisable'. To reinforce this advice, one of the men took out a pistol, opened the window of the office and fired a shot into the dustbin, with the words, 'Tell them it only barks once.'

At the Old Bailey trial all of the available witnesses were called but, as Mr Justice Edmund Davies told the jury, 'Their evidence had been highly unsatisfactory', and he felt that he could not ask the jury, on the evidence available, to convict on a charge of murder or manslaughter:

> It would be impossible on the evidence to point your finger at any of these men and say he did this or that. Somewhere, inside or outside this court, there may be a man or men with exceedingly bad conscience having regard to the way a young man lost his life.

The judge therefore directed the jury to return verdicts of not guilty on the four men, and on 8 March 1961 they walked free from court, their costs being paid out of public funds. The careers of both judge and defendant progressed: three years later, Mr Justice Edmund Davies went on to preside over the Great Train Robbery trial, and 'Big Jim' Tibbs became embroiled in near-homicidal gang warfare during the late 1960s and the early 1970s.

★

There were three sons in the Tibbs family: Robert Terence and John, both scrap metal dealers and James Edward Patrick 'Jimmy' Tibbs, a professional boxer. By 7 December 1968 his record was excellent: as a light-heavyweight he had won thirteen of his sixteen bouts. So on that date it was probably unwise of one Albert Nichols, aged twenty-five, to make a derogatory comment regarding Jimmy's pugilistic career to Jimmy's uncle, fifty-one-year-old George 'Bogey' Tibbs in the Steamship public house, Poplar. 'Bogey' reacted to this slight and received in return a punch in the face. But if Nichols had been ill-advised to make the remark, it was downright injudicious of 'Bogey' (who may have imbibed just a little imprudently) to have misplaced the homily, 'A still tongue keeps a wise head'. His response was, 'Is that the best you can do?'

– and he now received a black eye and lost two teeth.

This would be the catalyst for all-out warfare.

Three days later, retribution in the form of Jimmy Tibbs, his brother John and cousin George (the son of 'Bogey') arrived at Albert Nichols' minicab office in the East India Dock Road, close to the Blackwall Tunnel. According to a later version of events given by Jimmy Tibbs, he was in possession of a shotgun, not to shoot anyone, mind you, just to threaten them. He hit Nichols in the face with the gun's butt and, although he claimed he didn't know whether the gun was loaded, he discovered that it was when it went off. After he had carefully checked to ensure that nobody had been injured, a struggle with Nichols ensued, the gun accidentally went off again and the three men left the scene, leaving Nichols on the floor. Obviously he was in pain, but he had not suffered life-threatening injuries – at least, that was Jimmy Tibbs' recollection of the incident.

It was not, however an opinion of Nichols' condition shared by Detective Constable (later detective chief superintendent) Roger Stoodley, one of the first officers to arrive at the scene, who said, 'I thought he was not long for this world.'

So let's come back to reality. The shotgun blast had inflicted severe injuries on Nichols' legs and lower abdomen. He had also been beaten with a garden spade, the top of his head split open with the wounds resembling a star. There were cuts to his face, the tip of his nose was partially severed and the top of a finger was missing.

Stoodley had seen the brothers secrete the shotgun under a car parked in Bullivant Street, just off the East India Dock Road; they were arrested and taken into Poplar police station.

They were committed in custody to the Old Bailey, where before Mr Justice Lyell they all pleaded not guilty to charges of Nichols' attempted murder and wounding with intent to cause him grievous bodily harm. At the close of the prosecution's case they changed their pleas, which were accepted by the Crown.

Telling them, 'You have been guilty, apart from anything else, of the most appalling folly. I sympathise with your feelings but at the same time, living in the part of London where you live, there is a great deal too much violence,' on 6 March 1969, the judge (who mercifully retired two years later) sentenced each of the Tibbs family to 2 years' imprisonment, suspended for 3 years, for unlawful wounding, plus a £100 fine for unlawfully possessing a shotgun in a public place.

Albert Nichols was one of those who was not entirely sure that justice had been seen to be done; but be that as it may, Jimmy

Tibbs resumed his boxing career and during 1970 notched up four more decisive victories in the ring. But when he defeated Ray Hassan with a technical knock-out at the Empire Pool, Wembley on 24 March 1970, it was his final professional fight. He was twenty-three years of age and had the experience and ability to go right to the top of his profession. Instead, he chose to throw it all away.

*

It was a stupid, drunken disagreement, probably over football, that escalated out of all proportion in November 1970 at the Rose of Denmark public house at 78 Shirley Street, Canning Town. Frankie McDonald and Robert Tibbs had had an argument which culminated in a knife being produced. Micky Fawcett – the brother of Frederick Fawcett, who managed the Steamship pub and was a friend of the Nichols family – intervened, and in the ensuing fracas Robert Tibbs' throat was cut. No one was arrested and no one named the guilty party, but it was widely held in the Tibbs camp that Fawcett was responsible; something he strenuously denies to this day. Despite the wound to his throat, Robert Tibbs was heard to say, 'Some bastard will die for this.'

An attempt to make peace was turned down the following day, and although the matter was not officially reported to the police, they nevertheless got to hear of it. Commander John Lock QPM had a meeting with the father, James Tibbs, but was told, 'We don't want any police interference; we'll deal with it in our own way.'

It appears they did. On Christmas Day 1970 John Davies, an associate of Micky Fawcett, was attacked as he walked along a street near his home; he was beaten and cut. This was followed by Michael Machin strolling into the Steamship pub and firing a shotgun into the ceiling. In turn, Machin's brother Teddy (an associate of 'Big Jim' Tibbs) was in bed in his Forest Gate flat when a car drew up and shots were fired into his bedroom, blowing out the window and injuring him; within two weeks, brother Michael was approached by two men who fired shotguns at him.

Ronald Patrick Curtis, a friend of Micky Fawcett, was kidnapped by the Tibbs faction, who took him at knife-point by car to a garage, where with a gun held to his head he was beaten in an attempt to find Fawcett, but without success – Fawcett had prudently left for Spain.

Besides the animosity between the Tibbs and Nichols families and their associates, Leonard Kersey, the manager of the Black Boy public house, 169 Mile End Road, E1, had also incurred the Tibbs' displeasure. Over Christmas 1970 he had referred to the family collectively as, 'Dirty pikey bastards'. The pejorative usage of the term 'pikey' suggests that the family came from a gypsy background; satisfaction was demanded and it was taken in a particularly dreadful way.

On 30 January 1971, as Kersey left his flat, he was attacked by Jimmy Tibbs armed with a chopper and by John Tibbs, Stanley Naylor and Michael Machin, all of whom were armed with knives. He was struck over the head with the chopper and knifed; all four hacked at him, shouting 'Kill him! Kill him!'; only a later and prompt six-pint blood transfusion saved his life. As it was, he had been left in the gutter, bleeding and semi-conscious. He had sixteen wounds which would require a week's stay in hospital and the insertion of eighty stitches.

The most telling account of what happened would come from Kersey's wife, Diane, who was in the family flat with a friend, Mrs Linda Pearman, who was nursing her baby. Upon hearing the commotion, both women rushed out into the street, and this was the evidence that Diane Kersey gave to the court:

> I saw the men hacking at somebody on the ground and tried to stop the horrible thing. Then I saw it was my husband. His face was falling apart. I screamed the place down. My friend also screamed and dropped the baby.

But that evidence was not forthcoming immediately. Although the perpetrators were arrested and charged on 13 April 1971, 'Big Jim' Tibbs told Kersey, 'Get my boys out of trouble. You were hurt bad last time. If you don't go our way, it'll be worse next time.'

Tibbs also threatened to have acid thrown at Kersey's wife and children, and as a result, no prosecution witnesses appeared at court and the charges were dismissed. When it was heard that Kersey had been paid £1,000 for his injuries from the Criminal Injuries Compensation Board, he was provoked into a fight with Michael Logan and then the money was demanded with menaces.

Stanley Naylor, one of the Tibbs associates, was shot at, and then on 14 March 1971, as the Nichols brothers, Albert and Terry, were leaving the Rose of Denmark pub and approaching their car, Naylor tried, unsuccessfully to fire an automatic pistol at Albert Nichols. It was picked up by Jimmy Tibbs (he later said he did it to avoid somebody getting killed), who then attacked Albert Nichols with a knife; his arm and leg were slashed and he was also struck with a golf club wielded by Michael Machin, who shouted, 'Kill the bastard – he's a pal of Kersey's!'

Terry Nichols was shouting for the police and naming his attackers, which led Robert Tibbs to shout, 'Kill the fucking grasses!'; a shotgun was discharged, although fortunately no one was hit. Terry Nichols, the more seriously injured of the two brothers, was taken to hospital. When the police – in the form of Police Constable John Escott – arrived, Jimmy Tibbs tried to run him down in a car. The following month, Albert Nichols was threatened with a knife and a gun; he was lucky to escape. When Terry Nichols was punched and kicked and Stanley Naylor pulled out a knife, it was only the siren of a police car that frightened off the attackers.

On 13 April 'Big Jim' Tibbs threatened Terence Nichols by telling him that his brother's wife and children would have acid thrown over them if he gave evidence at the Magistrates' Court against the Tibbs family; no prosecution ensued.

George Brett, a friend of both the Fawcetts and the Nichols, was shot in the leg outside the Huntingdon Arms pub – and four years later, Brett and his ten-year-old son would become the murdered victims of an entirely unconnected gangland contract. David Storey, a friend of the Nichols, was also attacked.

The Tibbs faction must by now have believed that they could walk on water. In fact, Jimmy Tibbs decided to make a comeback in the ring. They could do as they pleased and no one would dare to give evidence against them. However, the tide was about to turn.

A bomb exploded in a yard belonging to the Tibbs family in Star Lane, Canning Town; Jack Cooper, who was a Station Sergeant at Plaistow police station, recalled that and other incidents:

> A café in Ordnance Road, Plaistow was blown up one morning – imploded is a better description, very skilfully done, it was put down to a gas explosion. A bomb was planted in the office hut at Hoadley's scrap yard by the Canning Town bridge, wired to the telephone. It was discovered and I attended; it was later dismantled. The Paul's Head public house in Silvertown Way was trashed, three times I think, until 'they' got a landlord who was willing to pay the weekly dues.

But a week after the bomb explosion in Star Lane there was a potentially horrifying incident.

Just before 9.00 am on 28 April 1971, Jimmy Tibbs, together with his four-year-old son (also named Jimmy) got into his Ford Thames van, which had been parked in Nelson Street, East Ham, in order to take his son to the nursery. As he turned the key in the ignition there was a tremendous explosion from under the bonnet.

Windows were shattered by the concussion and people rushed out of their houses. Jimmy Tibbs' wife, Claudette, later told reporters, 'I heard this tremendous bang. I thought two cars had crashed until my husband banged on the door, with Jimmy crying in his arms.'

It was only by a gracious dispensation of providence that neither father nor son was killed; in fact, neither of them sustained serious injuries. There was now no question of there 'not being any police interference'; furthermore, the possibility of the explosion in the Tibbs-owned café the previous week being due to a gas leak was ruled out, and the two occurrences were linked. House-to-house enquiries were made to see if anybody recalled seeing suspicious characters in the vicinity between 10.00 pm the previous night and the time of the detonation – but nobody had.

Jeff Edwards – later President of the Crime Reporters' Association – told me:

> I joined the *Newham Recorder* in the summer of 1970. One of the first big stories I had was the attempt to kill Jimmy Tibbs, with a bomb in his van. I can remember being told at the time the bomb had been made of nitroglycerine and had been wired into the distributor cap of the vehicle, so it exploded when he turned the ignition key. The explosion . . . was powerful enough to lift the engine up and over the houses where it landed in a back garden. The reason they were unscathed was the directional dynamics of the blast was forced back and up by the bulkhead separating the engine compartment from the driver's compartment They must have made them strong in those days!

A contributory factor to the blast going upwards may well have been that the bonnet on Tibbs' van had a defective catch, but there was no doubt that this was a sophisticated attempt to murder Tibbs. The police had no hesitation in classifying the incident as 'attempted murder', and for the 29 April edition of *The Times* to have claimed, 'The bomb was probably nothing more of a reminder that he is not liked' was stupid and irresponsible reporting.

Wickstead would later say that it was this incident more than any other which prompted him to personally intervene. But matters were not as straightforward as all that, not by any manner of means. At the time of the explosion, Wickstead was fully occupied (with a paucity of staff) in the Dixon investigation, and to suggest that he had been observing the situation with (as has been suggested) 'something of an Olympian detachment' is ludicrous. He had not investigated these matters, he had no idea who could say what about whom and the thought that he could rush around pulling everybody in without any evidence defies belief. More than anything else, with his lack of manpower and his full commitment to the Dixon enquiry, he had felt that he simply could not take on any more work at that time. But the explosion in the van changed all that. It was amazing that murder had not been committed; certainly, the attacks on Kersey and the Nichols brothers, then the bomb placed in Jimmy Tibbs' van, had been uncomfortably close to it. East Ham in 1971 was rapidly being transformed into the Chicago of the 1920s; something needed to be done, and sooner rather than later.

*

With the violence escalating out of all proportion, Wickstead had to draw up his battle plan. He came to the conclusion that of the various factions the Tibbs gang were the worst offenders, and if they were going to be prosecuted to conviction, the Nichols, Kersey and Fawcett would have to give evidence against them. But would they do so? Could they trust Wickstead and his men? Because it was widely believed that the Tibbs gang were protected by venal coppers in the very area where they lived and worked – and what was more, they were right.

So Wickstead's decision to come down on the side of other criminals to bring down the Tibbs gang was a controversial one, both at the time and since; there were honest, decent people in East Ham who admired the family. The Tibbs were high-profile in the area, and there were many who thought that whatever they had done was acceptable to defend the family name.

Wickstead spoke to the Nichols and Kersey; in the fight with Micky Logan, Kersey had apparently impaled his opponent's hand to a table with a knife, but Kersey was told that the incident between him and the Tibbs family would be re-opened. Then Wickstead put the word about that he wanted to speak to Fawcett, and eventually he came forward and agreed to assist. Of course, it was a fait accompli; Fawcett believed (with some justification) that the Tibbs family were after him, so he had to put his faith in the police – not the police at East Ham, but Wickstead. The word therefore went round that Wickstead could be trusted; but when he applied for extra staff, he was told that he couldn't have any – so he borrowed some more.

Statements were taken and strategies were worked out, but at the same time, plans were being put into operation for the imminent commencement of the Dixon trial at the Old Bailey. There were conferences with the prosecution counsel to be attended, last-minute statements to be taken, arrangements made for the high-security transportation of the prisoners from Brixton prison to court and the protection of the witnesses – but now, matters could wait no longer.

Ideally, Wickstead had wanted to make his move against the Tibbs family in mid-May, on the presumption that the Dixon trial would be more or less finished by then (that was a forlorn hope), but now he received some very pertinent information; what he had heard was that the Tibbs gang planned to make themselves unavailable, probably by vanishing abroad, after disposing of the Nichols brothers, Kersey and Fawcett. With eight days to go before the Dixon trial started, Wickstead decided that the Tibbs gang would have to be arrested, right now. Wickstead was very much like the legendary world champion heavyweight boxer, Jack Dempsey, who with a fight impending was usually in peak condition; but condition or no condition, he'd go straight ahead. On the morning of 4 April 1972 Wickstead did just that.

*

The first Detective Sergeant Roger Stoodley knew that he was being detached from his normal duties at Bow Road police station was when he was instructed to report to City Road police station at 2.00 am that morning, in conditions of the greatest secrecy. There he was astonished to discover that there were 159 other officers present: Divisional CID, officers from the Yard, Special Patrol Group officers, even some dog handlers. It was because of his previous dealings with the Tibbs family that Stoodley was there, purely for the arrests. In the four days that followed, Stoodley was one of the officers who worked eighteen-hour days, and he assumed that would be his total input; in fact, he remained with the Serious Crime Squad for five years.

But now, on the morning of 4 April, there was a full briefing by Wickstead: targets were given to the officers, no telephone calls were permitted and at 6.00 am the target premises were raided.

Stoodley's target was the Ground Rent pub in Rogers Road, Plaistow, where the licensee, Alexander Gordon Cousins, was said to be an associate of the Tibbs gang. Some shotgun cartridges were found in a bedroom wardrobe; under a mattress a shotgun was discovered which, Cousins stated, he was looking after for a friend. He neglected to name the friend and was arrested.

Michael Sidney Machin, aged thirty-five ('he was a nasty bit of work'), was arrested in bed at his home in Shrewsbury Road, Forest Gate, at gunpoint by Detective Sergeant Bernie Tighe.

Jimmy Tibbs was brought in and so was his father. Tony Stevens arrived at the bungalow in Lodge Lane, Romford with uniformed officers plus a dog handler. It was felt that this arrest might present 'a real problem', and consequently Stevens and other officers were armed. A quick entry was required, and this was before the days of battering rams. Stevens takes up the tale:

> I used a trick that I'd used before; get a uniform officer to knock on the door with us out of sight. The officer was, I think Sergeant Flynn; he was the biggest bloody sergeant I'd ever seen, about 6 foot 6 inches and he had to duck under the lintel at the front porch as he was even taller with his helmet on. He knocked on the door and old man Jimmy Tibbs opened the door. The sergeant said, 'Good morning sir, I am a police officer', which was pretty obvious to everyone. I fancy even Jimmy smiled. I went in with my team and the search warrant and began the search. In the kitchen I found a quantity of bullets, I think at least 20 in a cereal box in the kitchen cupboard and elsewhere three fur coats which I thought were iffy. As Mrs Tibbs must have known about both, I arrested her and the old man. She was bailed for further enquiries.

Under the code of the East End (which catered for anything and everything thought by its inhabitants to be disagreeable), the arrest of Mrs Kathleen Tibbs was considered to be beyond the pale. Reliable information was received that a bursary of £1,000 would be available to the person responsible for the removal of either Stevens, or Wickstead's legs (or the legs of both officers), preferably with the aid of a shotgun. Stevens was permitted to be permanently armed for some considerable time thereafter; for Wickstead it was the first of the threats made against him in this case and reinforced when 'Big Jim' Tibbs, following his arrest, told Detective Sergeant Clifford Paton of the Flying Squad, 'We'll fillet you lot out. You won't get away with arresting us.'

This spirit of optimism was shared by Stanley Naylor, because when he was arrested he told police, 'You won't get witnesses to stand up.'

In all, forty addresses had been raided, and rifles, shotguns, revolvers, knives, swords and pickaxe handles were seized. Twenty people had been arrested, of whom two were released.

However, 'Big Jim' Tibbs appeared fairly relaxed when he was taken into Wickstead's office for interview; after all, he had been interviewed by police many times before and therefore asked if he could speak to Wickstead alone.

Wickstead's reply was classic: 'Before we start this interview, let me tell you now, you have bought and sold your last policeman, so if that's why you've asked to speak to me, forget it.'

There was a stunned silence before Tibbs replied, 'Can I go now, please?'

But he wasn't going anywhere; neither were ten others. By the end of the second day, charges had been preferred.

'Big Jim' Tibbs was charged with possessing 600 rounds of .22 ammunition without a certificate and possessing an automatic pistol at the time of inflicting grievous bodily harm to Ronald Patrick Curtis. Additionally, together with Stanley Walter Naylor and Michael Gerald Logan, he was charged that they conspired to pervert the course of justice – and both Naylor and Jimmy Tibbs were charged with inflicting grievous bodily harm to Curtis. Naylor was also charged with grievous bodily harm.

Jimmy Tibbs, Michael Machin and Stanley Naylor were also charged with three counts of attempted murder, on Terry and Albert Nichols and also Leonard Kersey.

William Henry Birkeff, Ronald Sewell, John Connolly and John Arthur Clark were all charged with grievous bodily harm. Alexander Cousins was also charged with grievous bodily harm and possessing a shotgun without a certificate, and Donald Frederick Collinson was similarly charged with grievous bodily harm, plus possessing an automatic pistol and eight rounds of .32 ammunition without a certificate.

Bringing up the rear was George 'Bogey' Tibbs, charged with dishonestly receiving a quantity of goods, including tobacco, clothing, cutlery and shoes, knowing them to have been stolen; when the men appeared at Old Street Magistrates' Court on 6 April, 'Bogey' was the only one to be granted bail, in the sum of £300.

Not so the others, when they appeared in the dock in groups of three, with Wickstead telling the magistrate, Neil McElligott, that witnesses in the case were 'terrified'. Mr F. W. Baldwin, appearing for Naylor and Jimmy Tibbs, asked for reporting restrictions to be lifted, saying that he had been disturbed at the publicity given to the arrests, with wild talk of 'gangbusting', the Krays and the Richardsons; he hoped that people would take some note of the prejudice which had been created. Granting the application, Mr McElligott agreed that it was indeed 'unfortunate' and remanded the defendants (including Mr Baldwin's clients) in custody.

However, the round-up had not netted all of the gang; both John and Robert Tibbs were missing. Once their disappearance had been established, Frankie MacDonald and Micky Fawcett were brought in; they gave their accounts of what had happened at the Steamship pub eighteen months previously and were allowed to leave.

By the time the prisoners appeared in court on 20 April they had been joined in the dock by Mrs Kathleen Tibbs, accused of dishonest handling. She was granted bail, and Ronald Sewell had also been granted bail by a judge in chambers, in the sum of £2,000 with two sureties in similar amounts. Warrants had been issued in respect of Robert and John Tibbs.

'Anyone knowing their whereabouts', said Mr J. E. Leck for the prosecution, speaking more in hope than expectation, 'should get in touch with the police' – but nobody did.

The committal proceedings started on 15 May; the thirty-four charges were outlined by Mr David Tudor Price (later His Honour Sir David) for the prosecution. Lennie Kersey was permitted to write down his address, which was handed to Neil McElligott. He told the court:

> In conversation with my customers, I had called the Tibbs family dirty bastards. One Saturday afternoon in January 1971, I came out of my basement flat and two men appeared. John Tibbs said, 'What's all this about you calling us dirty bastards?' He pulled a knife and slashed me; Michael Machin did the same. I started to run, one of them grabbed my coat. Young Jimmy Tibbs, the boxer and Stan Naylor came up. Tibbs had a chopper, Naylor had a knife and stabbed me in the legs. Everyone was shouting, 'Kill him, kill him'.

Ronald Curtis described his car-borne kidnap, and the proceedings continued, some witnesses giving their evidence live, others having their statements read, until 22 May. It had been reported that Mrs Tibbs had received threats, but Wickstead told the court that he had no knowledge of them or of a letter which she had allegedly written to the commissioner of police. 'I know she has reported threats to the press,' he said, 'but not to the police.'

The charge against Tibbs father and son, Naylor and Machin, that they had caused grievous bodily harm to Ronald Curtis, was reduced to one of causing actual bodily harm, Naylor was further charged with conspiring with others to pervert the course of justice, and they were committed in custody to stand their trial at the Old Bailey.

But still no John or Robert Tibbs.

*

Station Sergeant Jack Cooper recalled, 'Wickstead based his squad on the top floor of the section house behind East Ham police station. Special security measures were put in to prevent access by non-squad officers; the place was locked off when not attended.'

But these security measures were not enough; Wickstead now started receiving death threats aimed at him and his family; he was also told his house would be bombed and acid thrown in his wife's face. He – and the rest of his team – took these threats very seriously indeed, bearing in mind what had happened with intimidation of the other witnesses over the previous twelve months. Matters were not helped by the fact that Wickstead and his family were living at 54 Norfolk Road, a terraced council house right in the middle of Tibbs territory, in East Ham; in fact, Wickstead's home was almost directly opposite the road in which 'Bogey' Tibbs lived.

Therefore, right in the middle of these enquiries – and the Dixon trial – Wickstead had to move, to a dilapidated house in Essex. In fact, the family were given a choice of five properties, but this was not a period in which they could afford the luxury of being choosy; time was of the essence. The ramshackle council premises in Loughton was spruced up, over a weekend when the courts were not sitting, by members of Wickstead's squad who provided expertise in their free time as carpenters, electricians, plumbers and decorators. However, once that was complete, members of the team were detached from their normal duties and were permanently armed to provide round-the-clock protection, taking Wickstead's wife shopping and his children to school.

On 16 August 1972, four months after the initial arrests, Robert Tibbs walked into a police station with a solicitor and was charged; he doubtless thought his belated surrender would be a bargaining point when it came to bail. No chance.

'I was prosecuting something at the Bailey and so they got me to do this bail application before my case resumed,' Stuart Moore (later Mr Justice Michael Stuart-Moore, Vice-President of the Court of Appeal, Hong Kong) told me. 'I well remember that they were threatening to blow up Chief Superintendent Albert Wickstead and to kill his family, which made it particularly easy to oppose bail on the ground that [Tibbs] was likely to intimidate witnesses.'

Judge Geraint Rees agreed, saying there was no doubt that there was a grave danger of intimidation to witnesses and that justice would not be done if bail was granted.

A week later, Wickstead opposed bail for three more defendants: Ronald Downes, a latecomer to the defendants' group (and one who would eventually be acquitted of all charges), John Clark and John Connolly. He spoke of the gang being involved with 'violence for the sake of violence' and added that he had been obliged to move home due to threats of violence by letter and telephone directed at his family. Unsurprisingly, bail was once more refused. And still John Tibbs could not be found.

The trial commenced at the Old Bailey on 30 October 1972, before Mr Justice Lawson. Michael Corkery QC prosecuted the eight men in the dock. These were Tibbs senior, his sons Jimmy and Robert, Naylor, Machin, Logan, Downes and George 'Bogey' Tibbs. Other original defendants had been the subject of pleas of guilty, separate indictments or no evidence offered, as in the case of a ninth defendant, Peter Lupson, who had pleaded not guilty to concealing ammunition and a bloodstained shirt belonging to Naylor and who would be now called as a witness for the prosecution.

The men in the dock had pleaded not guilty to an indictment containing eighteen counts: a miscellany of charges including attempted murder, wounding, assault, possessing offensive weapons, attempting to pervert the course of justice and blackmail. John Tibbs was not amongst their number, but it was John 'the Ferret' Farley who found him. He told me:

> I was asked to house him. I knew that Tibbs' child went to a playgroup near North Street, Romford and I discovered that the staff were concerned because the child hadn't turned up. I did a family tree of the Tibbs; I found the maiden name of John Tibbs' wife and that she had a sister living in a tower block in Leytonstone. Close by the flats, a housing estate was being built. I spoke to the site agent and I worked as a joiner on the second floor, with binoculars. On the fourth or fifth floor of the tower block opposite was a flat with a balcony at the back. I stayed on the site for four or five days. At about 9.00 pm I saw John Tibbs come out on to the balcony and I called up the arrest team. They radioed to say they couldn't find him; I told them to check the balcony, since he was hanging from the edge of it.

Mayhem in East London – the Tibbs Family

John Tibbs was arrested by Gerry Runham ('He wasn't a problem', Runham told me) and he later joined his family in the dock; two men accused of assisting in concealing Tibbs were later discharged at the Old Bailey.

Security was very strict. Police Constable Pat Collins drove the prison van from Brixton to the Old Bailey, accompanied by an armed officer. 'There were four routes to choose from, marked 'A' to 'D',' he told me. 'Whichever one was chosen, Information Room at the Yard was informed.'

Detective Constable Dave McEnhill, who had joined the Serious Crime Squad on the day that the trial commenced, was responsible for driving Lennie Kersey to court, but it was considered too dangerous to arrive at the front of the Old Bailey. 'I had an arrangement where I would park in the Lord Mayor's entrance at the back of the Bailey', he told me. 'I remember Kersey had a limp, as a result of the injuries he'd received.'

Micky Fawcett duly appeared for the prosecution, admitted knowing the Kray brothers and acknowledged going to James Tibbs' scrap yard, but denied collecting money on behalf of the twins and definitely denied that he had slashed Robert Tibbs' throat.

'I put it to you that your account is an absolute travesty', said James Burge, QC for Robert Tibbs. 'You were the man with the knife and it was part of a plan to collect protection from the Tibbs. You were the person who slashed Robert Tibbs twice, outside the public house.' This was denied.

But when Wickstead gave evidence, each of the barristers acting for the defendants declined to ask him any questions, knowing that to do so could cause untold damage to their clients. Instead, when Wickstead gave his evidence in chief, each barrister stood up in turn and said, 'I have no questions but I do not accept any of your evidence.'

Wickstead was furious and wanted to comment on this but he was not permitted to say one word in contradiction. Until, that is, the last barrister, the youngest and least experienced, repeated his fellow barristers' mantra but then added, 'And do you agree that the worst you can say about my client is that he was present, but took no part in the assault?'

Wickstead's face lit up and he replied, 'Actually, the worst I can say about your client is this . . .' then proceeded to tell the court of the most harrowing deeds of the defendant in question and in the space of the following fifteen minutes managed to include every other defendant in the dock, which was tantamount to involving them in a major conspiracy. The other lawyers spluttered protests to the judge, who gently reminded them that having been asked a perfectly reasonable question, Mr Wickstead was entitled to answer it.

But the allegations against the police came thick and fast, and as Christmas 1972 came and went, they intensified. On 15 January 1973 they led to Mr Justice Lawson telling the jury during his summing-up:

> I invite you to take a calm, clear look at allegations of a police conspiracy, made by members of a London family and their associates who, according to the prosecution, had imposed a rule of terror in the East End. The risks of such a conspiracy would be enormous. It was alleged that the conspiracy had been masterminded by Detective Chief Superintendent Wickstead and that its object was to protect people who were terrorising and committing offences against innocent victims. In other words, it was not just a conspiracy to convict innocent victims but at the same time to protect people who they knew were really responsible for the reign of terror under which members of the Tibbs family, friends and associates were alleged to be suffering. In more than forty years legal experience, it is the first time I have heard the suggestion made that one could get the Department of Public Prosecutions involved in a conspiracy of that kind.

After a 43-day trial, and after the jury had retired for ten hours, they returned their verdicts on 18 January 1973: the defendants were acquitted of some charges by the jury and of others on the direction of the judge, but on the remainder there were verdicts of guilty, and sentences were passed the following day.

James Tibbs ('The ruling head of this fraternity', Wickstead had called him) was convicted, together with Logan, of conspiracy to blackmail Leonard Kersey of £1,000, of conspiracy to pervert the course of justice by attempting to make arrangements to ensure that Mrs Linda Pearman, an eyewitness to the assault on Leonard Kersey, would not give truthful evidence and unlawfully possessing ammunition. Jeremy Hutchinson QC in Tibbs' defence told the judge that his client was not a man of violence. Since he had been acquitted of possessing an automatic pistol at the time of an assault on Ronald Curtis and a conspiracy to assault Fawcett and the Nichols brothers, it seemed fairly safe to say that.

He further told the court, 'Whatever his faults and qualities, he has an intense family loyalty' and he produced a petition signed by 350 East Ham well-wishers.

'I accept that you are a good father, family man and neighbour', said the judge. 'But there is the other side and that is the side which unfortunately has involved you in these offences. It is that man whom it is my painful duty to send to prison.' He then sentenced Tibbs to 15 years' imprisonment; Logan received 2 years.

Jimmy Tibbs, John Tibbs, Stanley Naylor and Michael Machin were all found guilty of attempting to murder Leonard Kersey, all of them were found guilty of wounding Albert Nichols and, with the exception of John Tibbs, they were found guilty of wounding Terry Nichols, as was Robert Tibbs. In addition, Jimmy Tibbs was found guilty of assaulting Police Constable John Escott by driving a car at him and of possessing a 9mm pistol and ammunition, as was Stanley Naylor, with intent to endanger life during the assault on the Nichols brothers and of possessing the firearm without a certificate.

Robin Simpson QC for Jimmy Tibbs stated that his client had been a professional boxer since the age of nineteen and added, 'The tragedy was that he was due to make a comeback and had a real chance of getting to the top.'

Indeed he had, but jailing him for ten years, the judge told him, 'You are a troublemaker who is prepared to join in acts of organized violence with weapons on people who are defenceless.'

'Family solidarity and affection is something which the East End of London may have something to teach the rest of the country about', said Charles Whitby QC for John Tibbs. 'It is a flame which burns brightly and which generates humanity and warmth. But when it goes wrong, it leads to vengeance and violence.'

'You took part in organized violence with weapons which took the form of a sudden attack in broad daylight on a wholly defenceless man against whom it is not suggested you had anything personal,' said the judge. 'Fortunately, the man did not die but that was due to the good fortune that he was taken to hospital in time' – and with that, he sentenced John Tibbs to 7 years' imprisonment. Robert Tibbs was sentenced to fifteen months for wounding Terry Nichols.

For his part in the attacks, Stanley Naylor was jailed for 12 years, and Michael Machin received 11 years, the judge telling him, 'You were playing a pretty active part, egging other people on to do violence.'

On the day of the sentencing, Mrs Kathleen Tibbs had collapsed from an overdose of drugs and was conveyed to Poplar Hospital. She discharged herself the same day and in the following day's edition of the *Daily Express* she informed its readers, 'They are not gangsters or godfathers. They are good, honest workers. The press and the court have crucified us.'

That was not a view shared by the judiciary, and Mr Justice Lawson went overboard on his commendation for Wickstead and his men, saying:

> Before we rise tonight, I think it is appropriate if I just say this. I do feel myself that the thanks of the public are due to Mr Wickstead and the members of his squad who quite obviously have been confronted with a very difficult task in the preparation and bringing of this case and whose work has resulted in the bringing of justice to people who, according to your verdict, ought to have been brought to justice, as they have been, and I think we owe a debt and the public owes a debt to Mr Wickstead and those who work with him in the detection and running to earth of what are really serious crimes and potentially much more serious than the crimes which they have in fact, according to your verdict, committed.

Wickstead – because of his rank – could not now be commended by the commissioner, but his officers were; instead, Wickstead received the written thanks of the Home Secretary, Robert Carr (later Lord Carr of Hadley PC). As the gang were put into the penal system, *The Times* speculated about a potentially serious security situation for the prison authorities because, they stated, 'The Tibbs family have enemies in practically every prison in Britain and many gang leaders have sworn revenge.'

Whether or not that was the case was a matter for the prison system; right now, with the Dixons and the Tibbs incarcerated, the East End of London was – for a period, at least – clear of organized crime.

One more matter. It became clear that before and after the arrests, witnesses – the families of the Nichols, Kersey and Wickstead – had been threatened; the 'alibi' witnesses for 'Big Jim' Tibbs who were told to give evidence were described as being 'terrified'. However, what was not generally known was that the judge, Mr Justice Lawson, was also threatened. Following the sentencing, he was escorted safely home.

The Serious Crime Squad were now dubbed 'The Untouchables' and 'The Gangbusters', and Wickstead became known as, 'The Old Grey Fox'.

But moves were afoot to thoroughly derail them; and when it happened, quite quickly after the verdicts and salutations, it came from an unexpected quarter.

★

Michael Machin served only nine months of his 11-year sentence, but before he expired from Bright's Disease he named names to Commander Reginald Arthur Davis, who since March 1973 had been head of the Inspectorate of the Metropolitan Police's No. 3 area.

Davis had seen wartime service with the Royal Navy as a petty officer before joining the police; he had been an industrious copper, commended on seventeen occasions, one a high commendation for displaying outstanding courage in the arrest of Günter Fritz Erwin Podola for the murder of Detective Sergeant Ray Purdy.

Micky Fawcett was the last of six men to be arrested; he was hauled from his bed and taken to City Road police station, where he was interviewed by Davis and Detective Chief Superintendent Frank Cater, who had been 'Nipper' Read's right-hand man on the Kray enquiry and was now seconded from the newly-formed complaints branch at the Yard, A10 Department. Fawcett was charged together with John Davies, Albert James Nichols, John Keith Enever, David Victor Storey and James Frederick Fleet with twenty-nine various offences, allegedly committed between 1961 and 1969. Fleet, Storey and Enever were charged with one attempted murder, Fawcett and Davies with another. Other charges involved causing grievous bodily harm, causing affrays and possessing firearms and offensive weapons. Fleet, Storey and Fawcett were all known enemies of the Tibbs gang. Was there a connection? All of them were remanded in custody when they appeared at Old Street Magistrates' Court on 27 August 1973, and three weeks later, two more prisoners joined their ranks: Charles Cook and Albert Nichols, both aged fifty. But on that date, all except Storey, Fleet and Enever were granted bail. What was going on? The Serious Crime Squad soon found out.

'You – all of you – you're all going to prison!' Those were the words used, with deadly solemnity, by Commander Davis after he had formed the officers from the Serious Crime Squad in a semi-circle in front of him. Each time he uttered the word, 'You!' he swung his arm, pointing at each of the officers in turn. Roger Stoodley told me that Davis added that all of the investigating team would be arrested for conspiring with the Nichols in perverting the course of justice to frame the Tibbs family.

'I remember it well,' Ed Williams – then a detective sergeant and later a detective superintendent – told me. 'Frank Cater stood to the left of Davis; he looked absolutely blank – no expression whatsoever in his face'. Williams, who had arrived on the Serious Crime Squad on the first day of the Tibbs trial, had taken no part in the investigation and was bemused by this strange scenario. He said, 'I went home and told my wife, "I'm going to prison and I don't know what for!"'

But Williams didn't go to prison, and neither did anybody else. After the Director of Public Prosecutions received the papers on those charges he realized that those witnesses who were still available were reluctant to give evidence, and on 19 October 1973 the charges against the eight men were dismissed at Old Street Magistrates' Court after the police threw the towel in and the magistrate, Mr Ian McLean, awarded each of them £100 each in costs.

'Spent that money, yet?' I jocularly asked Enever afterwards.

Failing to see any humour in the situation, he growled, 'It weren't enough!'

It was a humiliating end to a farce of an investigation and one, I suppose, best forgotten about by everybody concerned. But not Wickstead. He had not been on the receiving end of Davis' accusing finger but he never forgot what Davis had tried to do to his squad – and he never forgave him. A few years would pass before he would try to extract his revenge.

★

The Tibbs family were eventually released from prison and initially they went back into the family's scrap metal business and prospered. Later, Jimmy Tibbs became a trainer of promising young boxers, and then a born-again Christian.

In 1989 Robert Tibbs was arrested for masterminding a 1¼-ton cannabis smuggling operation worth £3,200,000, and after being convicted at Guildford Crown Court, was sentenced to 12 years' imprisonment. He appealed but at his retrial at the Old Bailey on 22 April 1993 he decided to plead guilty. Describing him as being 'in the premier division of drugs smugglers and a dedicated criminal', the judge sentenced him to 8 years' imprisonment as well as ordering him to pay £200,000 under the Drug Trafficking Offences Act within eighteen months or face a further 3 years in jail.

★

There's a footnote to this chapter. On the Monday following the Tibbs' sentencing I arrived at Forest Gate police station as a brand new detective constable. I lost no time in 'making my bones' as a detective and rushed about, making contacts, acquiring information and nicking villains. But quite apart from the foregoing activities, as well as investigating reported crimes I toured the metal dealers on the manor, and the reason for this was twofold. The first was that, as aids to CID, we were absolutely forbidden to indulge in this activity because it was felt that (a) as young, inexperienced coppers we might be corrupted or at least compromised by those tricky old dealers in non-ferrous metals; but also (b) because we feral young men were likely to nick anybody for anything, the first-class detective sergeant who traditionally inspected the yards and, it was said, received a bursary from the dealers, sought to keep the aids away from upsetting his investment.

The second reason was that now, as a fully-fledged detective, I wanted to lean on these characters, let them know that not all detectives who visited them were bent and hopefully find some crooked gear in their yards. 'Let's face it, Guv, 90 per cent of the gear that comes in here is bent', one such dealer told me and then added, 'and the other 10 per cent's iffy!'

So, yes, nick them and their customers if I could; if not, persuade them that providing me with good information was one way to get me off their backs, because if I was busy arresting villains they'd propped up, I couldn't be in two places at once, bothering them.

One of the yards I visited on a regular basis was minded by 'Bogey' Tibbs. At first, I was given a cautious welcome. 'Can I get you anything, Mr Kirby? A drink, perhaps? Er – anything else . . . ?'

'Just the books, please, Bogey', I'd reply. Only on one occasion did I arrest someone who'd brought some dodgy gear in; I arrested the manager as well, but it wasn't Bogey, who'd taken a day off. So my visits continued until it was clear that I'd become an encumbrance to Bogey.

'Right, I've had it with you, Kirby!' he shouted. 'I'm going to fix you for good!'

I smiled, went back to my car and drove back to Forest Gate. The CID clerk was in a nervous state; she'd received an irate telephone call from the most senior CID officer on the Division. He had said, 'When that fucking Kirby gets back to the office, tell him to stay there – I'm on my way over!'

'What's going on?' the clerk wanted to know.

I knew what was going on. He knew I was out of the office because Bogey Tibbs had told him so. I looked round at the office, which was quite full; they'd heard everything and I said, 'Right – when he gets here, everyone stay where you are.'

We didn't have long to wait. There was a squeal of tyres in the yard and the sound of footsteps pounding up the stairs. Seconds later, there he was, framed in the doorway, panting with exertion, his driver behind him. He looked at me, furiously – and I said, 'What was it you wanted to see me about, sir?'

He glanced around the office, to see a dozen pair of eyes staring back at him. Whatever he wanted to say to me, he didn't want to say it in front of ten detectives, the civilian CID clerk or the CID typist.

For a few seconds it seemed that he was tongue-tied, before he snarled, 'The next time you put in an application for annual leave, make sure it's put in quicker!' and with that he stamped out of the office.

He'd been a detective chief inspector on the division for three years from 1967, right in the heart of Tibbs territory; and since 1971 he'd returned as the top man. The Tibbs gang had been almost completely disbanded – and yet he could still be in fief to a member of that family, still upholding the good old traditions of the bent copper.

This was a time when the newly formed A10 department were really making themselves busy; a detective sergeant on the division had just been arrested for corruption and would later be sentenced to 2 years' imprisonment. And yet, here was the division's top detective determined to carry on in this disgraceful fashion, as presumably he'd always carried on.

It absolutely, utterly beggared belief.

CHAPTER 7

Norma Levy – Sex in Government

It's time to take a break from all the blood, snot and tears of the previous pages, just for a bit. They'll resurface soon enough, never fear.

In the late 1970s, as a member of the Serious Crime Squad – Wickstead had by now retired – I had locked up a bunch of troublesome Triads and their associates, and the office in which I was working had become too small to house the enormous amount of evidence I had accumulated. Another team had made arrests in a different investigation and were looking for an office from where they could carry out their enquiries. I therefore let them have mine and moved my evidence and all the attendant paraphernalia to an empty (and much larger) office on the top floor at Limehouse, where there was a sufficiency of filing cabinets to house my items.

I opened one of those filing cabinets and there I saw a pale green police correspondence folder. That was odd; normal Metropolitan Police files were buff-coloured, although those used by the Serious Crime Squad were maroon, marked 'Confidential' because our reports went straight to the deputy assistant commissioner. But green? Never seen one, never heard of one before. I picked it up and saw 'SECRET' stamped in red lettering at the top and then the subject of the docket: 'Investigation into possible breaches of security by Mr Lambton and Lord Jellicoe'.

Well, this looked a lot more interesting than anything I was dealing with, and if you believe that the thought, 'Oh, but I shouldn't be looking at *this*!' crossed my mind, you'd be a million miles wide of the mark.

So I made myself a cup of coffee, sat down and opened the docket . . .

*

The central character in this scenario was neither of their Lordships Lambton or Jellicoe (the anomaly between the 'Mr' of the docket heading and 'Lord' Lambton will be explained shortly) although of course they played an integral role in the set-up; it was a young woman who was born Honora Mary Russell in Limerick, Eire on 4 June 1947. She achieved worldwide fame – or notoriety – as a prostitute named Norma Levy, who almost brought down the British Government.

Leaving home (and temporarily changing her name to Mary Brown as soon as possible) she acquired a job as a bunny girl at a club in Middlesbrough and then progressed to performing as a stripper in Manchester. Two abortions later, she arrived in London, where, this time in Soho and at a variety of different clubs, she worked, once more as a stripper. Next came employment at the Embassy Club as a hostess and as a dancer at the Talk of the Town. This was followed by a job as a hostess at the Crazy Horse Club, where she met a company chairman who set her up in a flat at Regent's Park. There – and much to her embarrassment, she would later say – she was introduced to S&M clothing and practices; and apart from her benefactor, the apartment was shared with her regular boyfriend, as it was with whatever clients she brought home. The majority of them were wealthy; one bought her a Mercedes Benz.

She went to work for a Polish-born woman named Jean Horn, who acted as an agent arranging encounters for the prostitutes on her books (numbering anything from fifteen to twenty-five) and their clients. In this way, Russell had assignations with the old and the bold (although not necessarily the great and the good) whom she named as – amongst others – Sir Billy Butlin, Stavros Niarchos, the Greek shipping magnate, the Shah of Iran, Indonesia's President Sukarno and the oil millionaire John Paul Getty. During these meetings she provided whatever equipment and expertise was needed to meet the requirements of her clients' often grotesque desires.

She met Peter Goodsell, a small-time crook (who, she said, blackmailed her, although if it was true, he was never prosecuted for it), and after a fairly short-lived affair she met through him an even seedier small-time crook named Colin Levy, a one-time minicab driver, whom she married on 3 November 1972; Levy drank heavily, and it was a stormy relationship. It was shortly after her marriage that she would encounter Lord Lambton.

Lambton became one of Norma Levy's 60–70 regular clients. He was introduced to her as Mr Lucas and made it clear he wished her to dominate him. There were several assignations, and on the second occasion he paid not in cash but with a cheque. He neither made out the amount, nor did he sign it, but the account was in his real name.

Antony Claud Frederick Lambton was born in 1922. He was married with a son and five daughters, was the Conservative Member of Parliament for Berwick-upon-Tweed and a cousin of

Sir Alec Douglas-Home, the former Prime Minister and Foreign Secretary. He was briefly 6th Earl of Durham, and in February 1970 was styled Viscount Lambton. He had renounced his peerage since he was a member of the House of Commons, although despite a ruling by the Committee for Privileges he insisted on being addressed as 'Lord Lambton'. It might well be said that Lambton was a fairly arrogant character. Apart from taking drugs, indulging in S&M activity, enjoying a threesome in bed (which included a twenty-year-old male prostitute), he paid Levy with cheques and sent her a letter in his own handwriting. So he might be regarded as rather stupid as well. Taking all that into consideration, he was tailor-made for his position in the Tory Government as a Parliamentary Under-Secretary of State for Defence (RAF).

At that time, Norma Levy was living at 9 Marlborough Court, Maida Vale; the property was jointly owned by her and Bernard Davis, the chairman of the Atlas Stone Company, who, as he would later say, was 'absolutely horrified' to hear what had been going on there. Not a few of her clients would have been equally perturbed if they had known that she kept an A4 sized book which not only included all the names of her patrons but also details of when and how much they paid her, plus explicit details of who did what to whom.

Norma Levy would eventually say that she discovered (as did her husband) Lambton's real identity, plus his position in the Government. When her husband went on a mysterious trip to Morocco at the beginning of April 1973 and she found that the Lambton cheque and other items were missing, she went to the Yard and gave them a garbled (and as far as her activities were concerned, sanitized) version of what she and Colin Levy had been up to. She told the police the date and time when he was returning from Morocco, and they were waiting for him, expecting to find drugs; the official version is that they found nothing. Perhaps a little horse-trading had gone on. Colin Levy was a devious character; he told the police about the existence of the Lambton situation, but it's also extremely likely that others – Special Branch, MI5 and certainly the tabloids – were informed as well, and it could well be that he played one off against the others.

Deputy Assistant Commissioner Ernest Radcliffe Bond OBE, QPM had overall charge of the investigation. He had joined the Metropolitan Police after seeing wartime service with the Special Air Service and was a tremendous all-round detective. He had served with the Fraud Squad, the Flying Squad (twice), the Anti-Terrorist Branch and had helped set up the Criminal Intelligence Department. With him was Wickstead; two of the Met's top detectives reported directly to the Prime Minister. Wickstead suspected there was a leak and was furious; secrecy in this investigation was paramount, often spilling over into paranoia ('It was like working in a bubble', Ed Williams told me) and the waters became very muddied, indeed . . .

Wickstead had gone to work, it was reported, 'with a team of fifty detectives' and although he did not possess anything like that number of officers, this was not entirely press hyperbole, since Special Branch were certainly involved as well.

'I was involved in following Norma to the St John's Wood area', Dave McEnhill told me, 'and I was sure someone was following me, as well. I reported it, and got a call back, saying "leave it".'

Several such actions were unexplained. 'We did do some observations in the area of the Chinese Legation which was adjacent to Norma Levy's apartment', Bernie Tighe told me, 'but nothing ever came of that.'

When Colin Levy brought two anonymous men to her flat, Norma Levy said she had no idea of what was going on. On 5 May 1973 Levy and Goodsell had approached the *News of the World* with the story, and the newspaper was responsible for installing photographic, cine-film and sound-recording equipment in Norma Levy's flat. She and another prostitute, Kim Browne, had a threesome at the flat with Lambton, Norma Levy being unaware, naturally, that these frolics and Lambton smoking cannabis were being filmed and sound-recorded (the microphone was concealed in the nose of her teddy bear). When she subsequently found out that it was, 'Well', she would later say, 'I could have died.'

The Prime Minister must have felt much the same way after he was alerted regarding the situation by the Security Services and also later on 14 May by an MP, who told him that Rupert Murdoch was in possession of a 'Profumo-type' story, complete with photographs of sexual orgies involving a junior minister. Twelve years previously, of course, John Profumo, the Minister for War, had had an unwise dalliance with a young woman named Christine Keeler, whom our mothers in post-war England would have primly described as being 'no better than she should be'; but that in itself was not the problem. The difficulty was that Keeler was at the same time involved with a man who was a procurer of young girls for the so-called 'upper classes' and also with a Russian intelligence agent. The matter was exacerbated when Profumo was challenged about it; he lied to Parliament, which led to his resignation, followed by sensational world-wide revelations in the media, several court cases and Prime Minister Harold Macmillan having to step down due to ill health. A thorough investigation revealed that there had been neither security breaches nor blackmail; but would that still be the case now?

The implications were clear. Lambton was a service minister who had access to sensitive (as well as secret) documents. Was he being blackmailed? And even if he wasn't, had he blurted out any Governmental secrets to Norma Levy or any of her circle whilst he was getting systematically stoned and abused? It was a matter that had to be resolved, and quickly.

★

The material was kept by Goodsell and Colin Levy, who sold it to the *Sunday People* on 19 May. They produced seven pictures, a cheque and a tape and wanted £45,000. (They had tried to obtain £30,000 from another newspaper.) The paper later paid £750 initially and agreed a balance of £5,259 on publication for the material and statements, their argument being that it would be better to buy the material rather than leave it open to a blackmailer or a foreign embassy. The items were handed to the police.

'I saw the photo of Norma and Kim, the black girl in bed with Lambton who was smoking a big spliff', recalled Detective Constable Dave McEnhill. 'From the size of his member, I think Lambton should have been rechristened "Hampton"!'

Ed Williams told me:

> The photographic material came to the Serious and I was allowed to see it, prior to the search of Lord Lambton's address. Because of his status and the need to prove identity beyond doubt, not only were physical characteristics important, such as skin moles and scars, but so too were items of clothing shown in the photographs. Sex toys were also a feature in the search because Lord Lambton enjoyed extreme sex. In particular, we were looking for bulldog clips, metal spring-loaded, sharp toothed clamps, about four inches in length.

On 20 May the *News of the World* contained a report that 'political figures were involved in a vice ring', and the following day, the Levys left for Spain and Lambton was interviewed at the Yard by Bond and Wickstead.

Arrogance was Lambton's only defence, and it did not last long; it was quickly stripped away when he was shown the photographs, the cheque and the tapes. He admitted his sexual peccadilloes with Levy and Browne and also that he had smoked cannabis.

'I would not deny that', he said. 'Yes. I would not deny I have smoked marijuana.' Asked if Norma Levy had given him drugs, he replied, 'She has given me pep pills but I have never taken them. I have in the past taken marijuana and opium in China. I have never asked for them; it was a fetish.'

The officers accompanied Lambton to his house at 58 Hamilton Terrace, St John's Wood in order to search it; Lambton opened a small door in the skirting of his bedroom and took out a plastic box containing 5.84 grams of cannabis resin and ten pills and turning to Ernie Bond he said, 'You had better have this. I put it in there for safe custody. I did not want the children to get it. I accept responsibility for it.' A metal box was found in the bathroom containing 1.16 grams of herbal cannabis; a yellow tablet and part of a blue one were found in a bottle on a table. In total, the 11½ tablets were a mixture of amphetamine and barbiturate, amphetamine sulphate, amphetamine phenacetin and aspirin.

In addition, a Walther gas pistol and three cartridges were found; these belonged to Lady Lambton, and following an interview with her and a consultation with the DPP, the items were confiscated and no further action was taken.

The next day, 22 May, Lambton resigned from the Government and five days later, stated that he intended to apply for the Chiltern Hundreds immediately, despite appeals from his constituency to reconsider his position.

And the day following Lambton's resignation, George, 2nd Earl Jellicoe KBE, DSO, MC, FRS, Lord Privy Seal and Leader of the House of Lords also resigned. The name 'Jellicoe' had been discovered in a call-girl's notebook and since the police believed this referred the Earl of the same name, telephone intercepts revealed that he was indeed consorting with prostitutes. In fact, the 'Jellicoe' in the notebook was a reference to Jellicoe Hall, a community centre in North London, named after a second cousin of Jellicoe's. The Earl had been told by the Prime Minister, Sir Edward Heath KG, MBE, PC, that an unnamed minister had been photographed in compromising circumstances with a prostitute and he had heard that Jellicoe might be involved. There was going to be an article published in the German magazine *Der Stern* the following day, and whilst Heath did not know what it might say, he did not want Jellicoe to be caught unawares. Jellicoe thought it over, then admitted the following day that he had been consorting with prostitutes (although not Norma Levy) and he, too, resigned. It was a poor end to the career of a man who had served his country so well and so valiantly with the wartime Special Boat Service.

The tabloids had a field day: 'Vice Probe Sensation' was the *Sun*'s headline, although when 'Larry' Lamb, editorial editor of News International Ltd which controlled *The News of the World*, was asked if the newspaper had been involved in taking photographs of Lord Lambton in compromising situations, he replied, 'I'm not sure which pictures you're talking about' – which given the publicity that had been generated sounded slightly shifty. Winston Churchill MP, scenting blood, called the remark, 'equivocal and evasive'.

'Police seek men who tried to sell Lambton picture' reported the 24 May edition of *The Times* and went on to inform its readers:

> Scotland Yard detectives are anxious to trace two men who may have compromising material said to connect two other members of the Government with the Lambton affair. The men being sought, whose names are known to the police, have disappeared from their regular London haunts, after failing to sell to newspapers for £30,000 a dossier of photographs and information about Lord Lambton and his relationship with a West End call-girl and referring to two other ministers. The men are also believed to have a tape recording of a conversation between Lord Lambton and a woman known as 'Betty' who worked for a West End model agency. The two men, close associates of the woman, are believed to have photographed Lord Lambton walking into her flat. Several other photographs of a compromising nature were also taken inside the flat when Lord Lambton was with the woman. The flat was also 'bugged' and a tape recording was made. A report connected with the affair was handed to Sir Norman Skelhorn QC, Director of Public Prosecutions, at midday yesterday. A spokesman for the Director of Public Prosecutions said last night that the report was 'under active consideration'.

*

Lambton appeared at Marylebone Magistrates' Court on 13 June 1973 and pleaded guilty to the three charges of drug possession; but he was wriggling. David Tudor-Price for the prosecution told the magistrate, Rupert Rawden-Smith:

> Since the summonses were issued, Lord Lambton has made certain public statements indicating his possession

was technical. The prosecution are unable to accept this. The drugs were in three separate places. Enquiries have been made and statements taken. Lord Lambton asked a person with whom he was associated for drugs, asking them to give them to him and on one or more occasions, he was in possession of cannabis and smoked it.

Lambton's defence counsel, Edward Stephen Cazalet (later His Honour Judge Sir Edward Cazalet DL), sought to put a different light on matters, saying that the cannabis was an old, minute amount, that the drugs were not for his (Lambton's) use and that they had been confiscated from another person, whose identity he refused to disclose.

The magistrate said that taking drugs into custody was a different situation than using them, to which Cazalet replied, 'Lord Lambton says that on a limited number of occasions with the prostitute he smoked cannabis. On no occasion did he take cannabis or any other drug to or from the flat.'

The two counsel went into a huddle with the Magistrate, who said that whether the drugs were or were not for Lambton's use was a fundamental point and suggested that that line of mitigation might have to be withdrawn. There was a hurried consultation between lawyer and client, after which Cazalet turned to the court again, stated he would not be calling his client and asked for leniency. Since the Lambton family owned most of Durham, a fine totalling £300 certainly represented a large dose of clemency.

Both peers were interviewed by the security services – had they been blackmailed? No, said both of them. Had Lord Lambton taken any red boxes containing secret defence papers with him during his assignations with Norma Levy? No, said Lambton, and as Charles Elwell, MI5's investigator, rather bitingly noted in his report, 'Indeed, he had no need to, since he had so little work to do.'

Lord Jellicoe's position was slightly different because the prostitutes he had consorted with ('on five or six occasions') had come to his London flat during his wife's absence; but he stated that he had always locked his red boxes away in a cupboard. In contrast to Lambton, Jellicoe was very hard-working; the surprised reaction from the secretaries in the House of Lords was, 'However did he find the time?'

There had been no blackmail or any breaches of security. However, Jellicoe had been luckier than he knew. He had used Glamour International and Mayfair Escorts, agencies run by Joey Wilkins, a top London gangster. If I were to say that Wilkins had every crooked cop at West End Central in his pocket, it might be an exaggeration – but not, I assure you, by much. Fortunately, Jellicoe had used the alias 'Mr Jefferies' and, unlike Lambton, had always paid in cash. Two foolish men had been toppled from power, thanks to the greed of a couple of very greasy, second-rate crooks and the antics of a manipulative young woman.

'Norma Levy tried to come across as a poor little girl who had been cajoled into doing the things she did', was Dave McEnhill's opinion, 'when in fact she was very clever, indeed.'

*

Meanwhile, the Levys were in Spain – this trip had been funded by the *People* – then went on to Tangiers, Morocco, then Casablanca, after which, with Norma Levy disguised in a burka, they flew to South America for a single day, then came back to Germany. There poor exhausted Norma was shown photos of many men she had consorted with and, confused and weary, she signed a statement to that effect. With her passport in Colin Levy's possession, the couple flew to the south of France, then on to Spain where, since she learned that her London flat had been repossessed, Norma Levy decided to fully cooperate with the press as a way to earn an honest living. It was only when Colin Levy apparently tried to run her down in a drunken rage that she had him charged with attempted murder and on 15 July returned to England.

But on the day before the Levys left for Spain, Norma Levy and a friend, Brenda Harris, had gone to view a cottage, which she described as being 'just outside Colchester', and had decided to purchase it; she told the agent that she would telephone him the following day to make an offer. This conversation had been picked up, doubtless by means of a telephone intercept, and Wickstead sent Detective Sergeants Roger Stoodley, John Farley and Dougie Gowar to make enquiries about the premises, named Tom Swallow Cottage, at Plough Road, Great Bentley, Essex; it was up for sale at a price of £22,500 (currently valued at £712,000) and the estate agents were Bairstow Eves in Clacton.

'We were given strict instructions not to discuss our business with anyone outside of the immediate enquiry team', said Stoodley, adding, 'Believe me, when Bert issued instructions, they were followed to the letter!'

Posing as potential buyers, they went to the cottage to await the arrival of the agent, and upon hearing of their interest, the next door neighbour, who kept a key for the property, let them inspect the interior. They found correspondence in the name of

'Harrington', which meant nothing to them; however, as Stoodley later said, 'If Bert Wickstead had not been so secretive, we would have known it was an alias used by Norma Levy.'

Further enquiries with the estate agent revealed that 'Mrs Harrington' wanted to purchase the cottage without her husband's knowledge and planned to add a swimming pool and a paddock; and whilst the officers were unaware if she intended to keep it as a 'love nest' or for her own use, Norma Levy would later say she wanted it as an investment. Whatever the truth of the matter, the phone call to the estate agent was not made and the sale never went through.

★

Meanwhile, the Yard had not been idle. The 24 June edition of the *News of the World* declared that 'startling new evidence' had been obtained by 'agents' of Scotland Yard, who in turn denied the suggestion that the Levys had been visited by their 'agents' or people acting on their behalf. True, Detective Inspectors Joyce Cashmore (who with Bill Waite had been one of the first two officers Wickstead had selected for his squad) and Graham Howard had travelled to Spain, but whatever evidence might or might not have been uncovered, 45 years later Howard staunchly denied to me meeting with the Levys, so the Sunday paper must have been misinformed with regard to that aspect of their story. However, it was good to know the whereabouts of the Levys, because on 22 June Wickstead had obtained warrants to arrest both of them: Norma Levy, for attempting to procure a female for the purposes of prostitution, and her husband for living off immoral earnings.

Wickstead had arrested Norma Levy's employer, fifty-two-year-old Mrs Regina Jean Horn, who described herself as 'a property dealer' – which, whatever way one looks at it, was probably a fair assessment of her profession. He had obtained a statement from a prostitute who claimed that Mrs Horn had proposed a deal whereby the girl would charge a client £30–£50 and Mrs Horn would extract a commission of £5–£10 per transaction, having arranged the date, time and place. She was joined in the dock at Marylebone Magistrates' Court on 11 July by Mrs Roswitha Abray, a thirty-one-year-old German national known as 'Rocha' and described by Norma Levy as being 'a big, brassy peroxide blonde'. Both of them admitted two charges of influencing prostitutes for gain, with Mrs Abray taking Mrs Horn's place when the latter was admitted to hospital.

In response to a question from the defence, Wickstead agreed that the accused 'were not connected with a third woman whose name was not revealed and who was said to be out of the country' – which must be regarded as being fairly disingenuous. Mrs Horn, said to have played a major part in the agency, was fined a total of £200 with £30 costs. Mrs Abray, who also admitted unlawful possession of a teargas pistol and ammunition, was fined £130 with £20 costs.

★

As Norma Levy alighted from the aeroplane at Heathrow, so she was arrested by Wickstead, and he, together with Detective Inspector Joyce Cashmore, took her to Tintagel House.

Telling Wickstead, 'I'm going to tell you everything', she gave an account of just what she wanted to tell him in a 20-page statement, which included the words, 'I kept a record of all customers involved, their names and telephone numbers, who the girls were and the fee they received and the commission to be paid to Jean Horn. I also recorded the names of the girls concerned.'

At 2.15 on the morning of 16 July she was charged with attempting to procure a woman to become a prostitute – something she denied (and when she appeared at Marylebone Magistrates' Court on 31 July, that charge was dropped) – and she pleaded guilty to three charges of influencing the movements of prostitutes, while she ran the organization when Jean Horn had to go into hospital.

Robert Gibbons for the defence told the court:

> I should like to point out that as far as this young woman is concerned, she is not a principal in these matters. She is a girl who has been caught up in this particular web. She has pleaded guilty to these charges today, but she is not the head or even the member of any gang of swindlers or blackmailers.

Norma Levy, who at the age of twenty-six could not really be described as 'a girl' and by no stretch of the imagination as 'a housewife', which was how she described her profession, was fined £225 plus £25 costs.

'Despite considerable efforts to winkle Colin Levy out of hiding, he had, to all intents and purposes, vanished,' Ed Williams told me. 'I circulated him as "wanted" with CRO (Criminal Records Office), but now there is little doubt that nobody wanted him found. The nation did not need another political scandal. A year later, he had still not surfaced and I transferred away from the Serious.'

That was it; Ernie Bond went back to his office on the 5th floor of the Yard, and following the quickest enquiry ever carried out by the Serious Crime Squad, Wickstead and his men returned to work for which they were far more suited – gangbusting.

Peter Goodsell, one of the others involved in the filming of Lord Lambton, was convicted of helping to smuggle cannabis worth £40,000 from Jamaica into Switzerland in 1979. He was jailed for 3 years at Lincoln High Court.

The Press Council severely censured the *News of the World*, and following the scandal Lord Lambton left his wife and went to live at the Villa Cetinale in Tuscany. He died in 2006, aged eighty-four.

George Jellicoe could not be considered to be conventionally good-looking but he was extremely charismatic as well as immensely popular, and his friends and contemporaries rallied round. He had committed very foolish and indiscreet acts and paid for them; but his contemporaries wanted someone to blame. Not Jellicoe, certainly, or the prostitutes who brought about his fall from grace, so they selected the police to be their whipping boys. In the Lords on 6 June 1973 Baroness Gaitskell said:

> Why was it necessary to have detectives watching a flat, noting that Lord Jellicoe entered, identifying the number of his car and then passing the information on to the Government? Entering a prostitute's flat is not a criminal offence and unseemly behaviour need not be treated as criminal behaviour. I wonder who authorised that particular snooping?

And in a preposterously pompous statement, Jellicoe's biographer noted that, following the revelations, the Metropolitan Police invited Jellicoe to a lunch. This, it was suggested, was to 'salve their consciences over the mistaken connection they had made, since they had no other reason to put on a lunch for him'. No reason other than Jellicoe and Ernie Bond both being members of the Special Forces Club, having both been in the wartime Special Air Service, as well as Jellicoe and Wickstead having been members of the Special Boat Service – that's all.

Jellicoe – who died, aged eighty-eight in 2007 – took his transgressions on the chin; it's a pity his supporters couldn't have left matters like that.

★

Norma Levy divorced her husband, and in the four months left of 1973, following her conviction, had her memoirs published with breathtaking speed; then, before she could enslave the whole of the Serious Crime Squad, she went to live in the USA. She was married twice more, first to Jack Geiger, with whom she lived in Florida ('but he drank too much') and then Louis Macchione; they lived in a villa in New Jersey until his death in 1998.

She ran a call-girl agency on America's East coast but was sentenced to eighteen months' imprisonment at Danbury maximum security prison in Connecticut, her mansion and assets, valued at £1.5 million were seized and she was deported to Ireland; reports vary as to whether it was her third or fifth deportation. She ended up living in Toronto on benefits of £150 per month and staying in a hostel for the homeless.

Dave McEnhill told me, 'Norma Levy was the most beautiful woman'; but by now, her beauty had gone; fat, her looks fading fast, with arrests for drugs and being drunk and disorderly, she died aged sixty on 8 October 2007 from pancreatic cancer.

There was a third minister involved. Norma Levy named him, then retracted her statement. He has never been publicly named. In the files held at the National Archive it was not considered sufficient for the file to remain closed; the minister's name has been blanked out as well.

The Government had been concerned (and rightly so) that there could have been a breach of security, but when the enquiry chaired by Lord Diplock determined that that was not the case, the matter disintegrated into a comedy of errors.

The constituents of Berwick-upon-Tweed bemoaned the loss of their popular Member of Parliament who, perhaps surprisingly, had appeared on television to be asked by Robin Day, 'Why should a man of your social position and charm and personality have to go to whores for sex?'

To this Lambton replied, 'I think that people sometimes like variety. I think it's as simple as that and I think that impulse is probably understood by almost everybody', adding for effect, 'Don't you?'

Given those impenitent comments, the *hoi polloi* giggled when they read in the tabloids of the peer who had been photographed both wearing and taking off his red flannel underwear, as well as about other unnamed people who enjoyed being beaten, humiliated and urinated upon. The traditional black humour of the police was trespassed upon and was not found wanting.

'Back in those days, I drew the conclusion that I was leading an awfully boring sex life', one Serious Crime Squad officer ruefully told me, and another, referring to the compromising photograph of Lord Lambton said, 'if I'd been him, I'd have had that photo enlarged, framed and hung above my bed; I'd have been so fucking pleased!'

★

My coffee had gone cold. I closed the green file which, John Farley told me, 'We weren't allowed to look at' (although it was known to members of the Squad as 'The Saga of Lambton's Hampton') that contained so many secrets, to return to the more pressing business of my pestilential Triads. Was the name of the third erring minister contained in that file? As Francis Urquhart, the duplicitous minister in Michael Dobbs' *House of Cards* was prone to say, with a knowing look to the camera, 'You might well think that – I couldn't possibly comment.'

CHAPTER 8

The Porn Squad and the Maltese Syndicate

There can be little doubt that Wickstead's tenure as head of the Serious Crime Squad was a pretty busy time. While dealing with the commencement of the Dixon trial in 1972 he had also been obliged to arrest the Tibbs gang. But following on from there, the Commissioner dumped Wickstead's biggest, most complex case in his lap, one in which the investigation would go on for years. It involved organized gang warfare in the West End of London, prostitution, pornography and a whole collection of bent coppers.

It started in 1972, when Wickstead and a number of other officers from his squad, including John Lewis and Bernie Tighe, were summoned to the Yard to see Sir Robert Mark GBE, QPM, who had been commissioner since 17 April 1972.

Mark was a controversial commissioner. Much of his early service had been in Manchester and Leicester, and he had arrived at the Yard in 1967, becoming first the Assistant Commissioner 'D' Department, then 'B' Department, next Deputy Commissioner and finally commissioner. He had not liked what he had seen of the Criminal Investigation Department – the feeling was fully reciprocated – and, convinced that CID officers were corrupt, he set out to eradicate them, very much like an avenging angel wielding a flaming sword. Mark was right – but he was also wrong. Most CID officers were honest and hard-working (much later, he admitted this was so), but there was a cadre of officers, some of whom were attached to the Flying Squad and others who were members of C1 Department's Obscene Publications Branch – colloquially known as 'The Porn Squad' – who were very crooked indeed. They were hand-in-glove with some of Soho's most prolific pornographers and, as John Lewis told me:

> Mark told Bert that the only way he could end corruption within the Force was to rid the West End of Bernie Silver and Frank Mifsud who he believed were the two men dealing with senior police officers. As a result, we were given the task of investigating those running

prostitution and dirty bookshops in Soho and Mayfair. Bert did not want his squad involved with the investigation of police officers, so a separate squad was set up to do that.

Again, Mark was right and he was wrong. Silver had indeed been involved in corrupting officers, but it would not be his demise which would cause the bent coppers' whole rotten house of cards to come tumbling down; when the chips were down, Silver refused to implicate any crooked cops. Mark had not mentioned Jimmy Humphreys, who had become Silver's arch-enemy, but it was he who would provide the impetus to expose some very corrupt cops. And even then, it might not have happened had Humphreys not become thoroughly upset with 'Pookie', his wife's former lover, who got cut to pieces. This led to Humphreys fleeing to Holland on a false passport, Serious Crime Squad officers bringing him back and the dramatic production of some highly sensitive – and incriminating – diaries, which in turn resulted in some explosive, headline-grabbing trials.

But now I'm getting ahead of myself. Time to let you in on the build-up to this state of affairs, which also, sadly, led to the eventual destruction of the Met's Criminal Investigation Department, the tattered remnants of which can be seen to this day.

★

As the head of what became known as 'The Maltese Syndicate', Bernie Silver was something of an anomaly, because he was Jewish. Born in Hackney, London in 1922, he described himself as 'a café proprietor' but in reality he was a ponce. As the Messina brothers (who had run prostitution in Soho during the 1930s and the war years) faded from the scene, through imprisonment, deportation or death, Silver stepped in to fill the void and in doing so was quite successful. He ran an estate agency in Romilly Street, Soho, where twenty-four flats, which normally brought in a rent of £3–£5 per week each, were leased only to prostitutes, who were charged £25 per week and, in addition, had to pay £200 'key money' to permit them access in the first place.

It was a pretty lucrative business, which brought an income of £60,000 per year. Following a three-week trial, where Silver was one of eight male and one female defendants (the latter being Mrs Albertine 'French Betty' Falzon, whom Silver would later marry) charged with living wholly or partly on the earnings of prostitution, in a fairly scatty ruling His Honour Judge Maude QC decided there was no case to answer; on 9 February 1956 everybody in the dock walked free.

Pausing only to arrange – so it was said – the demise of Tommy 'Scarface' Smithson, who had imprudently tried bossing about some of the Maltese gangsters, Silver teamed up with an 18-stone former Maltese traffic policeman, 'Big Frank' Saviour Mifsud. They opened a strip club in Brewer Street and by the end of the 1960s they controlled nineteen of the twenty-four strip clubs in the Soho area. Silver's marriage to 'French Betty' came to an end when she committed suicide by jumping out of the window of her Soho flat in Peter Street in the 1970s. It was additionally upsetting for Silver since he had been living off her immoral earnings, but he married twice more and had a string of girlfriends. He also acquired two London homes as well as a number of Rolls-Royces and other expensive vehicles. Moreover, Silver and Mifsud became rather over-friendly with a number of police officers whose duties led them into Silver's area of Soho; but more of them later.

*

Although Bernie Silver's Soho domain became known as 'Silver City', James William 'Jimmy' Humphreys would become a far higher-profile character than Silver. Born in January 1930 in South London, he left school at the age of fourteen and began a life of crime. Aged fifteen, for housebreaking and stealing two fur coats he was bound over for two years to be of good behaviour, but such decorum was beyond his capabilities. The same year, he was sent to an Approved School, and then began a dreary pattern of more crime, more Approved School, Borstal and just before his twenty-first birthday, twelve months' imprisonment. During the 1950s two more terms of imprisonment were imposed for receiving and taking and driving away, and in 1958 he broke into a Post Office in Wales and stole postal orders with a value of £8,000. Having notched up his ninth conviction, he was properly regarded as 'a habitual criminal', and having received a sentence of 6 years' imprisonment, he served his time in Dartmoor.

In between times, Humphreys had met and married his first wife, June Driscoll, and started a family, as had a young woman named June Beryl Packard, later Gaynor, who due to the colour of her flowing hair would become known as 'Rusty'; she was someone who would play an important and decisive role in Humphreys' life. In fact, Humphreys had met Rusty, then aged sixteen, in 1951, and when Humphreys' 1958 prison sentence began, Rusty started an affair with a con-man and hotel thief named Peter 'Pookie'

Garfath; this became an on-off relationship which lasted through 1961/2 and beyond.

When Humphreys was released from prison, he formed Humphreys Entertainments Ltd and started a club in Old Compton Street, Soho; it was not a success. But now he bumped into Rusty Gaynor once more; both their marriages had failed, Rusty was a successful stripper (and according to one particularly asinine observation 'half the Soho Vice Squad was in love with her'). They started living together, with Rusty dancing at Humphreys' club, and in 1963 they married. Even with the glamorous Rusty enhancing Humphreys' manifestly seedy institution, it was still unsuccessful, until something happened in a distinctly odd way which propelled both of them on the road to success. Fate – in the form of Detective Sergeant Harold Gordon Challenor MM – intervened.

★

Challenor had been a brave and resourceful decorated soldier with the wartime Special Air Service regiment; he had fought behind enemy lines, had been captured twice and escaped twice. He joined the Metropolitan Police in 1951. Undeniably tough and unorthodox, like other members of the SAS, it was rumoured that his unconventionality went rather too far in his dealings with criminals, as in the story about how, it was rumoured, he and Humphreys first came into contact.

Humphreys was awakened one morning by a thunderous knocking on his front door; there stood Challenor, who invited Humphreys to accompany him to search his car. In the car's boot was a handsome collection of what were known as housebreaking implements – or 'HBI'. Challenor ignored Humphreys' protestations that he had never seen them before; he was charged and remanded in custody for one week. However, by the time he next appeared at the Magistrates' Court, a closer inspection had been made of the HBI. That they were implements used for housebreaking was not in dispute; unfortunately, they bore labels which revealed that they had been the subject of one of Challenor's previous cases.

It was not done to upset the police in those days; the matter was quietly dropped, Humphreys walked free from court and the HBI were forwarded to the Prisoners' Property Store for destruction; but a connection between the two men had been made – that is, if one accepts such a far-fetched tale.

Going one step further with tales which might be apocryphal, in April 1963 Challenor again approached Humphreys, this time with a much more harmonious suggestion; he suggested that the unprofitable Old Compton Street club be closed down and the business be shifted to Macclesfield Street, a short through road just south of the former premises, running between Shaftesbury Avenue and Gerrard Street. Although this club, too, was not a success, Rusty was a clever businesswoman and she suggested going into partnership in a club situated at 5 Walker's Court, a very narrow thoroughfare situated between Brewer Street and Peter Street. The location appeared not to be too tempting, dingy and off the Soho beaten track, except for one thing: situated at 11 Walker's Court was Raymond's Revuebar. Paul Raymond's club had been in operation for the previous five years, and as a member's only club was one of the few in London able to show full frontal nudity. Humphreys' club was an instant success; those unable to gain access to No. 11 flocked to No. 5. Rusty was the principal dancer, and the shows staged and the prices charged were very competitive compared to Raymond's Revuebar.

In the meantime, Humphreys complained to the Yard that Challenor had approached him for money and 'bodies' (i.e. persons available for arrest); he stated that he had given Challenor two payments of £25, but although the complaint was investigated it was found to be unsubstantiated. What was authenticated was that Challenor had planted bricks on members of the public during an unpopular state visit, and while three of his aids to CID were sent to prison, Challenor was committed to a psychiatric hospital.[1]

While Challenor raved in a psychiatric ward, the fortunes of the Humphreys soared. They purchased Frogs Hill, a 28-room property on the Kent/Sussex borders, he drove a white Rolls-Royce and within two years they had closed Walker's Court and were using it as a booking office for the Queen's Club. This was a much larger property in Berwick Street which housed many more strippers; then even more properties were acquired, including an apartment in Dean Street and a holiday flat in Ibiza.

Just seven years after Jimmy's release from prison, the Humphreys were an affluent couple, but now Jimmy wanted to diversify and found in pornography the way to expand his business interests.

However, matters were not as cut and dried as all that. Both the pornography and prostitution trades (as well as quite a few night clubs and clip joints) were run by Bernie Silver, and any attempt by

---

[1] For more details of this controversial cop, see *The Scourge of Soho*, Pen & Sword True Crime, 2013.

Humphreys to gatecrash the porn market was met by opposition from Silver's men or crooked police officers in Silver's pocket.

But Humphreys was nothing if not resourceful; although he and Silver hated each other, he managed to engineer an introduction to Wallace Virgo, then the Commander of C1 Department, and through him to some of his officers, especially Detective Chief Superintendent Bill Moody, the head of the Obscene Publication Squad.

It would become clear that the scale of corruption was staggering; Moody would provide Humphreys with a licence for his own bookshops – in turn, Silver would pocket a share of the profits, as would the police.

The meetings took place at the Empress restaurant; it was agreed that a bookshop at 55 Rupert Street would be managed by a Joey Janes (who had also been a front man for a similar bookshop in Walker's Court, owned by Silver) and the profits would be split 50-50 between Silver and Humphreys. As a result, Moody became richer by £4,000, this sum being split equally between Silver and Humphreys and for his introduction fee to Moody, Virgo received £1,000. Later, three more bookshops were opened, which resulted in another £6,000 for Moody.

Into this cauldron of corruption stepped Ken Drury, the commander of the Flying Squad. At just over six feet tall, this ex-military policeman had joined the Met just after completing war service and with thirteen commissioner's commendations to his credit, and (although he referred to himself as 'an over-promoted detective sergeant') he had shot up the promotional ladder. He had been reunited with the Flying Squad in November 1970 as the detective chief superintendent; promoted to commander the following year, he had remained as the head of the Squad.

Drury had met Humphreys at a police promotional party in 1971, the men and their families became friends, there was talk of them going into business together and on the fifty-eight occasions when the two men met at restaurants, clubs and sporting events, it was Humphreys who paid the bills.

But it could be said that Drury earned his money. When Humphreys started an affair with Silver's mistress, 'Dominique' Ferguson – which sounded rather more exotic than her baptismal name of 'Katherine' – whilst Silver was abroad, it became the worst kept secret in Soho; and Humphreys' friends told him to 'watch out'. Matters became critical when Dominique overheard a conversation between Silver and 'a senior detective' in which the fitting up of Humphreys was discussed. An urgent meeting with Drury was arranged, Humphreys was told not to concern himself, whatever skulduggery was planned was cancelled and Drury found himself better off to the tune of £1,050. This sum appealed to Humphreys' sense of humour; professional men i.e. barristers, surgeons etc. were always paid in guineas or multiples of 21 shillings. Nothing so common as a 'grand' was offered to Drury; the fee for his timely and qualified intervention was 1,000 guineas.

When the fall came, it was from four directions: a pretty piece of three-way grassing, Rusty's immorality, an ill-judged holiday and a gangland boss who objected to being fitted up. We'll deal with the last of those first.

★

In late 1971 there had been a robbery in Blackpool which resulted in a local police superintendent, Gerald Richardson, being shot dead by one of the robbers, Freddie Sewell. One of Sewell's associates was Joey Pyle, who had been acquitted of a gangland murder in 1960. His was one of many addresses to be turned over by the Flying Squad following the Blackpool robbery, and when he refused to disclose Sewell's whereabouts he was charged with conspiracy to rob, using as evidence a gun, ammunition and pickaxe handles found in Pyle's car. In vain, Pyle claimed that he had been fitted up, but while he waited for his trial date he was seething at what he perceived to be the injustice which had been foisted upon him. He was then approached by a reporter eager to publish a story about how innocent criminals had been fitted up by police. The reporter referred to a post office robbery in Luton where the postmaster had been murdered and one of the people convicted had been a Patsy Murphy; the case had been investigated by the then Detective Chief Superintendent Kenneth Drury. This was what the novelist John Buchan referred to as 'the cross-bearing'. Detective Sergeant Harold Hannigan was Pyle's alleged fitter-upper; he was a Flying Squad officer, Drury was, by now, the Commander of the Squad – and bingo!, that was the connection. Keen to know anything detrimental about Drury, the reporter was helped immeasurably by Pyle, who blurted out that Drury had just returned from a holiday in Cyprus with Jimmy Humphreys.

On the face of it, and to quite a lot of people, this appeared to be a straightforward piece of grassing, but Pyle strenuously (and understandably) denied it; as everybody knows, gangland bosses never grass. He offered two explanations for his comments: (a) that his statement 'just came out of the blue and bang, that was that', or (b) that it was 'to help a friend get off a murder charge'.

Whether or not Pyle's comments did assist, Patsy Murphy had his life sentence quashed at the Court of Appeal which was only half a result, since following the murder conviction he had been sentenced to 12 years' imprisonment for a robbery at Stoke Newington. Pyle got a better result when he was acquitted of the conspiracy to rob charge.

But leaving those two miscarriages of justice to one side, the cat was out of the bag with a vengeance. On 27 February 1972 the *Sunday People* published their exposé of the 'Police Chief and the Porn King'. It was true, said Drury, that he and his wife had accompanied Jimmy and Rusty Humphreys to Cyprus and had stayed in adjoining rooms in the same de luxe hotel in Famagusta, but he (Drury) had paid his own way and in any event, this was not a holiday since he was following up a lead as to the whereabouts of the escaped Great Train Robber, Ronnie Biggs. This implausible story – Drury had not told his immediate senior officer about this trip, and in any case there was no intelligence to suggest that Biggs was in Cyprus (he was in fact in Australia) – was supported by Humphreys; at least, to start with.

Unfortunately, Drury's improbable tale was coming apart at the seams, especially after it was discovered that the £513 bill had been paid by Humphreys; and little or no credibility could be put on the possibility that, hearing of Drury's presence, a desperate Ronnie Biggs had skipped off to Beirut, which the quartet from England visited on a two-day jaunt.

On 6 March Drury was suspended from duty, but before disciplinary proceedings could be instituted, he resigned on 1 May. And all might still have been well – Drury and Humphreys still continued to meet socially – until Drury, in an act of profound stupidity (and for a fee of £10,000) told his own story in the *News of the World*, naming Humphreys as his informant. Being labelled as a grass was not something that Humphreys was going to stand for; he struck back, saying that Drury had been living out of his pocket for some time.

Robert Mark, who two weeks prior to Drury's resignation had been appointed commissioner, was similarly not going to accept a bollocks story about Drury going to Cyprus to find Ronnie Biggs.

In the same edition of the *Sunday People* which had exposed Drury's relationship with Humphreys and which carried a piece on porn shops in Soho, one of the investigators was quoted as ironically saying that he had 'formed the opinion that some policemen are corrupt'.

It was sufficient for Humphreys, who now ducked out of the public spotlight and fled to Ibiza. It was said that in his absence

Peter Garfath and Rusty Humphreys resumed their long-running affair; and it was then that the last of the factors bringing about a calamitous finale for everybody involved fell into place.

*

Detective Inspector Bernie Tighe and Detective Sergeant John Lewis got to work in Soho on the prostitution investigation, with the latter taking up the tale:

> At first, Bernie and I had an old briefcase with a camera in it and we would walk around Soho and Mayfair, into cafés and bars and in the street, photographing those we thought were involved, without their knowledge, for later identification. This gave us an idea of who was doing what in the organization. We also visited prostitutes in their flats and got some information regarding who they were paying rent to, or who was taking money from them. Eventually, we managed to get an informant who we took to an East London police station and he gave us pages and pages of notes, setting out which properties were owned and by whom, who was living off the girls, who owned the dirty bookshops and the strip clubs. All this was recorded in a red book by Bert and the pages were later stapled together because Bert did not want any other police officers to know who the informant was, or what information had been given. The book was eventually put away with the papers, as far as I know, still stapled together. When we left the police station, the informant was scared that his name would get back to those he had grassed and started tearing up all his notes into little pieces and throwing them out of the car as we drove along. We then got pulled over by a police car for littering the streets and it took some careful conversation to put things right without letting on what it was about.

Dave McEnhill, too, toured the Soho area, also with a briefcase camera ('with the lens in the bottom right-hand corner', as he confided to me). He also obtained statements from the prostitutes and unpatriotically told me, 'The French were the best looking ones.'

One prostitute had to be brought in for questioning, and Roger Stoodley was despatched for this task. Following a sign bearing the legend 'French Lessons' he ascended several flights of rickety stairs, provoking the instant flight of three waiting customers when he revealed his occupation. After meeting the prostitute, he queried the use of an angled mirror above her bed and was rather nonplussed to discover that whilst she was entertaining a client, she would use the reflection of a nearby TV in the mirror to watch *Coronation Street*.

In the face of this police activity, it was not surprising that there were counter-attacks. Humphreys was going to use his allies, the villainous Nash brothers from North London, to act as muscle in taking over Silver's business interests; whilst they had been in Cyprus, Drury had told Humphreys that Wickstead had commenced enquiries into the Nashes – and what was more, he was right. Ed Williams was carrying out an observation with another officer when they were suddenly confronted by a very aggressive bunch of Nash supporters, and without any back-up they had to beat a hasty retreat. 'I can't believe we weren't set up', he told me – and he was right, as well.

Wickstead received a visit from Wally Virgo who, having been the commander of C1 Department since 1 April 1970, was Wickstead's immediate boss. Putting £500 on his desk, Virgo stated that Wickstead could expect a similar sum each week, providing he kept out of Soho. Wickstead threw Virgo and his bursary out of his office and from then on ensured that whenever his correspondence was sent to the Yard it completely bypassed the commander and went straight to the office of the deputy assistant commissioner. Perhaps Virgo sensed which way the wind was blowing; he resigned on 4 March 1973.

Wickstead's officers found themselves being 'chatted up' by various officers when they visited the Yard; in addition, as members of C1 Department, they were expected to carry out night-duty reserve at the Yard, to cater for any reports of serious crime being received from any part of the British Empire which might require C1's expertise.

'My men aren't fucking telephone operators' said Wickstead in the right quarters. None of the Serious Crime Squad personnel ever carried out that rather irksome duty, and visits to the Yard were kept to a minimum.

Meanwhile, witnesses were seen and statements obtained, with officers from the squad travelling abroad to amass information. This coincided with Wickstead supplementing his team with two stalwarts from his 'G' Division days, Detective Sergeants Terry Brown GM and Stan Clegg, both of whom were attached to the Flying Squad.

'I was a Second-class on 10 squad, an East End team', Clegg told me. 'I was only there for a few months, when I got the calling from Bert.'

The Porn Squad and the Maltese Syndicate

Clegg was one of the officers who went to Malta to trace witnesses who had been involved in the West End's vice trade. It was important to trace George Caruana; he had been beaten up and slashed by Tommy 'Scarface' Smithson and his cohorts prior to Smithson being lured to an address owned by Caruana where he was murdered. Later, Caruana became the centre of consideration for assassination by the Kray brothers, at the behest of Bernie Silver, first by dynamiting his car, then by means of a crossbow.

Stan Clegg now takes up the tale of the Malta expedition:

> On our first visit with John Lewis and Bernie Tighe, we had to go to the Police Headquarters which was situated on the other side of a football pitch. Totally unsuited for the climate we set off, suits and ties and briefcases in hand, we must have been a pretty picture to the locals. On arrival at the HQ we were ushered into the office of the head of the CID, a short, stout grey-haired Maltese. It was just like a scene from a 1940s film, it was dimly lit, one 40 watt bulb and a ceiling fan which rotated when it felt like it. It was a very social meeting, consuming a glass or two of the local brew. We were then introduced to Fred Calleja who was to be our escort on our many visits.
>
> We traced most of those we were looking for but one, George Caruana, didn't want to meet with us and he went on the missing list. As most of our work was in the evening, we were having a short break during one afternoon, so a friend of Fred's took us on a trip round the islands in his speedboat.

One of the many islands in an archipelago between Malta and Gozo is Comino; just 3.5 sq. km. in size, it's a paradise for snorkelers, divers, windsurfers, ramblers – and George Caruana, whom the officers met when, by chance, their speedboat arrived in one of the island's lovely bays. He failed to attend a meet that evening with the officers; instead, he left Malta bound for Germany and was later traced to a Frankfurt strip club, where he made a statement; but the slippery Mr Caruana never did give evidence in court for the Serious Crime Squad.

*

Rusty Humphreys was arrested on 31 August 1972 after she was found in possession of a Webley pistol and five rounds of ammunition at Heathrow airport. Her husband was in Ibiza and, it was said, she intended to 'threaten' him with the pistol; at Uxbridge Magistrates' Court on 25 September she was imprisoned for four months. Inexplicably, she was released on 20 October, just after Humphreys had been warned 'big trouble is coming' – a warning also received by Silver, who promptly left for France and Spain, as did Mifsud, for Eire, then Brazil, followed by Switzerland. But whatever that 'big trouble' was that awaited Humphreys, it could not have been the attack on Peter Garfath, because that had not yet occurred.

Having heard of his wife's alleged liaison with Garfath, Humphreys decided to teach him a lesson and impress upon him not to pursue the relationship. At 11.30 pm on 23 October 1972 Garfath was drinking at the bar of the Dauphin Club, George Street, Mayfair when Humphreys and four of his henchmen entered. Humphreys ordered a round of drinks, there was some whispered conversation and then they cornered Garfath in the men's lavatory. His face was slashed and, as he tried to escape, a hostess saw his bleeding face trapped while the door was banged against his head and he was kicked in the stomach. Humphreys mocked Garfath, chanting, 'Pookie, Pookie', which was Rusty's pet name for her lover; Ronald George Bergin was the knife-wielder and was egged on by Humphreys telling him, 'Cut his hands off!', although a more temperate gang member rejected that suggestion, saying, 'No, that's not our game; we're just here to cut him up.'

But that was not sufficient for Garfath to complain to the police; when he was admitted to hospital he stated that he had fallen down some stairs in a restaurant with a glass in his hand. It was not until a month later that police commenced their enquiries, and that was after Garfath had been attacked once more and sustained serious head injuries.

The enquiry was taken up by Wickstead's team. Jimmy Humphreys had fled to Holland together with his wife and a warrant was obtained for his arrest.

*

In the meantime, Peter Garfath was being minded by the Serious Crime Squad. The protection was carried out in two ways. Four temporary detective constables (TDCs) were seconded from their Divisional stations to the SCS, one of whom was Michael Hall from Tooting police station. He was paired with another TDC, 'Taff' James, and answering to Detective Chief Inspector John Bland they moved into the Norfolk Court Hotel, 315 Beulah Hill, SE19. He told me:

Garfath was an absolute cretin. He brought a kitten along with him; we were supposed to share a room with him but we couldn't – the smell was atrocious. He was never not smoking or drinking; I had to keep him supplied with booze and fags. One week, I put in a bigger expenses bill than Bert Wickstead – he went through the roof! Garfath would often go walkabout. He met someone in a pub who tried to bribe him not to give evidence. Surprisingly, he agreed to be wired up for another meet with this man. The result was very good and I believe the man was arrested.

The second form of protection was to use SCS personnel. One of the principal minders was Ed Williams, probably selected because he had previously formed part of the 'N' Division boxing team and was an authorized pistol shot. He was directed to go to the Leigham Court Hotel, Streatham Hill (the Norfolk Court Hotel, 1½ miles away, was under the same management) by John Bland, and Williams describes what must have been an onerous duty:

Peter Garfath had very thin hair, it was falling out, he wasn't good looking, he was unclean, a sloppy eater, very erratic and unstable. He was also an alcoholic so it was a hard job to mind him. The scars from the attack were very livid on his face; he was haunted by his ordeal which was why his drinking would never abate. I thought Rusty was very abusive and unpleasant but Garfath was still head over heels in love with her.

We stayed in a south London hotel, in the same room. I wanted the bed nearest the door, so that if somebody got in, I would be the closest to confront them. Garfath was drunk but he put up a very convincing argument that if that happened, they would expect the police officer to be closest to the door, so they would fire at the furthest bed. He'd been a hotel thief and knew that the locks could be picked.

I slept with a gun under my pillow. I heard a rattling sound in the middle of the night, turned the light on and saw Garfath, who was so drunk, he was pissing on the floor. I began to think that if he did get shot, at least I wouldn't have to share a room with him, any longer.

He complained that he was being kept from his girlfriend and being denied his conjugal rights; Bert directed that Roger Stoodley and I took him down to see her, somewhere on the south coast. We stopped at a hotel for lunch; midway through the meal, he excused himself, saying he wanted to go to the toilet. After five minutes, he hadn't returned so we went to look for him and found him in a corridor of the hotel, obviously about to break into a room. We marched him back to the restaurant but he thought this was hilarious, saying if he'd been caught later on, his alibi would have been that he was with two Scotland Yard detectives!

One night, a man named Eddie Machin came into the bar; he claimed to know me, although I didn't know him and wanted to buy me a drink. 'Want to see my party trick?' he said, and with that, he did a backflip. I was amazed.

Machin knew my name and where I was working. I can't tell you how unsafe I felt after that meeting and I went back to Bland to complain that my/our cover was blown; I was told to 'get on with it'.

Machin had demonstrated a great deal of dexterity for a fifty-one-year-old who had been shot in the buttocks the previous year during the Tibbs/Nichols gang wars, not that he would last much longer, because the following year, 'Terrible Teddy' as he was known was shot dead in the East End. But the reason for his being at the Leigham Court Hotel was because he was acting as minder/chauffeur to the owner, Charles Taylor. In fact, Taylor merits a mention later on, since this thoroughgoing crook had a corrupt relationship with a number of senior police officers, of whom the most junior would become a detective superintendent and his name was John Bland.

*

Bland was a rather odd character; he had served in the Royal Navy where he had successfully boxed in three different weight divisions. Just one-eighth of an inch over the (then) minimum height requirement of 5ft 8ins, he joined the Metropolitan Police in 1956 and it was discovered that he had a hair-trigger temper; instead of endeavouring to resolve differences amicably with his colleagues, he offered to fight them. He served a total of eight years with the Flying Squad and was awarded nine commendations for courage and ability, mainly in the arrest of armed robbers, including one for his input into the investigation of the world-famous kidnapping and murder of Mrs Muriel McKay.

He was promoted to detective chief inspector in January 1972 and posted to 'C' Division, right in the heart of Silver's and Humphreys' empires; but within three months he was transferred to the Serious Crime Squad which coincided with the commencement of Wickstead's investigation. So much, so far, for Bland. He reappears later on in this narrative.

*

Meanwhile, the pornographic bookshops were raided; altogether, 40 tons of material were seized. The pornographers and bookshop managers were scandalized; this was something which was simply not supposed to happen – this was what they paid protection money for, to prevent such a disgraceful state of affairs.

'We turned over lots of dirty bookshops and confiscated so much porn we couldn't keep it all at Tintagel; it wasn't structurally safe so it had to go to another office', John Farley told me.

A move was made to redress the balance. Farley was waiting on the ground floor at Tintagel House when the lift doors opened to reveal that the two occupants were Wickstead and 'Wicked' Bill Moody.

Farley recalled, 'Bert said to Moody, "Fuck off out of my sight and don't come back" and then, seeing me, he said, "Sergeant Farley, you're a witness". I thought, "A witness to what?" but I've no doubt it was to do with the porn we'd seized.'

Roger Stoodley was the office manager employed to check everything in and out, collate the evidence and pass the findings to Wickstead in a manner which could be formally presented at court. However, the workload was so intense that he often found himself part of the search teams. He said:

> We went out frequently to raid those premises. In one shop, Detective Sergeant John Lewis was puzzled by the layout of the shop in relation to the configuration of the rear of the shop. There was a blanked-out window at the rear of the building but he could not relate it to the interior. We delved around in the shop and discovered a trap door leading to a secret room under the floor. When it was opened up, it was filled to the brim with pornographic material. It took hours to recover all of the books and films. John was a very astute officer who uncovered an important illegal store.

*

The Serious Crime Squad now moved their headquarters to Limehouse police station (although an office was retained at Tintagel House) and the thirty members of the squad took up residence in the vacated married quarters there. It was ideal. Prisoners could be brought in to the police station, housed in the cells and charged. There were canteen facilities plus round-the-clock security. Relations with the uniform officers at the police station were magnificent, not least because when an operation was underway it meant large amounts of overtime for them as they worked their extended hours.

Alan Brooks was one of the Limehouse officers and he told me:

> Because of the sensitive nature of the investigations, all officers on Bert's team parked their cars in a nearby disused factory/warehouse with a police security guard monitoring access; Bert, however, parked his yellow Triumph in the yard. The charge room at Limehouse had two charge books: one for Limehouse jobs and one for Bert's. Sample charge from Bert's: 'On or before (date) you did conspire with a person or persons unknown to murder a person or persons unknown.'

By 28 January 1973 Rusty had returned to Britain, and Bernie Tighe and John Lewis arrested her at the Dean Street flat; as Bernie Tighe recalled:

> In early 1973, she [Rusty] became fairly vocal in the press and she moved around quite a bit but had a flat in Dean Street controlled by a phone entry system. We called her and thinking we were from the press, she remotely opened the ground floor door. She was somewhat taken aback when we walked into her flat and this resulted in a ruckus with John Lewis and self, restraining her on her bed.

'I had just returned from Malta and was very suntanned', John Lewis told me, 'and I can remember Bernie Tighe and I chasing her around the bed in her flat and her shouting, "Get that little half-caste bastard away from me!"'

Other important raids had been carried out, and as a result, eleven defendants appeared in the dock at Old Street Magistrates' Court on the morning of 30 January 1973.

Rusty Humphreys, together with Trevor Davies, a forty-five-year-old manager, was charged with conspiracy to pervert the course of justice by offering £2,000 to Garfath not to give evidence about his attack. Both of them, together with Gabor 'Hungarian George' Stresznyak, a forty-three-year-old butcher from Soho's Rupert Street, Patrick 'Coloured Pat' Dunn, a thirty-two-year-old shop assistant from Finsbury Park and William Murdoch aged twenty-six, a shopkeeper from Clapham, were charged with conspiracy, with others, to cause grievous bodily harm to Garfath.

Stresznyak, Davies, Dunn and Murdoch were accused of attempting to murder Garfath and were additionally accused of conspiracy to pervert the course of justice by agreeing that if police seized pornographic material, they would say that they were the true owners of the shops although the shops were owned by others, and that if they were fined they would be reimbursed.

Stresznyak and Davies, together with Lionel Gold, a thirty-two-year-old printer from Stamford Hill, James Goodere, aged thirty, a company director from Waltham Abbey, John Lawson, a thirty-four-year-old bookbinder from Southgate, Alan Miller aged twenty-eight, a company director from Tufnell Park and John Miller, thirty, a company director from Winchmore Hill, were charged with conspiracy to contravene the Obscene Publications Act by publishing obscene articles.

Gold, Goodere, Lawson and Gerald Citron, aged thirty-seven, a company director from Cobham, Surrey, were charged that they possessed pornographic material for gain, Alan Miller with publishing pornographic material for gain and John Miller with causing pornographic material to be published.

The Magistrate, Mr Ian McLean, granted June Humphreys and Gerald Citron bail in their own recognisances of £25,000, plus sureties totalling £50,000. Everybody else was given bail in the sum of £4,000 each, except for Stresznyak, Davies, Dunn and Murdoch who did not bother applying for bail.

Whilst this case was remanded until it could be committed to the Old Bailey for trial (and where the pornography charges would be split, to form indictments separate from the charges involving Garfath) Jimmy Humphreys wrote a letter to the Deputy Commissioner, James Starritt (later Sir James Starritt KCVO), a 6ft 4ins Irishman who had spent much of his career in Soho. In it, Humphreys protested that he had not taken part in the assault on Garfath and that he was being set up for the attack by Detective Chief Inspector John Bland, who had framed him in revenge for Drury being forced to leave the police.

Humphreys told Starritt that he had written to him since he felt that he (Starritt) would not reveal the contents of the letter to a certain Soho millionaire – this was obviously Silver – who was able to obtain copies of confidential police documents. Should he wish to continue this dialogue, said Humphreys, a coded message should be put into the personal column of *The Times*.

On 19 February 1973 Starritt passed this information to Gilbert James Kelland CBE, QPM, at that time Deputy Assistant Commissioner for 4 Area. Kelland stated that a warrant for Humphreys' arrest had been issued, no such message was inserted in the newspaper and the communications from Humphreys ceased.

But not from his wife. Acting, certainly, on her husband's instructions, on 18 April Rusty complained to A10 Department that her husband's diaries, taken from the safe at Dean Street at the time of her arrest, had contained details of illicit dealings with detectives and yet nothing had been done about it. Kelland was appointed to investigate the matter and went to Tintagel House to collect the diaries – a 1971 pocket diary and a 1972 Letts desk diary – from DCI John Bland, who stated that pressure of work had precluded the diaries being handed over, something which Kelland rather sniffily stated, 'I had always found difficult to accept'.

John Lewis – it was he and Bernie Tighe who had seized the diaries and handed them to Wickstead – puts a different aspect on the retention of the diaries:

> We were not involved with the police corruption side of the investigation; Bert deliberately kept us away from that and wanted us to concentrate on the Bernie Silver/Big Frank aspect of the enquiry. It could well be that Bert, who was paranoid about police association with Silver & Co, kept the diaries until he was sure someone would act on the information in them but again, that is just my guess and I have nothing to substantiate it.

In fact, Lewis' theory was authenticated; Kelland was not appointed as investigating officer until the day after Rusty Humphreys made her complaint.

Contained in the diaries were details of twenty-one detectives, with entries relating to meetings at well-known restaurants, and a few weeks later, Rusty obliged once more with an index book containing names and office and home telephone numbers of a number of detectives.

★

The trial at the Old Bailey of some of the participants, at least, in the Garfath slashing commenced, and Bland got a mauling in the witness box regarding what was said – and what was not – during his questioning of the defendants.

'Would it be right to say James Humphreys preoccupied the attention of a number of police officers for a considerable time?' asked Cyril Salmon, QC.

When Bland replied, 'I would not know about that', it did not sound particularly convincing.

Various charges were dropped, some on the direction of the judge, including on 9 July 1973, when Stresznyak and Davies were acquitted of attempted murder. Eight days later, William Murdoch changed his plea to one of guilty in respect of unlawful wounding. On 23 July Rusty Humphreys was found not guilty of conspiracy to pervert the course of justice, as was Trevor Davies who, together with Stresznyak, was found not guilty of grievous bodily harm with intent and also of wounding a certain Ibrahim Veli on the same date as Garfath's attack; and Dunn was cleared of all charges. However, Davies and Stresznyak were found guilty of unlawful wounding, and the following day, Mr Justice Nield sentenced both of them to 5 years' imprisonment, while Murdoch received a twelve-month sentence and was ordered to pay £100 legal costs.

But matters were far from over regarding Garfath. On 30 August 1973, at Old Street Magistrates' Court, George Bergin – also known as Ronald King – was refused bail when being committed for trial to the Old Bailey after it was alleged that he was responsible for inflicting two cuts, one measuring 7ins, the other 9ins, on Peter Garfath's face as well as other injuries to his face and body during the attack at the Dauphin Club. And coincidentally, on the same day, in the same court, Rusty Humphreys appeared and pleaded not guilty to a charge of being a party to keeping a brothel. The premises in Greek Street, Soho, said David Tudor Price for the prosecution, was leased by Mrs Humphreys for £6,500 per year. The basement was a club, the ground floor was a shop and the two upstairs flats were used for prostitution for which Mrs Humphreys charged each occupant £100 per week.

It was these girls who provided statements to Bernie Tighe and John Lewis, but afterwards, Rusty Humphries evicted both and replaced them with two others. Perhaps, given her not guilty plea, Rusty was working on the assumption that the prostitutes would not give evidence; if so, she was wrong. One of the girls, referred to only as Miss 'A', told the court that she had operated as a prostitute at the premises from January 1971 until February 1972 and went on to say:

> We paid a rent of £100 a week each to a man named Joe but later, Mrs Humphreys came to the flat and said the money had not been reaching her. We were to pay the

money into a bank account at Barclays Bank in Wardour Street. There was a girl doing the same thing upstairs in the other flat. We never took the day off together. Another girl came in as a relief.

It was sufficient for Rusty to change her plea to guilty, and sentencing her to three months' imprisonment, suspended for 2 years, as well as fining her £100 and ordering her to pay £300 costs, the Magistrate, Mr Tobias Springer, commented, 'It has been said on your behalf that you were really under the thumb of your husband', who Ivor Richards QC for the defence described with masterly understatement as being 'a man of certain notoriety'.

And the following day, 222 miles away, after an Amsterdam District Court heard that one James Humphreys had ordered an associate to cut off Peter Garfath's hands, he was recommended to be extradited to the United Kingdom. Let's see how this came about.

*

It began with the arrest of David Fitzgeorge, a thirty-one-year-old painter from Deptford. How did it happen? Maybe a top-rate informant, or an unfortunate telephone call that was subject to a Home Office intercept, perhaps just an overheard, injudicious comment in a pub – but it was enough to bring about Fitzgeorge's arrest and questioning. What was revealed was this: between 1 and 24 February Ronald Leigh, a forty-six-year-old lorry driver from Rotherhithe, was rather hard up; and during that period, for the princely sum of £20, he handed over to Fitzgeorge his birth certificate and driving licence, together with permission to use his details on a passport application form. Describing the applicant as an engineer and affixing Humphreys' photograph to it, Leigh's signature was forged, an insurance agent signed a declaration to confirm that these details were correct and a passport, valid for six months, was issued and sent to Humphreys at an address in Amsterdam. There we can leave Mr Fitzgeorge; his court appearance was sandwiched between the conviction of three men for the Garfath slashing and Rusty's brothel-keeping conviction, and he was sentenced to twelve months' imprisonment.

Bernie Tighe received information that Humphreys was using the Hotel Spaander, situated by the edge of Lake Ijsselmeer in Volendam, an old fishing village north of Amsterdam.

'At this time, Humphreys was frequently in contact with the press in London, decrying Scotland Yard, saying that we would never catch him,' Tighe told me.

This was right, although a *News of the World* reporter received a telephone call from Humphreys in May; he refused to say where he was but he did say that he did not intend to stay away from London, indefinitely.

'Although the information was vague', continued Tighe, 'we were in no uncertain terms told by Bert to find him.'

Together with Detective Inspector Brendan Byrne, Tighe slipped out of London quietly so as not to alert the press, who had been monitoring everything they had been doing. On a previous visit to Holland he had been harried by journalists who had heard of his presence in Amsterdam. They liaised with the Dutch police in Amsterdam, where they were assigned two officers, and they set off for Volendam. At the Hotel Spaander (which informs the visitors, 'We speak your language!') discreet enquiries failed to assist in the search for Humphreys, so the officers decided to keep an external observation on the hotel. Tighe takes up the story:

> We were casually dressed as holidaymakers and in order to cover the location, either Brendan or self covered the front of the hotel from a restaurant opposite during the lunchtime and evening or from a terrace at the rear of the hotel. One of us was with a Dutch officer and swapped around as dictated by the like of the menu.
>
> We did this for about ten days and when I happened to be in the restaurant opposite the Spaander Hotel, I said to my Dutch colleague that I fancied an ice cream that I knew was being sold outside another hotel, some 200 metres away. As we were enjoying the delights of the ice cream, Humphreys walked past us and went into this hotel (not the one we had been watching). His hair was dyed and he'd walked confidently into this hotel. I dispatched the Dutch officer to get Brendan who had been watching the Hotel Spaander from the rear terrace. Humphreys reappeared after about half an hour and went into a photographic shop and made a purchase. The area was very busy with holidaymakers, so we allowed Humphreys to walk towards a car park and the Dutch police officers stopped him and asked him his name. He said, 'Leigh' and after a few perfunctory questions, I said, 'It's all over Jimmy, I know who you are'. He said, 'Where the fuck did you come from?' I introduced Brendan and myself and told him we were from Scotland Yard and that he was being arrested and would in due course be extradited to the UK. He went quite limp and the blood literally drained from his face.

He had, in fact, been living in Rotterdam and hadn't been in Volendam for about three weeks. So it just shows that an ice cream was responsible for him being arrested.

The arrest occurred on Friday, 15 June 1973, but although the 17 June edition of the *Sunday Telegraph* stated that a Dutch police spokesman had predicted that Humphreys would probably be returning to London with the two British detectives the following day, this was more in hope than expectation. Humphreys resisted extradition, and it would take another six months before he was returned to the United Kingdom. Meanwhile, there were some interesting developments.

According to Humphreys folklore, he initially attempted an escape from prison, tunnelling through to an empty cell to reach the roof, where one of his sons would spirit him away. However, the proposed prison breach coincided with the Dutch Queen Juliana's birthday and the city was closed to traffic, thus thwarting the escape. It's a good story, except for the fact that the Queen's birthday was on 30 April; he had not been arrested until 15 June, and by the time Queen Juliana's sixty-fifth birthday came around the following year, Humphreys was back in dear old Blighty.

★

At the time of Humphreys' incarceration, Gilbert Kelland had served in the Metropolitan Police for 27 years, always in the uniform branch. Quite a lot of his service had been spent in Soho, but his experience of the club owners and other riff-raff had mainly consisted of serving summonses alleging breaches of the Licensing Acts which normally resulted in a 40 shilling fine. To show their contempt, the club owners launched expensive appeals, which were inevitably upheld. Was he the right man to investigate the criminal activities of someone as cunning and manipulative as Humphreys? Almost certainly not.

There are ways of tackling someone as devious as Humphreys, as all detectives know but (a) Kelland was no detective and (b) he had been appointed under the provisions of Section 49 Police Act 1964 to investigate the matter, so the die was cast.

First, Kelland put the ball well and truly in the Humphreys court by asking Rusty, who visited her husband once a week, if he wouldn't mind speaking to him. By September back came the answer: Humphreys would agree to see Kelland after receiving an assurance that he would not be prosecuted for corruption. Without one word being spoken between the two men, Kelland agreed to this stipulation, thereby putting Humphreys firmly in control.

Next, Kelland visited Humphreys, in the presence of his legal advisor, in the Amsterdam prison. Humphreys specified that no notes would be taken, and that the conversations would not be tape-recorded, and Kelland caved in once more. There was a conversation which Humphreys controlled, asking many of the questions, and having received the answers he required he agreed to a further meeting the following day. Kelland was initially elated; although rather less so the next day, when Humphreys' solicitor told him that his client had changed his mind and was refusing any further interviews. How Kelland's poor little face must have fallen at being so easily duped by a master manipulator. Humphreys now had a guarantee that he would not be prosecuted for corruption and he had received the information he had demanded, leaving Kelland feeling like the sole competitor in a one-legged arse-kicking championship.

Even though an Amsterdam District Court had recommended Humphreys' extradition on 31 August prior to the meeting with Kelland, it was not until 27 December 1973 that the Dutch Supreme Court approved the District Court's recommendation and Humphreys was returned to the United Kingdom, arriving on 9 January 1974. At City Road police station the same day he was charged with causing grievous bodily harm with intent to Peter Garfath, and upon his appearance at Old Street Magistrates' Court the following day he was remanded.

The trial commenced at the Old Bailey on 23 April 1974; joining Humphreys in the dock was George Bergin, who pleaded guilty to the charge; Humphreys did not. Outlining the case for the prosecution, Michael Corkery QC told the jury:

> The prosecution case is that here was a man who had clearly annoyed Mr Humphreys by taking up with his wife when he was out of this country and he arranged for retribution. He instigated the attack on Garfath, intending that he should suffer serious bodily harm. The knife was wielded by Bergin but the Crown will prove that it was the effect of an agreement between him and Humphreys. Humphreys egged-on the man with the knife.

Garfath gave his testimony, Humphreys offered no evidence in his defence and despite his being smartly attired in a navy suit, pink shirt and black tie, on 25 April the jury found him guilty. Although his barrister, Miss Jean Southworth QC, told the judge, 'If this was retribution, it brings the case four-square within what is sometimes described as a crime of passion', it was probably not the most appropriate phraseology to use in a plea for mitigation, because Humphreys and Bergin were both sent to prison for 8 years.

Time eventually ran out for Peter Garfath. In October 1975 he was found dead from an overdose of drugs at a flat in Devonport. He had converted the flat into a prison cell, with bars on the windows so that nobody – except, perhaps his demons – could get in.

Rusty left the courtroom in tears, shouting at Wickstead, 'You've convicted an innocent man. I hope you can live with that!' And to the press she said, 'The police are just having a go at Jimmy. He knows so much about them. Jimmy can't speak for himself now he's in jail, but I'm going to speak for him. I'm going to create a hell of a fuss.'

She wasn't the only one. Now he was on the back foot, Humphreys decided to play ball with Kelland and on 15 May 1974 he started a series of statements, but always, of course on his own terms. He acted like a prima donna. Humphreys wanted to pick and choose who he would give evidence about. He sulked. He pouted. He refused to give evidence at the committal proceedings of one of the porn trials, and Kelland simply stood for all this nonsense.

I know what I'd have bloody well done with him.

While all this was going on, Wickstead had been saddled with the Norma Levy enquiry; either the commissioner thought he was under-employed or, more likely, realised that he was the best detective for such an investigation. Be that as it may, we can leave Humphreys for now and return to what else was happening in Wickstead's investigations into the world of porn and what followed after Rusty's arrest in January 1973.

CHAPTER 9

Trials – and Some Dodgy Cops

It was an incredibly difficult investigation: witnesses were seen by the squad, statements were taken, then many of those witnesses were threatened and one of them – Frank Dyer – alleged that he was later kidnapped and, with a gun to his head, was ordered to give details of what he'd told the police. Several of the witnesses were seen in Malta; some did give evidence but others did not. And Bernard Silver let it be known that £35,000 was on offer for Wickstead to drop the investigation.

But there was a sufficiency of evidence to carry out a wave of arrests, and 'D-Day' was scheduled for 4 October 1973. It didn't happen. When a large-scale operation such as this one is going to be undertaken, police officers – usually surveillance officers from C11 Department – are tasked to check that those targeted for arrest are where they're supposed to be. Usually, this will commence the day before the arrests and will continue until the early hours of the morning of the raid, to 'put them to bed' and possibly stay in the vicinity of their homes right up until the time of the arrest, whereupon those faceless men and women can melt back into the shadows whence they came. But not on this occasion. The day before, they reported back to Wickstead that 'the birds had flown' – there was no sign of them in their natural habitats – and Wickstead knew why. One of his own men had betrayed him and his squad. There was absolutely no doubt as to his identity, but for a number of reasons there was no question of his being prosecuted or even having to face disciplinary proceedings; he was simply (and immediately) transferred.

The reason why Wickstead was aware, so quickly, of the betrayer was because there was a Home Office intercept placed on the public telephone box situated outside the White Horse public house, 16 Newburgh Street, Soho, run by former Detective Sergeant Walter 'Sandy' Sandison, who was a useful conduit between villains and bent cops; the pub was used by both Silver and Humphreys to pass illicit payments to police.

However, the intercept used was one of the 'lines' allocated to Special Branch and was therefore quite separate to the other intercepts used by the Metropolitan Police, which were controlled by C11 Branch. Wickstead felt that if a more conventional intercept had been used it would have been compromised; and he was not being fanciful. The head of C11 was Commander David Clarence Dilley, a friend of both Silver and Mifsud. He ordered surveillance photographs of the duo to be destroyed, plus Silver had been Dilley's personal guest at a police stag 'do'; Dilley was also a friend of Wally Virgo, whom he personally forewarned of his imminent investigation. Dilley – who entered C11 as a detective inspector and remained there for the rest of his service – regularly monitored the intercepts. Needless to say, he was as straight as a corkscrew. Any of his subordinates who queried his veracity were framed with disciplinary charges, transferred and returned to uniform. Known as 'The Kipper', due to his being two-faced and gutless, it came as no surprise to those who knew Dilley that just before he retired he was awarded the Queen's Police Medal for distinguished service.[1]

I know the identity of the crooked officer who warned the gang members and the extenuating circumstances which led to his betrayal and why he was not prosecuted; but for all that, I nevertheless feel that, at the very least, he should have been kicked straight out of the police.

But now Wickstead demonstrated why he was known as 'The Old Grey Fox'. He growled. He fumed. Muttering furiously under his breath, he went grumpily back to the courts who had issued the search warrants to have them withdrawn. All of the work carried out by the Serious Crime Squad in respect of 'The Syndicate' had been a complete waste of time; and what was more, the press informed their readers, the squad was now going to concentrate on raiding the porn bookshops in the West End. This had the ring of plausibility about it; after all, the squad had already accumulated 40 tons of the material. Therefore, it must have been true; hadn't the press said so?

Nothing was further from the truth. With the assistance of the Director of Public Prosecutions and the magistrate at Marlborough Street Court, further warrants were applied for, covert enquiries were carried out and the Old Grey Fox retreated to his den at Limehouse to await developments.

There's an old Fenland saying, 'All birds come home to roost', and that was certainly true regarding 'The Syndicate'. They had swallowed Wickstead's disinformation hook, line and sinker, and

---

[1] For further details of this officer's appalling behaviour, see David I. Woodland, *Crime & Corruption at the Yard*, Pen & Sword True Crime, 2015 and Jim Smith, *Undaunted*, Round Midnight Productions, 2009.

believing that the threat of arrest no longer existed, they returned to London.

The day before New Year's Eve 1973 became a red letter day for Wickstead; first thing in the morning, it was confirmed that in the New Year's Honours list he was to be awarded the Queen's Police Medal for distinguished service (*see* Appendix). And just when he thought things couldn't get any better, they did. That evening, John Lewis received a tip from an informant that Bernie Silver was back in town.

He telephoned the news to Bernie Tighe at home, and the two men rushed into the West End.

'We kept observation on Silver's flat at Wilton House, Knightsbridge', Lewis told me, 'we saw the light go out in his flat and moments later, he left, together with his girlfriend, Kathleen (Dominique) Ferguson, and they were arrested.'

Now that the pair were in custody at Limehouse, Wickstead immediately revised his earlier plans. The Scheherazade Club was the meeting place for members of the Syndicate, and Wickstead personally led the raid. Bernie Tighe strode on to the stage, relieved the blonde singer of her microphone and told the clientele, 'This is a police raid; everyone stay where you are.'

The star turn then took over from the compère; taking the microphone from Tighe, Wickstead roared, 'My name is Detective Chief Superintendent Albert Wickstead.' This brought a ragged cheer from the audience which died away as Wickstead continued, 'And everybody here will accompany me to Limehouse police station.'

'What do you think of the cabaret?' said a member of the audience to his neighbour.

'Not much', was the laconic reply.

When Wickstead said 'everybody would go to Limehouse' he meant just that; it included the band, who put on an impromptu show for their sixty fellow prisoners and their captors. Over the next few days the wheat was separated from the chaff, although three days after the initial arrests a sergeant at one of the overspill stations from Limehouse telephoned Wickstead. 'Guv'nor', he said. 'What d'you want me to do with these two RAF officers we've got in the cells?'

'What RAF officers?' growled Wickstead.

'The ones from the club', explained the sergeant. 'I mean, they were all right for the first couple of days, but now they're getting a bit grumpy!'

This was small beer for Wickstead; the RAF officers were later seen, told they were lucky not to be charged, and released. But this was a bit of levity in an ongoing and serious operation.

At the same time that the Scheherazade Club was being raided, Wickstead had dispatched 150 officers, made up with Serious Crime Squad personnel and uniform officers, to bring in the rest of the targets.

Geoff Turner was attached to Bow police station but recalled that during the 1970s he spent half of his time crewing the Area Car at Limehouse; as such, he was swept up into the Serious Crime Squad operations. He told me:

> I remember being briefed along with quite a few of my uniform colleagues to be part of a raid that was carried out at several addresses mainly, I think, around the West End. We were all sworn to secrecy about where we went, who we dealt with and where they were subsequently detained following the operation.
>
> I went with a DS and a couple of other officers to an address in the West End; the DS arrested an occupant, Tony Mangion, who I believe subsequently received a substantial prison sentence. All the raids were carried out by officers from the Serious Crime Squad and were all accompanied by uniform officers from Limehouse sub-division. For a week or so following that, apparently a cat and mouse game went on with lawyers visiting stations around the area trying to trace their miscreant clients. I remember being at Limehouse police station when a solicitor came in and demanded to see Mr Wickstead. He made a mistake of switching on a tape recorder and putting the microphone in Mr Wickstead's face. There was a loud crash, somehow the recorder ended up in pieces, followed by 'I'm Bert Wickstead, now what d'you want?'

The majority of the syndicate had been rounded up, with the exceptions of Emmanuel Collero, Anthony Micallef and Frank Mifsud. The latter had been living in a run-down Dublin housing estate; Eire's *An Garda Síochána* had previously been asked to carry out covert surveillance but it had not, it appeared, been done as judiciously as one might have wished. He vanished just prior to the raids, and it would take a long time before he resurfaced.

It's time to return to Detective Chief Inspector John Bland. Leaving the Flying Squad on promotion on 3 January 1972, he was posted to 'C' Division, right in the centre of the Silver/Humphreys empire; and yet a bare four months later, he was transferred to the Serious Crime Squad, on 15 May 1972. This was just about the time when Ken Drury was making his revelations known to the readers of the *News of the World*; and Bland had worked with Drury. There's a line of thought amongst former officers of that Squad that he was deliberately planted there to see how the West End enquiry was progressing – and then to report back. It may not be as far-fetched as all that.

'When John Lewis and I arrested Bernie Silver', Bernie Tighe told me, 'John Bland asked us to witness him speaking to Bernie Silver in the cells to deny all knowledge that they had ever met.'

John Lewis concurred. 'He was definitely not happy when we arrested Bernie', Lewis told me, 'because only Bernie Tighe, myself and Bert knew what information we had and who our informant was, so he [Bland] would not have known until the arrest. From that moment onwards, his attitude to us was very aggressive, and Bernie Tighe is correct, he asked us both to be present when he went to the cells and asked Bernie Silver if they had ever met. Make what you want of that, but why do it unless you have something to worry about?'

On the face of it, there wasn't much, because the following day, Bland was promoted to the rank of detective superintendent and he was retained on the Serious. But he was not liked. Ed Williams told me, 'He said the squad was circumventing him. He thought John Farley was not sharing information with him and that I was lazy. Everybody got threatened by Bland; he'd often take his jacket off to us.' But matters started to deteriorate even more because Bland was mistakenly blaming Lewis for his problems that were beginning to accumulate – and they would be considerable.

As John Lewis told me, 'I said to Bert, "This is becoming very difficult, as he's my superintendent and your head of operations". Bert said, "Don't worry, you're going to Malta for a couple of weeks with Bernie and when you get back, he'll be gone".'

And he was; on 15 April 1974, Bland was posted to 'A' Division, right by the Houses of Parliament – rightly or wrongly regarded as 'a punishment posting' – one week prior to the commencement of Jimmy Humphreys' trial.

★

Bernie Silver said, 'Mr Wickstead, what can I say? You obviously done your job. I can't say we were not expecting it, can I? I should have known about you and not come back.'

He was right, because his empire was starting to crumble. When John Farley searched his flat at Wilton Place he looked up at the high ceiling and realized a piece of coving was slightly at variance with the rest. As a former joiner, it offended his craftsman's eye; he climbed a ladder and discovered that behind it was a repository for a number of incriminating documents. These included substantial credit facilities in a Belgian bank, an interest in a flat at St Saviours, Jersey and 1,000 ordinary shares in a distillers company in the name of Bernard Hamilton. In addition, there was a receipt for £10,000, part-payment for a twin-diesel yacht which stipulated that the balance of £17,500 was to be paid within 30 days.

Tony Mangion told the officers he had helped 'Big Frank' and Silver collect money from the prostitutes, although he added that his weekly share from the takings was never more than £400.

When Joseph Mifsud's premises were raided by police, they found £2,100 in various currencies in a locked cupboard in his bedroom, as well as chequebooks drawn on different banks plus a book containing girls' names. Initially, he tried to bluff his way out of an alarming situation by saying that they were strippers who worked at El Paradiso Club, but he later changed his mind and stated that these were rents he collected on behalf of his brother. He added that the Syndicate had 25–30 flats in the Soho area, although most of them had been evacuated following the enquiries by Wickstead's squad.

Nazarene Galea told the officers that he collected rents from the prostitutes and handed the money either to Joseph Mifsud or Bernie Silver; this was not a statement guaranteed to endear him to the rest of the defendants.

Emmanuel Bartolo, who was arrested on 4 January, was known as 'The Landlord' but this, he explained, was only because all Maltese had nicknames. He denied having financial interests in prostitutes' flats, claiming, 'No. I have a flat in Alexander Road, Holloway and that is where I earn my living.' Asked how much he got for that, he replied, '£35 a week'. It was pointed out that elsewhere he had a smart house and a new Jaguar plus at least one other car, and he was asked how he could afford it on £35 per week? That, replied Bartolo, was because he had had a share in the Phoenix Club, but that was now finished. Asked if he had shares in prostitutes' flats in five streets in Soho, Bartolo replied that he could not tell them anything about it. However, after a prostitute's flat had been raided, letters which bore his name, plus the Holloway address and that of his house at North Finchley, had been found. When he was reminded that the prostitute used the name 'Janet Bartolo' it necessitated a substantial re-think but not a particularly convincing one; asked if he paid income tax, he replied, rather disingenuously, 'I think I do.'

The question of the kidnapped witness, Frank Dyer, was brought to Bartolo's attention. The circumstances were these:

Trials – and Some Dodgy Cops

Dyer had come to England from Malta in August 1973 because he had correctly heard that the Syndicate was selling off properties in Soho. Police investigations had commenced, there had been a rather explosive exposé in the *News of the World* and it was reasonable to assume that one of those properties could be had for a reasonable price. Dyer saw Victor Micallef, who told him that there was a property in Berwick Street for sale at £66,000. However, the deal could not be finalized because Silver and Frank Mifsud could not be contacted. Dyer returned to Malta, where he was questioned by the police; news of that interview found its way back to London, and when Dyer returned in November 1973 he was kidnapped, driven around in a van and finally taken to the basement of a house where he was roughed up, tied up, his glasses removed and a gun put to his head, in order to find out what he had said to the police. Dyer protested he had said nothing and that he was a friend of both Silver and Mifsud; eventually this was accepted, and he was released.

So Bartolo was asked if he had known that Romeo Saliba had put up £5,000 to have Dyer killed or hurt so that he would not give evidence. He replied, 'I have heard of it.'

'Where did the idea come from?' he was asked, and he replied, 'Don't ask me, please.'

'Where would Saliba get £5,000 from?'

'There was a pool.'

'Did you pay any money into the pool?'

'Sir, please. I was not going to do it. I am not a violent man.'

'But you agreed for it to be done?' he was asked.

'That', Bartolo replied, 'is different.'

Bartolo agreed that he knew of the arrests of other members of the Syndicate, and when he was asked if he knew who put them inside he replied, 'Romeo said it must be Frank Dyer. He knew him in Australia. He said he has always been a grass.'

Asked if it was then that he decided Dyer 'had to go', Bartolo ambiguously replied, 'It was a foolish thing that we have done.'

Victor Micallef denied having anything to do with Dyer's kidnapping but said it had been organized by someone known as 'Black Frank' (this was the nickname of Frank Spiteri). Joseph Mifsud was also questioned about Dyer and he replied, 'We've all heard of him; he's a grass.'

*

Out of eighteen people who had been questioned, seven men were charged with a variety of offences, including conspiracies to pervert the course of justice, cause grievous bodily harm and live off the proceeds of immoral earnings; they appeared at Marlborough Street Magistrates' Court on the morning of 8 January 1974.

Some months later, Frederick Henry Brett, a doorman from Upper Norwood, was arrested in connection with the Dyer kidnapping. He told the officers, 'All right, I'll tell you straight. There was a fellow who was causing some trouble and we had a frightener; I didn't have a gun, though.' He added, hopefully, 'I'm not a villain, you know.'

But even though the main protagonists were remanded in custody, there was still dirty work afoot. Witnesses were being paid large sums of money to 'forget' their evidence, and those who could not be bought off were threatened. That included Fred Calleja, the Maltese detective inspector who had been so helpful to the Serious Crime Squad officers; he was returned to uniform. The Syndicate had a strong pull in the island; Wickstead's team were no longer welcome there. Wickstead received the main threat; after a five-figure sum was put on his head, two hitmen were sent from Malta to dispose of him. His wife and children were also threatened, and as Wickstead told the press, 'I've had a few of these in my time but this one I'm taking very seriously. I think they mean business.'

The trial commenced at the Old Bailey on 19 September 1974 before Mr Justice Geoffrey Lane (later Lord Chief Justice of England and later still, Baron Lane AFC, PC, QC); this caused some concern to the defence since the judge was renowned for his pro-prosecution views. Eleven defendants appeared in the dock: Anthony Mangion aged forty-eight, a property developer, Romeo Saliba, aged fifty-six, Frank Melito, aged forty-one, Emmanuel Bartolo, Bernard Silver, Victor Micallef, Lawrence Charles Agious and Nazarene Galea, all of whom were charged with conspiracy to live off earnings from prostitution. Saliba and Bartolo were also charged with conspiracy to live off immoral earnings from premises in Berwick Street, and Melito was similarly accused in respect of premises in Half Moon Street.

Frederick Henry Brett and Vincent Saviour Stevens were charged with being concerned in a plot to deal with Frank Dyer, and Stevens alone was charged with attempting to pervert the course of justice by offering money to Dyer, in order that he should 'disappear'. Brett, together with Micallef and Joseph Mifsud, was accused of conspiracy to imprison Dyer between 11 and 16 November 1973, and Bartolo alone was charged with assaulting Dyer.

The dock was not as full as it should have been; three men had evaded arrest, and Joseph Medina had been arrested but, as Michael Corkery QC for the prosecution told the jury, had 'escaped the net, just before the trial'. In outlining the case to the jury, Corkery said this:

> For 18 years, Mr Silver and Mr Mifsud had made rich pickings; they acquired leasehold and freehold properties in the Soho area and often ran striptease clubs or 'near beer' establishments in the basement or ground floor of the premises. The floors above were where the prostitutes worked in separate flats. They paid what were clearly inflated rents, more than £100 a week; that was about average for one room or possibly two. Prostitutes working full time could earn between £200 and £600 a week. There were replacements as one prostitute went off somewhere else. Indeed, it would appear that sometimes there was almost a shift system. A room would be rented out to a prostitute on the basis that she worked from noon until 1.00 am, and when she left, someone else would take over the premises.

On the second day of the trial the number in the dock was reduced by one; Romeo Saliba changed his pleas to guilty and was remanded until the conclusion of the case for sentencing.

Michael Corkery had succinctly detailed a fairly seedy picture to the jury; but no seedier than some of the characters who gave evidence for the prosecution. There was Frank Vassallo, a ponce who knew most of the defendants and their illicit dealings; Paul Inguanez, a homosexual known as 'Paul the Priest' since he had once studied for the priesthood, had quarrelled with the Syndicate in 1968 and provided evidence for the inner workings of the gang; then there was Frank Dyer, known as 'The Snake', who gave evidence, including the fact that he had arrived in London from Malta in 1947 and was married to a woman who was a Soho prostitute between 1953 and 1960. Dyer was twice imprisoned for living off her immoral earnings, and when he hurriedly left the country for Malta in 1959, a warrant for his arrest was in existence, once more for living off immoral earnings.

One morning, a figure turned up at the Old Bailey oddly dressed for an autumnal British day. Wearing white canvas shoes, white drill trousers and a splendid Hawaiian-type shirt, a Chinese gentleman named James Hing had read of the case in a newspaper whilst holidaying in Guyana. Realizing he could give crucial evidence, particularly to the detriment of Anthony Mangion, he had simply boarded the next available plane to London.

Hing had lived in a flat above a strip club; the Syndicate wanted him out, so that he could be replaced with a tenant who could provide a rather more lucrative rent. Hing refused, and after he returned to the premises one evening with his wife and family, he discovered that the stairs leading to their flat had been chopped down.

Hing made a statement and gave evidence, and the judge directed that his return air fare plus his night's accommodation in London should be fully reimbursed.

John Lewis recalled:

> There was an occasion during the trial when Bert was in the box and in answering a question from a defence barrister, said that Bernie and I spoke fluent Maltese. We had to follow him in the box but were not asked if we did; probably following the sensible advice that, 'if you don't know the answer, don't ask the question' – nobody has been happier than Bernie and I with that advice!

There was a deal of double-dealing by the defence in the case: shadowy Soho figures were introduced into court to intimidate prosecution witnesses; approaches were made to witnesses to give false evidence, and a solicitor forced (by the judge) to provide documentary evidence regarding the ownership of a number of Soho properties actually tried to hide, whilst he was in court, an exceedingly incriminating document; a solicitor's representative was found, in an otherwise empty court, looking through Michael Corkery's prosecution papers; and, worst of all, three senior Metropolitan police officers gave Bernie Silver a character reference.

It was clear amongst all the defendants that come what may and whatever else might be admitted none of them were going to confess to being the landlords of the properties which housed the prostitutes. As we know, Bartolo's nickname was 'The Landlord', so that did impose certain difficulties, and this was aggravated by his being defended by Sir Harold Cassel QC. The kindest comment offered on Sir Harold's character was that he was eccentric; however, it was generally held, with some justification, that he was as mad as a bag of bollocks. As a judge, Sir Harold was adored by defence barristers ('What an irrepressible old darling he is!' was an oft-repeated comment) because of his unduly lenient sentencing, and he was loathed by police (whom he would contemptuously refer to as 'Mr Policemen') for the same reason. As a defence counsel, his peculiar talents were problematical because he was such a loose cannon; when he cross-examined a prostitute who had given evidence for the prosecution he asked her, 'It is true, is it not, that for the past nine months you have been living, rent-free?'

'Well, yes,' replied the witness. 'That's true.'

'Of course it's true!' cried Sir Harold. 'It must be true because all the landlords are in the dock!'

There was a collective groan from all the other defence counsel, one or two of whom buried their face in their hands.

'Oh, Harold!' one of the defence team was heard to moan. 'You *cunt!*'

But after thirteen weeks the trial came to an end. Inevitably, some charges were thrown out, some defendants acquitted. On 19 December 1974 seven men stood in the dock to be sentenced.

Bernard Silver, Anthony Mangion, Emmanuel Bartolo, Victor Micallef and Joseph Mifsud were all convicted of conspiracy to live off immoral earnings between January 1964 and December 1973. Silver was sentenced to 6 years' imprisonment and fined £30,000. Bartolo and Mangion were each jailed for 5 years and fined, respectively, £15,000 and £10,000.

Micallef was sentenced to 3 years' imprisonment, admitted two charges of possessing firearms without certificates and was sentenced to concurrent terms of three months' imprisonment.

Frank Melito was acquitted of the main charge but was convicted of the offence in Half Moon Street; he was sentenced to 4 years' imprisonment and fined £5,000.

Joseph Mifsud received 2 years and Romeo Saliba who had pleaded guilty on the second day of the trial (and had only returned to England because he erroneously believed he would be called as a prosecution witness), was given a remarkably lenient sentence. After hearing he had spent the last three months in solitary confinement for his own safety, the judge sentenced him to concurrent sentences of nine months' imprisonment which more or less coincided with his release.

Wickstead received a fulsome commendation from the judge, who said:

> It is quite obvious in this case to anyone who has sat through it that the amount of work done by the police and the extent of their enquiries has been quite extraordinary. Insofar as it may lie outside their line of duty, they are to be congratulated for what they have done.

In the next available edition of the *News of the World*, Wickstead in turn paid tribute to his officers, saying, 'They were so helpful in these enquiries because of their expert knowledge of the Soho area and the people concerned that I could never have brought this case to a conclusion without them.'

★

This was not the end of the enquiry. Back in 1956, Tommy 'Scarface' Smithson had been murdered; two men, Philip Ellul and Victor Spampinato, were charged, and although Spampinato was acquitted, Ellul was sentenced to death. Two days before his intended execution he was reprieved and served 11 years of a life sentence. However, there was more to it than that. When Wickstead started his enquiries, it was said that the murder had been arranged by Bernard Silver, Frank Mifsud and Tony Mangion.

Ellul was traced to San Francisco, and Detective Chief Inspector Ken Tolbart and John Farley brought him back; Bernie Tighe and John Lewis brought Spampinato back from Malta. Both men made statements (as did Frank Dyer) incriminating Silver, Mifsud and Mangion and gave evidence at Old Street Magistrates' Court; it was sufficient to commit Silver and Mangion (Mifsud still being absent) to the Old Bailey to stand their trial.

But in the intervening period both Ellul and Spampinato melted back to whence they'd come, the former suddenly becoming £60,000 the richer and the latter, £30,000 better off. However, there was other evidence; Silver and Mangion stood trial and while Mangion was acquitted, on 8 July 1975 Silver was convicted and received a life sentence for murder with a concurrent 10-year sentence for plotting to murder Smithson. But thirteen months later, Silver's murder conviction was quashed on appeal, it being held that it was neither safe nor satisfactory.[2]

In March 1976 Frank Mifsud stood trial at the Old Bailey after John Lewis had traced him to Switzerland and had him successfully extradited; on 22 March he was acquitted of Smithson's murder but on 13 August 1976 he was found guilty on a separate charge of perjury.

This charge arose from incidents going back eight years; after a spate of petrol bombings on three of Frank Mifsud's premises, he believed that a rival club owner, one Tony Cauci, was responsible. Cauci and his doorman, Derek Galea, were charged with conspiracy to cause explosions. Harold Stocker, who ran a hot-dog stand, testified that he had seen Galea running from the club after it burst into flames, and then Galea gave evidence against his co-accused, Cauci. It resulted in Cauci being sentenced to 5 years' imprisonment and Galea, in recognition of his spirited grassing, to 2 years.

---

[2] For full details of this case, see *London's Gangs at War*, Pen & Sword True Crime, 2017.

But what in fact had happened was that both Galea and Stocker had committed perjury, Stocker at Mifsud's behest; both admitted doing so but only because they were terrified of 'Big Frank'.

Now, with Mifsud back in the United Kingdom, to all intents a sick man and a spent force, the tentacles of the Syndicate nevertheless reached out again. Mifsud was charged with suborning perjury, with Harold Stocker as one of the prime prosecution witnesses, and Stocker – who had been promised £100 for his perjured evidence in the previous trial but only received £15 – was now approached by Mifsud's brother, Joseph, with a more tempting proposition. He was offered £2,000 to go away on holiday so that he would be unavailable for Mifsud's trial.

Stocker reported this to the police. The meet was arranged outside Stockwell underground station, with Stocker – who had been fitted with a covert recording device – travelling to the rendezvous by Tube.

Stocker had scarcely emerged from Stockwell station and stepped into Clapham Road before he was approached by his contact; the incriminating statement was recorded on tape, the money was handed over and suddenly Detective Sergeant Terry Brown appeared out of nowhere and made the arrest. I was part of the surveillance team and it was the quickest piece of work I'd ever seen, so much so that it bordered on the supernatural. First, Brown wasn't there – then he was; a heavily-built man, his fleetness of foot demonstrated why he had been awarded the George Medal, ten years previously, for his part in the arrest of gun-toting Walter 'Angel Face' Probyn.

On 21 February 1977 Joseph Mifsud, Joseph Feenech and Emmanuel Borg all pleaded guilty at the Old Bailey to conspiracy to pervert the course of justice. Mifsud – who had not long been released from his 2 year sentence – and Feenech were each sentenced to 3 years' imprisonment, Borg to two.

This was not the only conspiracy to come to trial; on 15 June 1976, Carmelo Sultana, a 45-year-old cook was jailed for 5 years at the Old Bailey for plotting with others to pervert justice in relation to the Tommy Smithson murder.

On 13 August Frank Mifsud was sentenced to 5 years' imprisonment and fined £50,000 for suborning Stocker to commit perjury, but he, like Silver, had his conviction quashed on 21 November 1978. He returned to Malta with his Irish wife, son and daughter and lived a comfortable life on the Sliema seafront; he died, aged ninety-one on 3 December 2017. After Silver was paroled in 1978 he also lived quite comfortably. He died in 2002, aged seventy-nine, but following their 'retirements' neither ever wielded the same amount of power again.

★

Now, you could be forgiven for thinking that I'd forgotten about Gerald Citron. Remember him? He appeared in the dock at Old Street Magistrates' Court on 30 January 1973, together with Rusty Humphreys and other luminaries, and was remanded on bail totalling £75,000 for possessing pornographic material for gain. Citron – like so many other ne'er-do-wells in this chapter – deserves a closer look.

Gerald Citron was born in 1936, the son of the owner of a washing machine factory which was successful enough to enable him to send his son to Repton. He obtained a degree in law at Manchester University but, tiring of the work of a solicitor's clerk, decided to start publishing magazines which had a reputation for being 'saucy'.

The business was so successful that he became a gambler, speculating heavily at the tables and the race tracks, before becoming a supplier to the London hard-core pornography scene, where Jimmy Humphreys was his biggest customer.

Now Citron became even more successful; he married a glamorous model and moved into Thornhill, Eton Park Road, Cobham, Surrey – then worth £150,000 and at 2018 prices around £3m – a mansion complete with swimming pool. To complement the residence were a number of rather expensive cars, including a Rolls-Royce. Fewer than 10,000 S-type Jaguars were ever manufactured, but Citron acquired one of those as well. He also invested some of his money into a wine importing business.

In 1971 he rented a cowshed from a Mr Skinner, the owner of Highway Model Farm, for £20 per month. The farmer could not help but notice that, particularly at weekends, there was a great deal of coming and going of lorries, loading and unloading. In the middle of 1972 Mr Skinner's curiosity got the better of him and he visited the shed, where he discovered a quantity of obscene books.

When the cowshed was entered by officers from the Serious Crime Squad they seized 18 tons of obscene articles for gain which were awaiting distribution, of which 75 per cent was hard-core porn and 15 per cent, obscene. This included 42,500 magazines as well as 57,800 pornographic books imported from the United States. There were also 30,916 indecent books and magazines, the importation of which was prohibited. Altogether, this seedy

BW in his office

Gangbusting

(*Above left*) George Dixon

(*Above right*) Jimmy Tibbs

(*Above left*) Micky Fawcett

(*Above right*) BW; not in a mood to take 'no' for an answer.

The Norma Levy Case

(*Above*) BW arresting Norma Levy

(*Right*) DAC Ernie Bond

(*Above left*) Earl Jellicoe

(*Above right*) Lord Lambton

(*Above left*) Rusty Humphreys

(*Above right*) DI Brendan Byrne and DS Bernie Tighe in Holland, searching for Jimmy Humphreys

(*Left*) 'Big Frank' Mifsud

(*Below left*) Bernie Silver

(*Below right*) Jimmy Humphreys with Terry Brown, having been extradited from Holland.

Three Dodgy Commanders at Scotland Yard

(*Above left*) Dave Dilley (C11)

(*Above right*) Ken Drury (C8)

Wallace Virgo (C1)

(*Above left*) A red book 40

(*Above right*) Alec Eist

(*Above left*) Reg Dudley

(*Above right*) Bob Maynard

(*Right*) L-R: DS John Lewis, DI Fred Calleja, DS Bernie Tighe

(*Below*) BW's leaving function from Limehouse.

Top labels (L–R): John Corner | Ruth Corner | ? | Brendan Byrne | Graham Wickstead | Stephanie – Graham's girl-friend, now his wife | ? | Brenda Wickstead, wife of Ian | Ian Wickstead | Aunt Vi

Bottom labels (L–R): Dave McEnhill | Andrew Wickstead | Bert Wickstead | Jean Wickstead | Neil Wickstead | Jean's mother | The Wickstead brothers' cousin, Cheryl

(*Above*) BW and Jean having re-affirmed their wedding vows at St John's Church, Loughton.

(*Below*) BW's medals L-R: Queens Police Medal, 1939–45 Star, Burma Star, Defence Medal, War Medal, Police Long Service and Good Conduct Medal.

collection was valued at £500,000. It was the largest single batch of pornography ever seized.

Citron was released on bail in respect of those matters, until he was re-arrested and appeared back in the dock at Old Street Magistrates' Court on 27 June 1973, charged with attempting to pervert the course of justice. No bail this time, and he was remanded in custody.

By the time he appeared at Wells Street Magistrates' Court on 3 October 1973, the magistrate decided that there was insufficient evidence to proceed further with the charge of attempting to pervert, and that was dropped. Nevertheless, he was committed to stand his trial at the Old Bailey on the porn possession charge, plus two more: between January 1972 and January 1973 that he had conspired with James Humphreys to publish obscene articles for gain in the West End of London and elsewhere; and also conspiring with an Albert Edward Crighton and others to publish obscene articles. Notwithstanding these heavyweight matters, he was again allowed bail, which this time totalled £100,000.

When he appeared at the Old Bailey on 21 May 1974, Citron pleaded guilty to possessing 18 tons of obscene articles for publication for gain, plus keeping the prohibited books for gain. The two conspiracies in respect of Humphreys and Crighton were dropped, as was the charge of having obscene articles, books and magazines for gain during July 1972; this was after Aubrey Myerson QC for the defence told the court that Citron had been interviewed by senior Metropolitan Police officers 'and what he has told them will greatly assist their fight against corruption in London'. Consequently, Citron was fined £50,000 or twelve months' imprisonment and was given six months to pay.

Indeed, what Citron had to say about bent coppers was quite damning. He told of one case where an officer and his wife had dined with the Citrons and the Humphreys at the Clockhouse Restaurant, near Ripley, Surrey, and then named five more officers with whom there had been illicit dealings. It was a long, detailed statement, and Gilbert Kelland was thrilled with it. He was less pleased when questioning the named detectives, all of whom gave 'no comment' answers during their interviews. Additionally, he felt that matters had become calamitous when Citron took himself off to the South of France, then to the United States, where he was eventually found to be a Rolls-Royce salesman in Los Angeles. Deported to the United Kingdom, he disappeared again.

He never did give evidence against the bent cops, nor did he ever intend to. He didn't settle the £50,000 fine; he hadn't proposed to pay that, either.

There was one hint of humour to be had out of the whole mishmash of the internal investigation; it came when Citron was with his solicitor whilst awaiting trial and wearing his Old Reptonian tie. An elderly man who had attended the same school spotted the tie and engaged him in conversation, asking him what business he was in. 'Oh, me?' replied Citron artlessly. 'I'm in publishing.'

Comical or not, it detracted nothing from the fact that once more, Gilbert Kelland had been royally shafted by a clever, manipulative criminal.

However, Wickstead and his men had achieved staggering success with the battle against pornography, as can be judged from the following statistics: in 1970, when the Porn Squad was at its height, the number of seizures of pornographic material amounted to 71,053. Perhaps this was regarded as a success by their masters at the Yard, because that represented over double the number of seizures of the previous year – 35,390. But when the Serious Crime Squad got to work, in the first ten months of 1972, the amount of pornography grabbed by them amounted to 871,468 items.

*

On 28 February 1976 the arrests of the detectives were carried out. From the time of Humphreys' allegations being first made to Kelland it had taken three years; during this time fifty meetings had been held with him, an average of one meeting every three weeks. Humphreys' evidence had resulted in 74 officers being investigated. Of these, 12 resigned, 28 retired, 8 were dismissed and 12 stood trial.[3]

There were three separate trials. Six officers stood trial in the first; each was accused on twenty counts of accepting £4,680 in bribes, and while one was acquitted, the remaining five were sent to prison for a total of 36 years.

At the second trial, six officers were accused on twenty-seven counts of accepting bribes to the amount of £87,485. A horrifying picture of corruption emerged: payments to operate porn shops were handed out to the police, pornographic material seized from one shop would be sold to another, and holidays, social functions, clothing, cars and home improvements were lavished on the crooked cops. 'Wicked Bill' Moody told a colleague that he was going to organize bribery 'as it had never been organized before'

---

3 For fuller details of this matter, see *Operation Countryman – The Flawed Enquiry into London Police Corruption*, Pen & Sword True Crime, 2018.

and also accepted the biggest single bribe – £14,000 – to help get a pornographer's manager off a criminal charge. Money was thrust into the pockets of honest officers in an effort to compromise them; those officers who were horrified at the blatant corruption on 'The Dirty Squad' and requested a transfer were told that such a posting would cost them £500. Moody was sentenced to 12 years' imprisonment, as was Virgo (although his conviction was later quashed on appeal), while other defendants were sentenced to a total of 24 years' imprisonment.

Finally came the trial of three Flying Squad officers; Ken Drury fought back, his barrister George Shindler QC suggesting to Humphreys that the reason for his accusations stemmed from two grudges. The first was because Drury had exposed Humphreys as being his informant in the *News of the World* article, and the second was because he held Drury responsible for his present plight – that of serving an 8-year sentence for slashing Peter Garfath. Irrespective of Drury's guilt or innocence, both of these accusations had the ring of truth about them. But they were cleverly countered by Humphreys who, in denying both allegations, stated that he did not hold Drury responsible for his conviction, of which, he was quick to state, he was wholly innocent. He told the court, 'Drury is a great friend of Superintendent John Bland who framed me. It is no fault of Drury's when Bland takes revenge on me. Drury resigned over me and that is why Bland took revenge on me.'

This, of course, was nonsense; whatever faults Bland possessed, he was not responsible for framing Humphreys for a crime which he claimed he did not commit, when Humphreys was patently responsible. There were moments of humour during the trial when it was claimed that due to the opulent lunches which he had been fed, Drury had been obliged to acquire an exercise bike to rid himself of excess poundage.

Nevertheless, Drury was found guilty of accepting bribes of £5,000 and was sentenced to 8 years' imprisonment (later reduced on appeal to five) and ordered to pay £2,000 towards his legal aid costs; one co-defendant was sentenced to 4 years and the third was acquitted.

★

One month after Drury's conviction, Humphreys received – with no pun intended – his thirty pieces of silver. On 25 August 1977 his sentence became the subject of a Royal Prerogative of mercy, and having served 2 years and 4 months of his 8-year sentence, he walked free from Maidstone prison.

Thereafter, he sent Christmas cards to Kelland at the Yard. This was a gesture like that of the club owners who launched appeals against their 40-shilling fines to show their contempt. In Kelland's shoes, most detectives would have kept quiet about those Christmas cards and not mentioned it in their memoirs; but then, as we know, Kelland was no detective.

The Humphreys went to Eire; he became involved in horse and greyhound racing, but in 1982 he made himself unavailable after a warrant for his arrest was issued for manufacturing amphetamines. They travelled to the United States and Mexico before returning to London, where they set up a prostitution ring which, in the space of twenty months, netted them at least £100,000. Rusty acted as a maid to the prostitutes and forced them to pay such high rents that they had to work twelve-hour days, seven days a week. During a nine-hour period, police observed twenty-six men go into one of the brothels. If the girls failed to pay up, Rusty would shout and scream at them and threaten to throw them out of the three upmarket houses from which they operated in Central London and for which they paid rent of £900 per month.

The couple were arrested in November 1993, and although Humphreys asked the arresting officers if 'anything could be done', he was curtly advised, 'This is 1993, not 1973, mate!'

They pleaded guilty at Southwark Crown Court on 1 July 1994; Jimmy Humphreys was jailed for twelve months, Rusty for eight. The opulent house at Aberdare Gardens, West Hampstead, which they had rented at £1,000 per month, was vacated; following their release, they relocated to the south coast and ran a removal company.

They were in discussions regarding the possible filming of their life stories, reunited despite their often tempestuous relationship, when the Grim Reaper intervened. Jimmy Humphreys – whom the press had dubbed 'The King of the West End' – died in Hastings on 22 September 2003, aged seventy-three.

*

The trials of the police officers were the beginning of the end of the Metropolitan Police's CID. The commissioner flooded the senior ranks of the CID with mainly inept senior uniformed officers, the rank and file were subject to 'interchange' between uniform and CID upon promotion and Gilbert Kelland was promoted to Assistant Commissioner (Crime). The man who had permitted some of the underworld's most prolific and manipulative criminals to thoroughly bamboozle him was now in charge of all of London's detectives, a body he knew next to nothing about.

Trials – and Some Dodgy Cops

John Lewis perfectly summed up the situation, 40 years later:

> The arrests set off a series of events which did change the way the CID was managed. A great deal of those events were not for the better in my opinion, and the Force has suffered since the loss of the CID as we knew it. It's sad that in order to put one thing right, we lost so much.

*

Wickstead's time on the Serious Crime Squad had come to an end, and it had been crowned with glory.

'I've had four hard years and now, I'm looking forward to a rest', he told the *News of the World*, who added, 'Mr Wickstead is expected to be given a key administrative job at Scotland Yard, next year. But first he will move to an outer London division.'

The second part of the newspaper's prediction was correct; on 6 January 1975 he was back at his old job, as Detective Chief Superintendent of 'J' Division – but not for long. Four months later, he was promoted to Commander and appointed head of the No. 3 Area Inspectorate.

Both he and the *News of the World* had got their forecasts for the rest of his career slightly wrong. He was not going to the Yard in any kind of an administrative job, and he was not going to have a rest. Wickstead was going to be involved in the most controversial case of his career, but before that happened, he had an old score to settle.

*

Charles Taylor has already received a brief mention; he's going to be given a slightly expanded discussion now, but not by much. A revoltingly sleazy character, it's not so much who he was but what he did which will be of interest to the reader.

He was born Alfred Taylor in 1916, and with the death of his brother Charlie, adopted his name for fraudulent reasons. Prior to the Second World War he served Borstal and prison sentences and became a bookmaker. Following the outbreak of war, he was called up to serve in the Royal Sussex Regiment, married, went AWOL from the Army, got caught, escaped, got caught again, was sent to the military prison at Shepton Mallet, was divorced and dishonourably discharged from the army.

In the post-war years he was a spiv and a conman, married for a second time, was a gambler, a thief and defrauded his own family. He bought up boilers and radiators from demolition sites, renovated houses, drove a Rolls-Royce but often had no money to pay for the petrol. He was involved in long firm frauds and in 1963 opened a gambling club at 1 Inverness Terrace, Bayswater.

Taylor had been a heroin user since the 1950s. Now he supplemented his drug intake with amphetamines, barbiturates and amyl nitrate. In 1965 he opened an illegal casino at the Leigham Court Hotel, Streatham Hill. It was round about that time, when John Bland was a detective inspector on 'L' Division (which covered the Streatham area), that he and Taylor first met; Bland allegedly started accepting bribes from Taylor and became a go-between for criminals and the police.

In 1972 Taylor had a meeting with Detective Chief Superintendent Reg Davis, who, Taylor later alleged in court, swindled him out of £30,000 – or it might have been £40,000. Taylor must have been a magnanimous swindler, because the following year, he paid for Davis to accompany him on a holiday around Eire in a Rolls-Royce Phantom.

Taylor became involved with a security guard at London Heathrow airport regarding batches of krugerrands, gold coins imported from South Africa. In 1976 the guard appeared in court charged with the theft of krugerrands worth £250,000. Taylor contacted Bland, who said that assistance would cost £5,000, which apparently was paid.

Taylor also made the acquaintance of Leonard Ash, in respect of whom Bland told Taylor that a fraud was being carried out in Lincolnshire; he was asked to watch Ash. A few days later, Taylor went to the Fraud Squad office and received a reward of £500, signing for it in the name of 'Trainer'. Between August and October 1976, Taylor would say, he had gone again to the Fraud Squad office, where he was asked if Ash was rich. Saying that he was, Taylor was told that help could be forthcoming to help Ash 'if he comes across'.

It appears that he didn't; Ash was duly arrested for a long firm fraud.

Taylor had his finger in every conceivable criminal pie; he now became involved in what was known as a 'Dollar Premium Fraud'. Taylor reported this to Bland; he was both involved in the offence and acting as an informant in the hope of receiving reward money.

Believing Taylor had set him up, Ash complained to Gilbert Kelland, telling him everything he knew about Taylor and his police associates. At the same time, Kelland also received information from Police Constable Frank Pulley BEM, a very astute officer who had been informed of Taylor's activities regarding the

Dollar Premium Fraud and his association with corrupt detectives. Wickstead was ordered to make enquiries. He was permitted to choose his own staff, but Davis, now a Deputy Assistant Commissioner from 'C' Department, demanded to know what use they were being put to. Therefore, Wickstead had those officers temporarily transferred to A10 Department, where they would officially be under the control of the DAC 'A' Department, thereby cutting off that avenue of enquiry.

Wickstead now received a call from Betty Ambrose, the wife of Billy, who was at present on remand charged with a huge multi-million pound fraud as part of a gang who became known as 'The Hungarian Circle'. During his involvement with the Pen Club Murder in 1960 Wickstead had dealt compassionately with Ambrose and his wife; now Ambrose informed him that he had been approached in prison to set Wickstead up. He had been told, 'Wickstead's rocking the boat', and Ambrose would be supplied with dates and places where illicit monetary transactions had taken place. Wickstead was in no doubt that this was true.

By now, Taylor was no longer the slim, immaculately dressed spiv of yesteryear with a small, neat moustache. A police informant and a seedy lecher, drugs and drink had taken their toll; eating all the wrong food, he had piled on the pounds; he was a heavy smoker with a heart condition; he was lethargic, his teeth had fallen out and he stank. 'Taylor was greasy', Michael Hall, who knew him from his time of minding Garfath at the Norfolk Court Hotel, told me. 'You couldn't believe a word he said.'

On 17 November 1976 Taylor was arrested. Dies for making gold sovereigns were found, as was $7,000 in forged notes; both of these, he would whine, were planted. He was driven to premises in Mortlake, where gold half-sovereigns were being counterfeited. Taken to Loughton police station, he was interviewed by Wickstead, who allegedly told him, 'Knock that fucking grin off your face' and who questioned him with regards to his dealings with corrupt police officers. Taylor trembled and was charged with a number of serious offences.

He appeared at Epping Magistrates' Court on 20 November 1976 together with others and was remanded in custody.

By mid-December more arrests had been carried out, the men had appeared in court and had been remanded, and by 14 January 1977 nine men appeared in the dock at Bow Street Magistrates' Court charged with the Dollar Premium Fraud. These included a Bank of England official, two solicitors, a solicitor's managing clerk, an economist, a company director and a commodity trader. Most were granted bail. Taylor and Ash were not.

From his cell in Bedford prison Taylor began to make statements regarding his dealings with crooked police officers. These statements were passed to Barry Pain, the Chief Constable of Kent, who had been appointed as the investigating officer under Section 49 Police Act 1964.

Matters moved quite quickly. On 17 June 1977 Bland was suspended from duty and on 28 April 1978 he resigned on an ill-health pension, the reason given being 'severe agitated depression'. He had completed 21 years and 273 days service. Remarkably, his conduct was rated as 'exemplary'. Few of his contemporaries from the Serious Crime Squad would have disputed his mental condition; none would have agreed with the character assessment.

Four days after Bland's suspension, Reg Davis resigned. On 1 August 1977 John 'Jock' Wilson, who had been Assistant Commissioner 'C' Department, was reassigned as the head of 'B' Department – or traffic.

The trial at the Old Bailey for the Dollar Premium Fraud got underway on 4 April 1978 with Taylor, Ash and four others in the dock.

The details were set out by David Tudor-Price, who told the jury that attempts were made to borrow vast sums from foreign banks – in fact, £60m was mentioned – so that the gang could pretend it was the proceeds from the sales of non-existent securities on which they could claim the dollar premium. To qualify for the dollar premium under exchange control regulations, it was necessary to prove that the investments had been held in an authorized depository since 23 June 1972 and that the owner was resident in the United Kingdom on that date. Firms of solicitors were authorized depositaries, and the conspirators persuaded employees in the offices of two firms to falsely certify that the securities had been held by them since before that date and that their client had been resident in the United Kingdom since then. Also essential to the scheme was the Bank of England official; a file was found in his office which contained a letter, signed on behalf of the Bank of England, stating that a fictitious 'Mr Guardien' qualified for the dollar premium. It was, in fact, a licence to print money. The amount which the conspirators planned to pass through the system varied between £2.5m and £20m. Taking the lower figure, had the plan succeeded, the gang would have netted more than £1m.

It was an impressive case for the prosecution; in his defence, Ash came out with all guns blazing. He stated that he had provided information on a daily basis regarding corrupt police officers, some of whom had been suspended, and including an assistant

Trials – and Some Dodgy Cops

commissioner who had been transferred and two who had resigned. This was the reason, said Ash, for the police framing him on these charges.

Then it was Taylor's turn. Examined by his counsel, Victor Durand QC, regarding the alleged comments made in the Fraud Squad office in respect of Ash, he was asked, 'That is, in one word, bribery, is it not?'

Rather surprisingly for one who had let the cat out of the bag, Taylor coyly replied, 'It might be.'

Durand also mentioned the holiday his client had taken in Eire with Reg Davis and suggested that he was a close friend of Davis. Referring to his children's drug dependency, Taylor wailed, 'I had to be because of my children. He used to help them get out of trouble. This happened ten or fifty times.'

'In plain English', said Durand, 'do you mean he helped by squaring something?'

'That is right', replied Taylor and then went on to say that Davis had collaborated with him in a fraudulent scheme and induced him to pass £40,000 'of my hard-earned money' to a man named Stanton.

'Do you mean that Davis and Stanton defrauded you?' exclaimed Durant and received the reply, 'Yes, and I have proof of that.'

He was asked about a hand-written document which Taylor stated Ash had given him at the commencement of the trial, in which he detailed the evidence he should give, including a suggestion that Davis and Bland were involved in frauds and had asked him to finance them; Mr Tudor-Price said he would have the document examined by a handwriting expert.

It was a real 'dog-eat-dog' trial; and Taylor's testimony was not the most illuminating or persuasive of evidence.

Taylor was on his way home to Sheen Lane, Mortlake on the evening of 24 May 1978, when he collapsed at Waterloo Station and died later in hospital. Naturally, the conspiracy theorists had a field day. Did he fall or was he pushed? Murder or suicide? The arresting officer went straight to the mortuary, to ensure that Taylor wasn't pulling a fast one. But there was no mistake: the mess on the slab was Taylor, whether he called himself Charlie or Alfred; no error there. An autopsy proved that, irrespective of the hypotheses of the conspiracy lobby, he had died of a massive heart attack.

The trial continued; the remaining defendants were found guilty and were sentenced to imprisonment. However, on 3 December 1979 those sentences were quashed by the Court of Appeal, who criticized the judge's summing-up, which was variously described as 'unusual', lacking 'proper balance', 'defective' and 'unduly prejudicial'.

The counterfeiting trial followed but without Taylor's presence; and with the highly publicized resignation of a number of high-ranking police officers, there were allegations of police malpractice galore and the proceedings collapsed, with the defendants being acquitted of all the main charges.

★

The investigation by Chief Constable Barry Pain into the allegations of corruption by police officers was considered by the Director of Public Prosecutions, who decided – probably because of Taylor's demise – that no criminal proceedings would be instituted. There were disciplinary offences aplenty, but those who had committed them were gone, clutching their pensions.

Wickstead had taken no part in the Dollar Premium Fraud since the prosecution had been undertaken by the Treasury and had displayed little enthusiasm for the counterfeiting trial. Both these prosecutions had been a means to an end, because what Wickstead was after were the scalps of crooked police officers; he had never forgiven Davis, who had threatened his subordinates after the Tibbs trial.

However, he was denied even that, and Davis' resignation was only a pyrrhic victory; nevertheless, he was gone and out of the way. At least the Serious Crime Squad had been vindicated.

Now, it was time for Wickstead's last – and most controversial – case.

CHAPTER 10

Legal & General

This is the case that will never go away; whenever miscarriages of justice are mentioned, the Dudley and Maynard case will be trumpeted, in the same way that when police shoot an innocent man, the name 'Steven Waldorf' will miraculously be blazoned across the headlines. The 'Legal & General' case started in 1974 and came to rest 28 years later; it still attracts controversy.

But was it really a miscarriage of justice? Let's take a look at the main protagonists, all of whom, to a lesser or greater degree, had links with criminality in North London in this highly complicated (and highly charged) investigation.

Robert John Maynard – known as 'Fat Bob' – was a thief and a burglar, who was born in 1939 and grew up in Holloway. He possessed quite a marked speech impediment due, it was said, to having taken a severe beating in a West End club. One tale, which might well be apocryphal, had him enquiring after a friend's health, only to be told he had a problem with his prostate.

'W-w-what's a p-p-prostate?' asked Maynard, only to be told, 'It means he pisses like you talk!'

Reginald John Dudley was born in 1925, and by the time he was fined in July 1957 for obstructing police during the arrest of one John Ernest Clark for the theft of gold bullion valued at £20,119, he had already been convicted on nine occasions. Thereafter, he received a string of serious convictions and prison terms (including a 6 year sentence for slashing his wife's face); he was also a thief and receiver. He and Maynard often worked together in the Hatton Garden area of London, fencing stolen jewellery (Dudley was nicknamed 'Diamond Reg'), and the two men were known as 'Legal and General' since they wore identical overcoats, as did the actors in the Legal and General Assurance Company's television commercial.

William Henry 'Billy' Moseley had been sentenced to a term of imprisonment for theft in October 1973 and was released from Bedford Prison on 18 September 1974. He and Maynard had been friends since childhood – they had once been convicted together – but he had learnt of Maynard's association with Dudley, whom several of their ilk suspected of being a police informer. During his eight days of freedom, Moseley met up with Maynard, returned to his Stoke Newington flat (where Maynard had been paying the rent during Moseley's enforced absence) and visited several friends: his mother, his estranged wife Ann and their three children and, on 26 September, Phil Luxford, a car dealer and friend, who agreed to lend Moseley a Rover car, since Moseley mentioned that he had some business to attend to.

The business referred to was a meeting with a man named Ronnie 'Ginger' Fright. Whilst Fright had been serving a 7-year sentence at Chelmsford prison for armed robbery, Moseley had had an affair with his wife Elaine (known as 'Frankie') Fright. Their association had lasted for several years, and Frankie had visited Moseley on a number of occasions during his prison term. Her husband had discovered their relationship in August 1974 and was understandably furious. With Fright's release, it was now necessary, if possible, to clear the air, since to undertake a liaison with the wife of an incarcerated man was considered, in the rules which govern the underworld, beyond the pale.

The meeting between the two men was arranged by Frankie Fright to take place outside the Victoria Sporting Club, Dalston at 6.30 on the evening of 26 September 1974.

Ronnie Fright later said that he arrived at the rendezvous slightly late; and although he waited, Moseley did not arrive. When Luxford's car was not returned, it was reported missing to the police the next day, and although a search was made then and during the following day in the area of Luxford's garage, there was no trace of it. Maynard would later say that he had seen the car in that area, the day it was reported to police, but it was eventually found on 30 September outside a nearby public house.

On 3 October Maynard and his brother Ernest went to a funeral, where they were heard to say to a friend, George Thomas Spencer, words to the effect that Moseley would not be seen alive again. Shortly afterwards, Bob Maynard, George Arnold (the half-brother of Moseley) and Frankie Fright went on several occasions to Moseley's flat and took possession of money and property hidden underneath a carpet, together with a small key. Although both Arnold and Fright claimed that they saw Maynard pocket the key, this would be strongly disputed by him much later in court. Additionally, Maynard pointed out to Arnold the spot where Moseley and Fright were supposed to have met. After Moseley's disappearance, Ronnie Fright left his job and disappeared also; he and Frankie were later reconciled.

Between 5 and 15 October 1974, five parts of Moseley's body were found over a wide area in the Thames, ranging from East

London to near Rainham, Essex. The head and hands were missing, and although initial identification was by no means certain, it appeared that he had been tied up and tortured. Marks on his thigh and the fact that his toenails had been pulled out confirmed this, and he had been burnt with a naked flame, but neither the shock of this nor the additional injuries to his breastbone and ribs would have been the cause of death.

The pathologist, Professor James Cameron, believed 'a head injury of acute origin would appear to be the most likely cause of death' and that his body had been dismembered after – or possibly before – death. However, by the time the inquest was held on 17 November 1975, on the basis of a gallstone condition which had been registered on an X-ray in prison, plus blood samples which were matched with his children's blood group, Professor Cameron was able to state unequivocally to the Walthamstow Coroner, Dr Harold Price, that the remains were Billy Moseley's.

A murder enquiry was launched at Romford police station, and when the police went to Moseley's flat they did so in the company of his widow, Ann, plus Maynard, who told them of his sighting of the Rover. Another person interviewed was Michael Henry 'Micky' Cornwall.

On 18 October Cornwall, a serial criminal, had been released from Hull prison, having served a 9-year sentence for robbery. He and Moseley had been close – Moseley had regularly visited him in prison – and Cornwall was extremely upset to hear of his friend's death.

It's now time to introduce another of the interested parties in this case, and that is Reg Dudley's twenty-four-year-old daughter, Kathy. She had been married to a John Dann, but the marriage had floundered; early in 1974 she had become involved with a robber named Ray Baron, who in 1962 had been convicted with Cornwall and a man named Colin Saggs of a bank robbery. But with Baron now back in prison, once again for armed robbery, Kathy allegedly had a brief affair with Cornwall during December 1974; it was short-lived, and she returned to Spain, where she worked in a club in Lloret del Mar. In fact, she had arrived home from Spain with her father on the afternoon of Moseley's disappearance.

Since January 1975 Cornwall's base had been the Islington flat of the Saggs family. His rent was necessary to them since Colin Saggs and Moseley's half-brother George Arnold were back in prison, having been convicted of an attempted robbery in November 1974. Also occupying the flat was fifteen-year-old Sharon Saggs, her mother and three brothers. It appeared that between January and July that year Cornwall and Dudley had met, and there had been a great deal of hostility between the two; Cornwall believed that Dudley was a police informant, and Dudley may have been suspicious of Cornwall's association with his daughter, Kathy.

In between times, Cornwall moved on and moved in with twenty-one-year-old Gloria Hogg; even if she was unwilling to admit it, Cornwall was clearly planning a big robbery, possibly in the Blackpool area, to where the couple had travelled. Cornwall said so to a fellow armed robber, John Moriarty, who was not well liked. His nickname was 'The Target' because he had been shot twice, the first time ten years earlier when the occupant of a passing car in Highcroft Road, N19 had discharged a shotgun at him, resulting in serious injuries to his thigh. So it was injudicious to say the very least of Cornwall to mention his plans to Moriarty, since the latter had the reputation of being an informant (this was confirmed when he later turned supergrass); indeed, it was shortly after Cornwall's incautious comments that he was put under observation by the West Midlands Crime Squad and was followed to London.

The last Gloria Hogg saw of Cornwall was on 5 August, when he left saying he would return in a couple of days. But according to Sharon Saggs, Cornwall had hurriedly left the Islington flat on 7 August since he believed that someone was coming to see him. Within fifteen minutes of his leaving, two men did arrive; and Sharon Saggs would later identify them as being Maynard and Dudley.

Cornwall was apparently seen at a bus stop in Highbury on 22 August by John Moriarty, and although Gloria Hogg saw Maynard in a public house shortly afterwards and enquired regarding Cornwall's whereabouts, he told her he was unable to assist.

Between leaving the Saggs' flat and being seen by Moriarty, where Cornwall had been living was a mystery.

On 30 August 1975 turf was found to have been cut back in woodland at Lord Salisbury's estate, near Hatfield, Hertfordshire, but the person who discovered it noticed nothing else amiss. However, it was later established that this spot was the area of Cornwall's grave, prepared – at the time of its initial discovery – either before his demise or shortly afterwards, because on 7 September a schoolboy out blackberrying with his family discovered Cornwall's body there, wrapped in a bedspread. He had been shot in the head at close range; he had also been violently kicked in the back and, like Moseley, he had been tied up. It was thought that he had been killed sometime between 22 August and 1 September, and Hertfordshire police commenced a murder enquiry.

The investigating officers believed that Kathy Dudley had been Cornwall's girlfriend and on 10 September they saw her at her home address in the Holloway Road. She denied the relationship, saying that she had last seen him some two months earlier – she was later interviewed and, interestingly, thought she might be able to say why he had been killed. In addition, items which were identified as belonging to Cornwall were found in a garage adjoining her address.

Just over a week later, both Maynard and Dudley were seen by police in a pub. Dudley was apparently furious because the police had had the utter impertinence to speak to his daughter; he threatened the officers, screaming that 'The poor little cow ended up in mental 'ospital afterwards!' Moreover, Maynard was also angry because of a letter sent to the *Islington Gazette* which was signed with his nickname, 'Fat Bob'. It concluded with the words, 'It's been said that Mick was asking too much about Bill's death. The police seem to have forgotten Billy. They may forget about Mick.'

The piece was published under the heading, 'Underworld Tip Gives Police Gangland Killing Clue', but Maynard denied that he was the author of the letter; the newspaper published an apology. However, both Maynard and Phil Luxford received .22 bullets through the post.

The prosecution would later allege that both the letter and the bullets were sent by those responsible for the murders, intending to divert attention away from themselves, and it's right to say that this is a common ploy used by criminals. They deliberately draw attention to themselves so that – and always in the presence of witnesses – they can noisily proclaim their innocence at the top of their voices. It's known as the 'Market Trader's Defence'; they feel if they shout loudly enough, someone's bound to buy their wares. Sometimes – not always – juries believe them.

Then again, 24 years later in a *Rough Justice* television programme, it was suggested on the most nonsensical of evidence that the police were responsible for both writing and posting the letter and the bullets.

It certainly appeared that the murders were linked, and there was an amalgamation between the two Forces: Hertfordshire Police and the Met. The Hertfordshire contingent was under the control of Detective Chief Superintendent Ron Harvey (later Deputy Assistant Commissioner Harvey QPM), who as his contemporary, former Deputy Assistant Commissioner Neil Dickens QPM, told me, 'was a well respected and acknowledged investigator'. This was a view widely held. His reputation for integrity was rock-solid; two years later, as the commander of C11 Department at the Yard, Harvey was responsible for bringing to the attention of the commissioners of both the Met and the City of London, plus the Home Office, allegations of corruption within those two police forces which would result in the investigation known as 'Operation Countryman'.

The Met was represented by Wickstead, who since 17 May 1975 had been Commander of No 3 Area, which covered the region of Rainham. The hub of the enquiry was Loughton police station, an outpost station of the Metropolitan Police, close to the border of the Essex Constabulary and near enough to Hertfordshire to be accessible for their officers. It was also easy to get to for Wickstead, since he lived just half a mile away.

The co-ordinated enquiries were investigated, and when it was decided that the arrests would be carried out, the arrangements were made with Wickstead's usual military precision; Ken Dellbridge had been seconded to the enquiry team and he told me, 'The night before the arrests were made, we were outside the suspects' addresses to make sure they were there and then we reported back to Loughton. Everybody who was to have been arrested, was arrested; I was so relieved!'

The administrative arrangements in respect of the prisoners would have to be immaculate, and the best person to describe them is Mick Carter, who at that time was a uniform sergeant stationed at Chigwell police station:

> In January 1976, I was aware that Bert Wickstead was operating a murder squad from Loughton. I was seen by Chief Superintendent Randall Jenkins, who told me that he had recommended that I, Police Sergeant Terry Norman (Woodford police station) and Police Constable Gerry Mockford (Loughton) were to be seconded to the murder squad for an indeterminate period, to deal with a large number of prisoners. We were told we mustn't speak to anybody as security was a matter of priority.
>
> We were told to parade at Loughton at 4.00 am on 22 January 1976 to receive our instructions. Knowing of Bert Wickstead's fearsome reputation, I decided to go out and buy a new alarm clock to make sure that I was woken at 2.00 am and got to Loughton at about 3.30 am. At 4.00 am, Bert and other senior officers briefed dozens of CID and uniform officers (I think from the Special Patrol Group). Suspects' addresses in North & East London, Hertfordshire and all over East Anglia were to be raided at the same time and suspects arrested. Search warrants had been taken out to be executed at all the addresses. Other officers were already keeping observation on the suspects'

addresses to make sure they were in. I recall one DC saying to Bert, 'Guv'nor, what do we do if the suspect isn't at the address?' and Bert, in his usual gravelly voice replied, 'Don't fucking come back here until you've nicked him!' The point was taken by all present and no other questions were asked.

All prisoners were to be brought back to Loughton to be processed by Terry and myself. Gerry was the jailer for the next week or so. Once processed, the prisoners were put in the cells at Loughton whilst the majority were farmed out to other police stations all over East and North London until they were brought back to Loughton to be interviewed. Terry Norman was to deal with all the prisoners on arrival at Loughton and entered all their details in the Book 12A.

My function was to record all the seized property on the property sheets and make sure they were sealed and put in the property store. My other function was to record in the Murder Squad Occurrence Book all the movements of suspects from and back to the cells/detention rooms for interviews, examinations by Divisional Surgeons, visits to prisoners and anything else affecting the suspect's detention. When suspects were moved to other police stations or returned from a station to Loughton (invariably for interviews) these details were also recorded in the occurrence book. In the occurrence book, I showed a page for each suspect. Whenever I made an entry, I always signed and dated it. These entries included what I saw and also what I was told by officers dealing with suspects, especially going to and from other police stations. Gerry Mockford was the jailer and looked after the welfare of all suspects when they were in at Loughton, which also included making sure they were adequately fed. All three of us uniform officers were located in the charge room at Loughton so could easily monitor the movement of suspects to and from the cells, etc. All entries were made in the OB as they occurred and not at some later time – as alleged in the subsequent complaints. At no time did Bert Wickstead or any other officer instruct me to record anything which I knew to be untrue.

And that succinctly details the procedures which were set down and meticulously carried out in respect of the prisoners at Loughton police station. There we can leave it, for the time being at least.

Much later on in this narrative, those procedures will come under detailed scrutiny.

*

With a keen disregard for accuracy, the *Sun* told its readers, 'Four Killings Linked As Yard Grab 50', but more precisely, at 5.30 on the morning of 22 January 1976 eighteen people were arrested and taken to Loughton police station; eleven of them would subsequently be released. Various admissions by some of the prisoners were said to have been made, both on the way to the station and during subsequent interviews. On one such journey, Dudley, referring to Moseley, said, 'The cunt had it coming. He tried to fuck me, so I fucked him good and proper.' Later, referring to Cornwall and to his own daughter, Dudley was recorded as saying, 'I told him if he ever had sex with her, I would kill him.'

Cornwall had apparently written to Ray Baron whilst he was serving his sentence and bragged of his affair with Kathy, which elicited the reply from Dudley, 'Yes, but Ray never mentioned it to me. If he had, I would have given Cornwall his last rites earlier.' Still referring to Cornwall, Dudley said, 'He was a no-good loser. Take it from me, he's not on my conscience. He deserved what he got, and that's it.'

Wickstead asked, 'Did you murder Moseley?' to which Dudley replied, 'Prove it'.

And when Maynard was arrested at his address at Nettlecome House, Agar Grove, Camden, he told the officers, 'It's about time you came for me.' When questioned by Wickstead, he admitted going to the Saggs' flat looking for Cornwall, saying, 'It was business.'

Then he was asked this: 'Did you tell Ronnie Fright to be late at the meet and did you meet Moseley yourself?'

The answer given was, 'I'm not answering that, otherwise I'm finished.'

Wickstead said, 'You were going to kill him, weren't you? Weren't you?'

And when asked, 'Were you present when Cornwall was killed?' Maynard replied, 'You know he was asking for it.'

Unsurprisingly, all of these admissions would be later strenuously denied.

Mick Carter was responsible for preparing and typing the charge sheets; formally reading the charges to the prisoners took an hour. Dudley and Maynard were charged with murdering Cornwall and

Moseley, as were Spencer and Ronnie Fright in respect of the second charge.

Dudley and Maynard were also charged with assaulting and being concerned in Cornwall's false imprisonment, as well as being involved in causing him grievous bodily harm.

Dudley and Maynard, together with Spencer, Fright, Ernest Maynard and Charles Edwin Clarke, a fifty-two-year-old-greengrocer from Hazelville Road, Upper Holloway, were charged with conspiring with others to imprison Moseley against his will and conspiring with others to cause grievous bodily harm to Cornwall.

Dudley and Maynard were charged with being concerned in causing grievous bodily harm to Moseley, as was Spencer; and Dudley and Maynard, together with Kathy Dudley and Clarke, were charged with conspiring with others to falsely imprison Cornwall.

Dudley alone was charged with two charges of inflicting grievous bodily harm on a 'Miss X' in January 1969, one case of causing her actual bodily harm in 1973 and attempting to pervert the course of justice between January 1973 and February 1975.

Bob Maynard was charged with assaulting and imprisoning Moseley.

All of them appeared at Epping Magistrates' Court on Monday, 26 January and were remanded in custody; in addition, two men had been charged on the Saturday with conspiracy to offer imitation jewellery with the intention that it should be accepted as genuine – they were bailed to appear at court on 30 January.

Ken Dellbridge, who was part of the security detail for those remanded in custody, told me:

> We got up early and drove to Brixton. Two of us were in the van with the prisoners; this was before the days of SO14(2) Special Escort Group, so we had two Traffic Patrol cars, one in front, one behind, both with authorised shots on board and we drove straight through London to Epping Court, without stopping – then afterwards, the same again, back to the prison.

The committal got underway at Epping Magistrates' Court on 26 April 1976, and Michael Hills for the prosecution outlined the case to the Bench, telling them that the two murders were linked:

> If what happened to the second victim was anything to go by, Moseley was probably killed by being shot in the head. I talk in terms of probability about the actual cause

of death because – probably after death – his body was butchered and various parts of it cast into the Thames, somewhere around September 30 1974. One of the significant pieces of evidence was that Reginald Dudley, Robert Maynard and Mr Spencer knew that Mr Moseley was dead on October 3 1974 and Mr Maynard and Mr Spencer made a special journey to notify Ernest Maynard of that. That was two days before the first piece of Mr Moseley's body was washed ashore.

The case for the Crown was that both murders were ordered by Dudley and Robert Maynard, in the case of Moseley because he was accusing both of them of informing on criminals and because he had something they wanted: cash and valuables in a safety deposit box. This led to speculation about the small key that had been taken from Moseley's flat. In addition, his affair with Frankie Fright was known, not only to her husband but also to Robert Maynard, and two hours before Moseley had been lured and seized in Dalston, Dudley and his daughter had returned to England. Moseley had fought with Dudley in the late 1960s, the latter coming off worse.

'In his position of gang leader', Michael Hills told the magistrates, 'Dudley could not afford to leave the defeat unavenged.'

Cornwall had also accused both men of being police informants, had made extensive enquiries to discover Moseley's murderers and had established a sexual relationship with Kathy Dudley which her father found to be intolerable, since he regarded her as the girlfriend of Ray Baron, a serving prisoner.

So it appeared that the common denominators were greed, affront at being labelled grasses and revenge for affairs with wives/girlfriends of persons who were serving sentences.

Committal proceedings lasted until 18 May 1976; some charges were dropped, others imposed, but the magistrates were satisfied that there was a sufficiency of evidence upon which the defendants could be sent for trial. Kathy Dudley was granted bail, but she and the rest of the defendants, who were in custody, were committed to the Old Bailey to stand their trial.

However – and with no pun intended – a wild card was about to be added to the pack.

Within a few weeks of their arrest, at the end of February 1976, some of the accused men had been joined at Brixton prison by Anthony Wild, a prolific thief with eight previous convictions, who had been arrested for a robbery on a Securicor van in Redhill, Surrey, during which shots had been fired. It appears that he had got into conversation with Dudley, Maynard and Clarke.

Dudley had apparently told Wild, 'We're Murder Incorporated, we are,' and boasted of his involvement with Cornwall's murder, saying, 'He went up in the air, didn't he, boys?'

Wild added that Maynard had said, 'I didn't know guys would squeal like a pig.'

Most damaging of all were the remarks made when Dudley told Wild that he had taken Moseley's head in a polythene bag into Oliver Kenny's pub, the Horse and Groom in Brighton (in which Dudley had a business interest), adding that Kenny 'had almost died of fright when he saw it'. The head had then, allegedly, been thrown into the sea.

Wild added that Dudley had told him that a friend of his had been having trouble with his wife and said, 'We sorted the cunt out and I got his head to prove it'; he then described their involvement in murdering Cornwall.

Meanwhile, Ronnie Fright had been remanded to Pentonville because there had been an altercation between him and Bob Maynard; a prisoner named Frank Read stated that Fright had told him, 'We done one, we sawed him up.' Two other prisoners were later produced by the defence to say that they felt sure that Read was perjuring himself.

However, although Wild had written to Wickstead on several occasions, it was not until October that he was taken from Brixton to Loughton to make his damning statement.

*

The trial commenced on 11 November 1976 before Mr Justice Swanwick, who had served during the war years with the RAF Reserve, had been Mentioned in Dispatches and appointed a Military MBE. He had also been a formidable advocate, leading the prosecution in the highly controversial James Hanratty murder trial. So with a judge described as 'scrupulous and fair-minded' at the helm, the trial got underway. With Michael Corkery QC (who else?) prosecuting, the jury – who received police protection and were screened from the public gallery – was told, 'The story I have to tell is a terrible one. The evidence will disclose no shortage of cruelty and no shortage of sheer evil.'

It was unfortunate that press hyperbole went over the top – 'Gangland Executions By The Legal & General', 'Two Victims Of Sex, Murder, Torture Plot', 'Torture Unlimited', 'The Torturers – Court Story Of Sex, Murder And Violence In London's Gangland' and 'Gang Torture Ended With Two Murders'. On 14 November Mr Justice Swanwick demonstrated his fairness when he summoned the editorial executives of the *Daily Express, Daily Mail, Daily Mirror* and *Daily Telegraph* before him for their imprudent reporting. The judge accepted the Press Association's sincere apologies but issued a warning that any further infringements might not be so lightly treated; he also warned the jury to pay attention only to what they heard in court and not what they read in the press.

Not all of the same defendants faced the same charges (except Maynard and Dudley, accused of both murders), and there were further accusations facing the others in the dock: murder, conspiracy to murder, inflicting grievous bodily harm and conspiracy to assault and imprison both victims.

The allegations of police impropriety flew thick and fast, with denials of the alleged admissions. It appeared that Wickstead had a tape recorder concealed in a telephone on his desk. Why then, he was asked, were the interviews not taped?

'I am a police officer who believes in police methods', he stolidly replied, 'and tape recorders are not used in police interviews.'

This was true; tape recorded interviews would not be used by the police for another eight years, and Wickstead explained the tape recorder's existence by stating it was used when informants were supplying information.

Sharon Saggs' photographic identification of Maynard and Dudley arriving at her parents' flat was criticized, the defence saying that an identification parade should have been held; but the defence case was not helped when Sharon fainted twice while giving evidence. The Saggs family were later given fresh identities and relocated. Katherine Dudley declined to give evidence, whereas Anthony Wild gave compelling evidence in a series of lively exchanges. In cross-examination it was put to him that the defendants would hardly have supplied what amounted to a series of full confessions to someone whom they regarded as 'a disgusting homosexual', but the fact remains that criminals – especially when in the company of fellow law-breakers – do tend to boast of their accomplishments to enhance their standing in the twilight world of lawlessness. If corroboration of that statement is required, witness the number of present-day criminals who post rock-solid evidence of their unlawful accomplishments on social media sites, something which inevitably leads to their downfall.

However, having provided his enlightening evidence, on 7 December 1976 it was Wild's turn to stand in the dock in another of the courts at the Old Bailey, where he was one of four men accused of a series of armed robberies, which had netted more than £60,000. The ringleader was sentenced to 20 years' imprisonment, two of the others got 15 years each, and Wild, who admitted

Legal & General 161

ten charges, received 11 years. Perhaps he thought that because of his testimony in the murder trial he deserved a little less.

Pete Condon was a police constable at Plaistow and one of many detailed for jury protection, present at the Old Bailey to see the safe return of the jury members. Speaking from memory, he recalled a Ford Granada allegedly owned by Dudley which was supposed to be at the villa in Lloret del Mar at the time of the murder of Moseley: 'There was a lot of speculation on how long it takes to drive from Spain to the UK and back again. A gentleman from HM Customs and Excise was produced who remembered checking over the car on a certain date at Dover. This was obviously well received in court!'

In his summing-up (which lasted twelve days), the judge said this to the jury:

> In the case of every accused and every charge in this case, I think it is fair to say that without the evidence of the alleged oral confessions, there would not be evidence on which the Crown could ask you to convict. Where this is so, I tell you that does not mean that you cannot convict. It does mean that you must be very, very careful before you do. I am going into more detail, but let me say at once that you must be careful to be sure firstly, that the evidence of what was said is truthful evidence, and accurate . . . The most crucial decision you have to make is whether you can trust the confessions. It is suggested that there has been willing and enthusiastic compliance by all ranks from commander and chief superintendent down to detective sergeant and below in disgraceful conduct which, if detected should at least involve dismissal, disgrace and prosecution. If you think it really may be so that the confessions were fabricated, then it must mean that all those police officers are either very wicked or very weak men and it would undermine the whole prosecution case . . . In no case here, none of the cases against any of the accused, is there any physical evidence directly connecting any of them with any of the crimes charged. There is no evidence of where or exactly when either Moseley or Cornwall died. There are no eyewitnesses of any crime; there was no forensic evidence, no fingerprints, no bloodstained clothing, no murder weapon to connect any of the accused with either killing and no written and signed confessions. The evidence against the accused consists largely, and in some

cases almost wholly, of alleged oral confessions to police and others. So you must consider – such questions by themselves would not be sufficient – motive and opportunity, relationships, previous and subsequent conduct and see whether in each case they support and confirm the alleged confession or make it less likely to have been made or to have been intended as a confession.

On 15 June 1977 Ronnie Fright was acquitted of Moseley's murder and of causing him grievous bodily harm, but Bob Maynard was convicted by majority verdicts of the six male and six female jurors of the two murders, 11-1 in Moseley's case, 10-2 in the case of Cornwall; the judge discharged the jury from giving a verdict on causing Moseley grievous bodily harm. With that, the jury was sent to spend a second night in a hotel and told to resume their deliberations the following day.

On 16 June the jury unanimously cleared Ernest Maynard of conspiracy to cause grievous bodily harm to Moseley. Leaving the dock, he solemnly informed the court, 'They're all innocent'; but although George Spencer was cleared of murdering Moseley and causing him grievous bodily harm, he was the last to be acquitted.

Kathy Dudley was convicted of conspiracy to cause grievous bodily harm to Cornwall and was sentenced to 2 years' imprisonment, suspended for 2 years. Charles Clarke was unanimously found guilty of conspiracy to cause grievous bodily harm to both Cornwall and Moseley and was sentenced to 2 years' imprisonment on each charge, the sentences to run consecutively.

Reg Dudley was found guilty of both murders; he and Maynard were both sentenced to life imprisonment, with the judge stating that he would recommend to the Home Secretary that neither should be released for at least 15 years. Maynard shouted, 'I am still innocent, sir', while Dudley bellowed at Wickstead, 'Are you happy? You have fitted us all up but don't worry – you'll be fitted up in the end by your own kind.'

As we know, strenuous attempts had been made to do just that – without success.

The trial – at that time – was the longest in legal British history, lasting 135 days and entering the *Guinness Book of Records*; it had cost over £500,000, and the court transcript ran to over 3½m words.

★

On 28 July 1977 Moseley's head was discovered by a shocked roadsweeper, Harry Bromley, wrapped in a copy of the *Evening News* dated 16 June 1977 – the date the jury found Dudley guilty – in a public lavatory in Richmond Avenue, Barnsbury, North London. There was no gunshot wound to the head, and the Dudley/Maynard supporters went wild with delight, since that, they said, was one of the main features of the prosecution's case. Not so.

At the autopsy, the cause of death, was given as 'a head injury of acute origin'; and the bench at Epping Magistrates' Court had been told that judging by Cornwall's demise, Moseley's death was also 'probably' due to a bullet in the head. Due to the absence of Moseley's head at that time, the words had been carefully chosen.

However, the head was said to be in 'extremely good condition'; there were traces of car paint on it and it had been both buried and kept in a deep freeze. Once extracted from its frigid condition and wrapped in the newspaper, it had started to thaw. There was no indication that the head had been thrown into the sea, as Wild had said Dudley had told him.

The implications to the Dudley/Maynard camp were clear: the head could not have been placed there by any of the accused since all were in custody and had been for some time. Ergo, they were plainly innocent and would be released immediately. That was not the case, said the police – it was obviously placed in the lavatory by associates of the accused, with the intention of casting doubt on the jury's verdict.

Next, Tina Maynard, Bob wife, started what became known as the MDC (Maynard/Dudley/Clarke) campaign, and badges, slogans and T-shirts were printed bearing the slogan 'MDC – Not Guilty, Right✓'. Some supporters marched from Camden Town to Hyde Park Corner; a more strident group picketed Scotland Yard. 'Doan go in there, mate!' bellowed one of the group to me, too late, since I was leaving the building. 'They're all fucking liars in there, they are!'

In an attempt to defuse this hostile situation, I humorously replied, 'I'm afraid I'm one of them, Madam!'

Given the prevailing circumstances, this was probably the wrong comment to make, and I had to beat a hasty retreat to the sanctuary of the east-bound District Line platform at St James' Park underground station.

The demonstrations, plus the fact that both the convicted and acquitted took truth-drugs and lie detector tests and passed them with flying colours, generated some publicity; but since the findings of those tests were not acceptable in an English court of law (as those advising the participants must have known), it took their cases no further forward.

★

What of Oliver Kenny, the licensee of the Horse and Groom public house in Brighton, to whom Moseley's head had been shown? The newspaper headlines had been sensational: 'Severed Head Was Shown To Publican', 'Publican "Nearly Died Of Shock"'. A fisherman who was sure he had seen a human head bobbing about in the sea was called to give evidence.

Of Kenny it has been said, 'He was not available to the defence' – but is that right? No, it's not. Following Wild's revelations to Wickstead in October 1976, Kenny had been arrested by members of Wickstead's squad. He had been charged with the theft of diamonds valued at £1.5 million from Carrington's, the London jewellers, and in November 1976 he was committed for trial from Epping Magistrates' Court. At the time of his death from acute alcoholism, on 20 October 1977, he had been on bail awaiting trial at the Old Bailey five weeks later on 26 November – so why wasn't he called? There had been plenty of time; the trial had finished over four months previously. The second excuse put forward was that he had been prevented from giving evidence due to the conditions of his bail – this, and the first excuse, not to put too fine a point on it, are complete and consummate bollocks.

This is what Dudley's barrister, Jonathan Goldberg QC, had to say about it when he was interviewed in the 1998 *Rough Justice* programme.

> My memory is that Kenny was a terrified man who was coming up on trial himself. He told the defence solicitors that threats had been conveyed to him by [name deleted in the programme], that if he helped Dudley it would be very serious for him on his own trial and neither he nor his wife wanted to know at that time. Of course, we explored all these avenues but we met a wall of silence at every stage.

So here we have three separate explanations as to why the jury never heard Kenny's evidence: because he was not made available to the defence; because the conditions of his bail would not permit him to travel to London; and lastly, because Kenny was threatened by an unknown person, who by imputation must have been a very nasty police officer.

Right. Let's examine the question of witnesses at the time that this case was being tried. When a witness was called for the prosecution, a copy of his or her statement had to be served on the defence; therefore, the defence would know what that witness was going to say in advance. Usually, the defence would know months previously; however, sometimes a witness had been uncovered at a late stage, perhaps even the morning that he or she was going to give evidence. In that case, the witness's statement would be served on the defence, and if the defence then requested an adjournment in order to discuss the evidence with their client, that would be granted by the trial judge. In all cases the prosecution would have checked on the witness, and if he or she had previous convictions, details of them would also be given to the defence.

However, if the defence wished to call a witness, there was no necessity whatsoever to give notice of this to the prosecution. A defence witness could suddenly appear in the box and the police then had to rush around trying to formally identify the witness, whilst he or she was giving evidence, and try to discover if it was possible to obtain details of previous convictions, without having the advantage of a fingerprint check to establish that that person was who they said they were. It was all rather one-sided. It also required a goodly amount of puff to race out of court and up to the police room in the hope that a telephone was available to make the necessary checks.

Now let's return to the matter of Oliver Kenny. He had been interviewed by the police and a copy of his statement had been served on the defence; but since – for whatever reason – the prosecution decided not to call him, they were obliged to offer him to the defence to call as a witness so that he might be cross-examined by both prosecution and defence. However, the defence was under no obligation to call him. In cases such as this, if the defence were of the opinion that a witness might weaken (or cause irreparable harm to) their case, neither they nor any of the other defendants' barristers needed to call him, nor did they have to explain why they hadn't.

The case for the defence was that Dudley had not taken Moseley's head to Kenny's pub. Wild had given evidence that Dudley had told him that he had, which was strongly disputed. Kenny was the one person who could have said 'Yea' or 'Nay', and yet the suggestion was that he had been threatened by a rogue, unnamed police officer and that ill would befall Kenny at his forthcoming trial if he did give evidence. In that eventuality, one would have thought that an immediate investigation would have been launched, upon the directions of the trial judge, with Kenny and the unnamed officer both being questioned; but it appears that that was not the case. In fact, matters went much further than that. If perfidy on the part of the reprobate police officer could have been strongly alleged – not necessarily proved – it would almost certainly have led to the prosecution throwing in the towel at Kenny's forthcoming trial.[1]

In that eventuality, Kenny would have been freed from the toils (and possible consequences) of his trial, a venal police officer would have been exposed and, with the fabricated evidence against him unmasked, Dudley would have been vindicated and in all probability, would have walked free from court. In fact, matters go rather further than that. When a review was carried out, two years after the *Rough Justice* programme, no such allegation was made to the senior investigating officer. 'Had that been the case', he told me, 'I would certainly have immediately investigated it.'

*

On 26 March 1979 the four convicted persons sought leave to appeal against their convictions before Lord Justice Roskill, Lord Justice Ormrod and Mr Justice Watkins. The appeal was based on a large number of grounds: that the trial judge should have allowed two separate murder trials; criticism of the judge's summing-up; that the defendants were disadvantaged due to the length of the trial (which was a bit rich, since the adjournments and delays had been at the instigation of the defence); that the oral confessions which had not been corroborated were insufficient for the jury to be asked to convict; that the verdicts were inconsistent; that photographic identification of Dudley and Maynard by Sharon Saggs should not have been allowed; that the case of Kathy Dudley should have been withdrawn from the jury; that the security measures had robbed the defendants of receiving a fair trial; that the publicity surrounding the case had been highly prejudicial; and because of what was referred to as 'the hostile nature of the charges'.

Michael Mansfield for Dudley said:

> The murders were of a class which would horrify anyone who read about them and that a jury would approach their task on the basis that it would be utterly wrong if at the end of the trial they were to reach a conclusion that no-one was to be punished for these murders.

---

[1] Classic examples of this happening may be found in *Operation Countryman – The Flawed Enquiry into London Police Corruption*, Pen & Sword True Crime, 2018.

This cut no ice with the Appeal Court Judges:

> There are plenty of examples of horrifying crimes going unpunished because the Crown has been unable to adduce proper proof of the guilt of the particular alleged criminal who, on the evidence, has been rightly acquitted.

Felix Whaley QC for Maynard stated that Sharon Saggs had been given an armed police guard:

> When she came to court, she was in such an unfortunate state that when I asked her to look at Maynard, she would not. She turned away and burst into hysterical tears . . . The impact of that on the jury was disastrous for Maynard.

In order to discredit the police interviews, the services of the Revd Andrew Queen Morton, a Church of Scotland Minister, were sought. Morton believed that writers – or speakers – identify themselves by the use of frequently employed words and that it is therefore possible to determine if more than one person has contributed to a particular sentence. His CV was impressive; he had discovered, beyond a reasonable doubt, that the New Testament had been written on five different sizes of paper – this, apparently had been authenticated by Pliny the Younger – but the reverend gentleman's arguments regarding documents written some 2,000 years later failed to convince the Court of Appeal of any duplicity in the interview notes, and on 2 April 1979 all of the appeals were dismissed.

In 1980 Wild was released from prison. He met the *Guardian* reporter, Duncan Campbell, in a pub in Hove, Sussex, and having ensured that the conversation was not being recorded, then said that his evidence regarding Moscley's head was untrue and that he had followed guidelines given to him by the police. He stated that he could get Maynard and Dudley out of prison 'tomorrow' but would not do so, 'even for £50,000'. However, when he was interviewed by the police, he retracted these claims.

It was not too long before Wild was up to his old tricks again. Between April and October 1981 he participated in five armed robberies, where once again shots were fired. He escaped the police twice before his arrest on 9 December 1981, and on 23 April 1982 he was sentenced to 10 years' imprisonment.

In 1989, when documents in other cases said to have been miscarriages of justice were subjected to ESDA (Electrostatic Document Analysis), it was decided to subject the original interview notes to that process, only for it to be discovered that they had been destroyed.

In June 1992 the *Observer* published a piece on the case, and a report was sent to the Home Office in which attacks were made on the reliability of both the oral confessions and Wild's admissions. In 1994 a further appeal was refused.

But in 1995 Wild got in touch with journalists again, telling them that as a born-again Christian he wanted to tell the truth and claiming that his reason for giving false evidence in court was so that he would get a shorter sentence. This made a front-page story in the *Guardian*, but when he was again interviewed by the police, Wild, on the advice of his lawyer and facing an almost certain charge of perjury, said nothing. Dudley's lawyers wrote to the Home Secretary asking for the case to be reviewed; seven months later, the review was refused.

On 5 August 1997 Dudley was released from Ford open prison. He was now seventy-two and had spent 22 years in prison; Maynard remained in Elmley Prison in Kent.

As the years went by, there were television documentaries about the case, including BBC's *Rough Justice: The Jigsaw Murder* in 1998; Sharon Saggs was traced and said that she 'had doubts' about the evidence she had given at the trial. Anthony Wild, like Sharon Saggs, had his face obscured, in his case apparently to save him from the depredations of those whom 'he had fitted up'. He stated that following his interview with Wickstead he had been taken away by an unnamed officer (who, it was said, was 'unconnected with the investigation') and they conspired together to fit up at least some of the defendants. Yet despite this Machiavellian intrigue, Wild illogically stated, 'I never thought it would get to court.'

But an important point was not mentioned. It was Wild who – before even seeing him – wrote Wickstead a series of letters, entreating him to listen to what he had to say. It does tend to debunk Wild's story – which by his own account contained so many lies – of going off to collude with an unnamed, unprincipled police officer who had no connection with the case, rather than one who simply wrote down Wild's statement. It's not known if this dodgy police officer was the same one who had apparently threatened Oliver Kenny not to give evidence; maybe not. Perhaps Wickstead had a whole cupboard-full of dubious cops whom he could trot out whenever the course of justice needed to be perverted. Nevertheless, at the end of the programme, Kirsty Wark triumphantly strutted before the camera to announce, '*Rough Justice* has found that their convictions are unsafe.'

In July 1998 a request was put to the Criminal Cases Review Commission (CCRC) by the defence for the police notebooks to be tested scientifically (or photocopies if they were available). In turn, the CCRC instructed a leading forensic document examiner, Dr Robert Anthony Hardcastle, in order to examine the speeds of the handwriting, and in September 1999 he produced a detailed report.

Meanwhile, in May 1999 the Crown Prosecution Service decided to give immunity from prosecution for perjury to fifty-three-year-old Wild, 'in the interests of investigating a possible miscarriage of justice'. In April 2000 a statement was obtained from Wild in which he claimed his testimony had been fabricated in collusion with the police, although in his later judgement, Lord Justice Mantell said, 'It may be said that the discovery of the head after the trial provides some retrospective support for his (Wild's) credibility.' In June 2000 the CCRC referred the cases of Maynard, Dudley and Bailey (this was now Kathy Dudley's surname) to the Court of Criminal Appeal, Maynard was released on bail in 2000, and the following year, Clarke's widow (he had died in 1995) applied for leave to appeal against her late husband's convictions and was granted it.

However, the CCRC had commissioned a review into the case and this was carried out between 2000 and 2002 by the Directorate of Professional Standards Internal Investigation. The senior officer in charge was Detective Chief Inspector Neil Basu. He told me:

> All of the prosecution papers, all pertinent documents and a transcript of the court proceedings were read and I wanted to put them into the HOLMES (Home Office Large Major Enquiry) computerised system but not all of the documents were A4 size, so they were copied onto disk by a private company. It took three months and cost thousands and thousands of pounds. In short, I reinvestigated the case; the prosecution witnesses were re-interviewed.

The hearing commenced at the Court of Appeal (Criminal Division) before Lord Justice Mantell, Mr Justice Holman and Mr Justice Gibbs. Wild's revelations were an important part of the appeal process, but bearing in mind the number of times his testimony had changed in the 26 years since he had first delivered it, it really did need particularly careful scrutiny. 'I spent many hours with Wild', Basu told me. 'I was unimpressed with him.'

An equally important aspect concerned the alleged confessions, especially – in the light of Dr Hardcastle's findings – in respect of Dudley.

For some considerable time Wickstead had used the red Home Office Stationery Office 'Books 40' measuring 12" × 8" for recording interviews. Alf Marriott was a uniformed sergeant from 'W' Division who was supplied to the Old Bailey to act as a court sergeant and provide security in the corridors. He recalled going into court when Wickstead was giving evidence:

> Mr Wickstead had a Book 40, with markers down the side for each prisoner; a QC jumped up and challenged what was going on, saying something like, 'Mr Wickstead, that is not your pocket book.' His reply was, 'I anticipated that this would be a long trial and would take some time, and I would be cross-examined about my dealings with each prisoner and a great deal of time would be wasted by me searching through my pocket book. I felt I could facilitate my answers by using a larger book with markers and would be prevented from making a mistake when answering.' The QC made long submissions but the judge said that Mr Wickstead had been very thoughtful and helpful by his actions. I had to leave then, but returned several times in the following days and although I was a committed, experienced copper, and well used to dealing with aggressive questioning, I had a master class.

Thus, it was Books 40 which were used during the Dudley/Maynard trial. This was denied by all the defendants; they stated that during their interviews, notes had been written on sheets of paper and had obviously been transferred to the Books 40 at some later stage. Criticism was levelled at the police for not inviting the interviewee to read through those notes at the time and sign them. But this was said in the light of the provisions contained in the Police and Criminal Evidence Act, 1984. At the time of making those notes, they were a record kept by police, for the police only; if a prisoner wished to give a written account, he or she was perfectly entitled to do so, by making a voluntary statement.

Dr Hardcastle examined all the records of interviews to determine if they could have been written at the time in the time stated; and, with one exception, he accepted they could, and in several cases, that they had been written with ease.

The exception was Dudley's first interview on 23 January 1976. This had apparently been recorded between 4.28 pm and 5.18 pm. In this period of between 49 and 51 minutes, Dr Hardcastle concluded that the 11,325 characters simply could not have been written; the fastest speed that could be achieved in that time was 190 characters per minute, and if these times were correct, it meant that the writer had got down between 222 and 231 characters per minute. This, he stated, was a physical impossibility, and if the times of interview were correct, there is no dispute about that.

But it's necessary to get back to Mick Carter, who at Loughton was responsible for the booking in and out of the prisoners. Interestingly, he had never been called by the defence to give evidence at the trial. Even more interesting were Lord Justice Mantell's remarks when he stated that the Squad Occurrence Book 'has only very recently come to light'. This was not the case; documents prove that Carter was interviewed about that book by the Police Complaints Department as long ago as 1983 and again during the review in 2001. He told me:

> On 22 January Reginald Dudley was brought into Loughton at 5.50 am and after being booked in, in the Book 12A, he was then removed shortly afterwards to Walthamstow police station. On 23 January Dudley was returned to Loughton and I recorded in the Occurrence Book that he was interviewed by Detective Chief Superintendent Harvey (Hertfordshire Police) between 4.05 pm and 5.20 pm. I can't recall now who else was in this interview. The interview took place in a room on the first or second floor.

According to one officer, he took Dudley from the charge room – at 4.10 pm, he said – to be interviewed, then waited outside Wickstead's office for about a quarter of an hour, believing that Wickstead would interview Dudley; but it was in fact Harvey who conducted the interview. It's also very confusing, because Carter wrote in the thick, sand-coloured 15" × 10" Occurrence Book that Dudley was going to be interviewed by Harvey, not Wickstead, at the time of making the entry. In a statement made to an investigating officer in 1983, Carter, who had been provided with photostat copies of his entries in the Occurrence Book, said, 'I have recorded that the interview was by DCS Harvey . . . The interview would have taken place on the 1st or 2nd floor at Loughton and therefore when Mr Dudley was removed from the cell, I can only record what the purpose of his movement was for.'

There is little doubt that Carter's version is accurate and that it's possible that the officer who conducted Dudley upstairs was mistaken regarding the sequence of events.

According to the evidence given at the trial, the interview commenced at 4.28 pm, with the caution being given at 4.29 pm. From personal experience, I know that these timings (and what follows) are often scribbled, and it is quite possible that the times recorded were in fact, 4.08 pm and 4.09 pm respectively and that when the officers' statements were typed up from the notes, the mistake was made then. This was a view shared by Neil Basu, who told me, 'I believe the disparity of the times during the Dudley interview was due to the times being incorrectly recorded; I could find no evidence of corruption.' This would mean that in a 70-minute interview those notes were written at a rate of 162 characters per minute – fast, certainly, but within Dr Hardcastle's parameters. The finishing time of 5.18 pm was corroborated by Mick Carter's note that Dudley was returned to his custody at 5.20 pm.

This just goes to show that no matter how good a typist may be, mistakes can still be made, and therefore it is essential to check the original against the typescript, otherwise it can lead to embarrassing consequences. I once interviewed an armed robber and at the conclusion of the interview he read through the notes made at the time, agreed with the contents, initialled each of his answers and signed each page. After I interviewed him for a second time, I asked him to check the notes for their accuracy and sign them if they were correct. Possibly realizing his folly in speaking to me at all, he refused, saying, 'No, I'm not signing them; I was mad to sign the first lot.'

When the notes were typed up, I checked them and to my discomfort, they read, 'I was *made* to sign the first lot.' Moral: check everything.

Certainly, at the trial DCS Harvey and the note-taker, Detective Chief Inspector Trevor Lloyd-Hughes, gave evidence that the timing of the interview was from 4.28 pm to 5.18 pm in the erroneous belief that those times were correct when, quite patently, they were not. In fact, it is highly likely that they were led into their evidence by the prosecutor – and this was quite common – saying something along the lines of, 'Is it right that you commenced the interview of Dudley at 4.28 pm?' and the officers, believing this to be true, replied, 'Yes' before continuing with their evidence.

One very interesting point is that Dudley would later allege that he had never met Ron Harvey but this, as Neil Basu told me, 'was nonsense. Harvey was an accomplished painter – he had several of his works exhibited – and knowing that Dudley was also a painter, he mentioned this during the interview. The fact that this was mentioned was never disputed during the trial.' In fact, Dudley, 'a talented and self-taught artist', later told the BBC that he hoped to use his compensation to realise his dream of opening his own art gallery to exhibit his own work and those of young students.

The matter of speed had been mentioned by Dudley's barrister, Michael West QC, both in cross-examination and in his closing speech, but he had never suggested that this was a physical impossibility. Perhaps Lloyd-Hughes could have given a logical explanation, but by the time this discrepancy was discovered, 22 years after the event, he was dead and the original notes destroyed.

But there was enough uncertainty for Lord Justice Mantell to rule that Dudley's convictions were unsafe and he allowed his appeal, quashing them. The position of the other appellants was different, because the interviews in their case certainly could have been written in the times stipulated; also, there was arguably more evidence against Maynard independent of the interviews, and although Kathy Dudley had not given evidence, her barrister had attacked the police testimony. However, the 'hard-backed' book system was central to the issue against every appellant. Had the jury been affected by the evidence of Dr Hardcastle (if, of course, he had been there) then that would probably have caused them to look more cautiously at the integrity of every other interview; and therefore on 16 July 2002 the convictions of the other appellants were considered unsafe and were quashed.

Whilst the amounts of compensation were discussed (which later resulted in six-figure sums being awarded), Dudley told the BBC why he believed Wickstead had fitted him up.

'Wickstead hated me', he said, 'It stems from years ago when a local villain had been arrested for a break-in and my wife gave evidence on his behalf. Wickstead never forgave her, or me.' Two weeks previously, Dudley had told the *Observer*, 'Wickstead had tried and failed several times to recruit me as a grass.'

So that's two diverse reasons why Wickstead fitted him up for a double murder. Sounds reasonable? Right. Take your pick.

In the same *Observer* interview Dudley described himself as 'a fence, a buyer and seller of stolen property' and made reference to a bent detective with whom he had 'a close relationship'. He named him as Alec Eist and said, 'My friends knew that if they were in trouble, for a few grand channelled through me, Alec would do what he could to make evidence "disappear".' The suggestion was that Eist was acting as a conduit – a practice known as 'middling' – a go-between, vis-à-vis police and criminal.

So let's take a look at Alexander Antony Eist, who joined the Metropolitan Police in 1948. He was certainly an energetic and well-informed cop, who spent a total of eight years with the Flying Squad. He was also courageous, winning a BEM for gallantry in 1966 for tackling a vicious prison escapee, who was in possession of a loaded firearm. However, he was very much a law unto himself; at the conclusion of a successful case he would disappear for days to go horse-racing. This provoked the ire of the martinet head of the Flying Squad, Tommy Butler, who demonstrated that nobody is indispensable by kicking Eist right off the Squad. There were those amongst his contemporaries who described Eist as 'a loveable rogue' and others who felt he was, as Dudley put it, 'a bent detective'.

One of the practices that Eist adopted was the use of 'mugs', and the way it worked, was this. A thief would steal a lorry-load of goods and remove at least 50 per cent of the cargo. He would then inform his crooked police counterpart as to the whereabouts of the lorry, and the cop would keep observation on it. Not for too long, though, because the thief would have contracted a dupe – or mug – and not one overburdened with brains, to drive the lorry to a given location. En route, the lorry would be intercepted by the police and the driver arrested and charged, and the case cleared up. The crooked cop would then submit an informant's report, and the informant, i.e. the thief, would receive a small bursary from the Yard's Informants' Fund, plus a reward from the loss adjusters for 10 per cent of the value of the recovered goods which would be split with his crooked counterpart.

On one occasion Eist was summoned before a senior officer to be upbraided for something he had done, or perhaps neglected to do. Far from apologising, Eist went on the offensive, pointing out the number of stolen lorry-loads he had recovered.

'Alec', replied the other wearily, 'before you came we didn't *have* any fucking stolen lorry-loads!'

At the time of his third and final parting with the Flying Squad, Eist was posted to Holloway police station on 4 February 1974 as a detective chief inspector, the highest ranking CID officer there.

Eist was certainly in cahoots with Dudley; Allan Rowlands, who was a police constable at Holloway, told me, 'I recall seeing a photograph, obviously a surveillance photo, showing Dudley, Maynard and others on the deck of a cruise ship. Skulking in the shadows one could see the unmistakable features of Alec Eist. This photo was held by [the late] Charlie Carter, collator at Holloway, and shown to a few select people.'

Graham Hickson was an aid to CID at Holloway and described to me how he and his partner used to visit the small car workshop in Durham Mews, run by Philip Luxford:

> Now and then, we used to see Billy Moseley there, who was a friend of Luxford's. Sometime towards the end of 1974 Luxford spoke with us and said, 'Something's happened to Billy, he borrowed my car, went to a meet and not seen him since.' Well, nothing unusual, we thought at the time. Then Luxford contacted us and said his car had been returned and left outside the garage with the keys in it. It was an old 3-litre Rover. But still no Billy. Luxford said, 'Something has happened to him because I can't contact him.'
>
> It was shortly after this that some body parts appeared in the River Thames at Rainham, i.e. torso, no head and no hands. You get this gut instinct and we got our detective sergeant to contact Romford, where a murder squad had been set up, to inform them of Moseley's disappearance. Needless to say, we heard nothing, and as far as I can remember, no enquiries were made at our end. There seemed to be no movement at the Holloway end by the Romford murder squad. I later found out that Moseley had borrowed Luxford's car to go and keep a meet somewhere in Dalston with a person named Ginger Frith or Fry. There was a rumour Moseley was shagging someone's wife, not confirmed. I subsequently found out that early that year (1975), a bullet was received in the post by Luxford.

In January 1975 Hickson was appointed detective constable and was posted to Forest Gate police station, but his previous partner, who had paired up with another aid, was certain that the body parts were those of Moseley, and the two continued to make themselves busy. Suddenly the two aids were returned to uniform, apparently without reason, and Hickson's former partner was very bitter about the whole business.

'If I had still been at Holloway', Hickson told me, 'there's no doubt I would have gone the same way.'

As the DCI at Holloway, Eist would have been responsible for his subordinates' return to uniform. Did he think they were getting too close to something? Difficult to say, but consider this: as we know, Micky Cornwall's body was discovered on 7 September 1975. The following day, after just nineteen months' service at Holloway, Eist was transferred to Ilford police station on 'J' Division.

Coincidence? Possibly. He stayed on 'J' Division for ten weeks ('Where', Peter Binstead caustically told me, 'I expect the number of lorry-draggings rose dramatically!') before being returned to uniform posted to the Traffic Division, where it was expected that his time would be spent supervising the investigation of collisions involving police vehicles. However, it's doubtful if he tarried long enough to be fitted for his uniform, for he hot-footed it to Wellington House for a swift examination by the Metropolitan Police's Chief Medical Officer, who decided that, given his fragile mental state, it would not be desirable or necessary for Eist's tenure in the police to continue. He imposed the statutory ninety days of sick leave, and within one month of Dudley & Co appearing at Epping Magistrates' Court for their initial appearance, Eist had resigned on an ill-health pension, suffering from obstruction of the airways and depression.

Mind you, to say that Eist was controversial was rather like saying that Errol Flynn was flirty. He took on the Green Man pub at Six Mile Bottom, Cambridgeshire, but that was a brief respite, since he was arrested, stood trial and was duly acquitted at Middlesex Crown Court on 12 June 1978 for allegedly arranging an alibi for two London thieves. Next, three months later, he was hauled up by the House Assassinations Committee in the United States who were re-evaluating the evidence which Eist had supplied when he had arrested James Earl Ray in London. Ray subsequently pleaded guilty to the murder of Dr Martin Luther King Jr but then later decided that he wasn't guilty, and the Congressional Committee admitted that they were 'deeply disturbed' regarding Eist's evidence. They weren't the only ones, because Eist was quite concerned when Ray's attorney told the committee that he had received a telephone call from a London barrister saying that Eist 'had been fired from Scotland Yard after being charged with theft and perjury and was later found guilty of corruption'. I can't help but wonder what would have happened if a police officer stood up in court and described a barrister's character in such an inaccurate fashion?

Eist died on 27 January 1982; I passed this news on to one of his contemporaries. 'Alec? He ain't dead', was the contemptuous comment. 'He's middling in Limbo!'

So is there a connection here? Difficult to say, really. Just a lot odd goings-on in and around the Holloway area in the mid-1970s. Nothing at all to corroborate the suggestion that a senior, venal cop did anything wrong to protect a close associate who was a vicious North London gangster and who, of course, had nothing whatsoever to do with a barbaric double murder.

Nobody else has ever been charged (or even arrested) for those murders. But of course, the main thing is that the Court of Appeal ruled that MDC were Not Guilty – Right✓.

It's interesting to note that at the time of Maynard and Dudley's convictions, Wickstead sourly but correctly noted that the 'do-gooders' would claim that it was a miscarriage of justice; and he was right.

It was not a view shared by Neil Basu who told me, 'By the conclusion of the review, I was convinced there had been no miscarriages of justice at all; I said so in my report.'

And then, he said this:

> However, there is one matter I want to make clear. During the review, I interviewed both Bert Wickstead and Ron Harvey. I was so impressed with both of them and I came to the conclusion that they were remarkable detectives. It was after I met them – not before – that I decided I would become a murder investigator. It was their inspiration that made me the officer that I am, today.

That officer is Assistant Commissioner Basu QPM, BA (Hons), the head of the Anti-Terrorism Branch, New Scotland Yard.

Epilogue

Wickstead's critics would often say that not only would he not survive as a police officer today, but neither would his cases. They're right on both counts, but let's examine those statements.

First, when Wickstead joined the police, they were low in numbers and welcomed ex-servicemen because they had been part of a disciplined force. However, given Wickstead's legendary rudeness, it's highly doubtful that nowadays he would have survived training school. He was a one-off; he hated criminals as much as he loathed bent cops, and there is nobody nowadays who could come even close to his bull-in-a-china-shop style. In the modern-day 'let's-be-nice-to-everybody' Metropolitan Police, Wickstead would have disappeared in a puff of smoke.

Wickstead's era was in the days prior to the Crown Prosecution Service (CPS) and the Police and Criminal Evidence Act 1984, both of which have been responsible for favouring the criminal and making lawyers very rich indeed. With the representatives of the CPS and the defence lawyers demanding every scrap of paper penned by the police, even in the most trivial of cases, one remand at court would follow another, and this has dragged criminal justice down to a snail's pace. Unlike the police, criminals do not have a set of rules and regulations governing their behaviour; in many cases, neither do their legal representatives. In addition, let's not forget that in Wickstead's day there was no DNA profiling, no CCTV and no instant number plate recognition. What a bonus the last two would have been in tracing Billy Moseley's last movements – and the identities of those he met.

Consequently, it's pointless for Wickstead's detractors to judge his methods of investigation by today's standards, just as it is to make any other comparisons between 'now' and 'then'.

Wickstead's health might have suffered after he was attacked on the night of Saturday, 16 August 1975, when he tackled an intruder who had broken into a neighbour's house; he was coshed over the head with an iron bar which necessitated the insertion of eight stitches, and to add insult to injury, the burglar escaped. However, after a period of sick leave and the discovery of Micky

Cornwall's body three weeks later, Wickstead went straight back into the fray.

But now those days were gone, and Wickstead's career came to an end. He retired from the Force on New Year's Eve 1977, having served 30 years, which included 73 days' war service. For the latter half of his calling he had packed more work into those years than most detectives could have done in a dozen careers, and aged fifty-four, he was worn out. It was a good time to go; Wickstead's champion, Commissioner Sir Robert Mark, had retired in March 1977. He knew that Wickstead was a straight cop. In the same way that the Assistant Commissioner (Crime), Sir Ronald Howe KBE, CVO, MC, had told the embryonic members of the secretive postwar Ghost Squad, some 30 years before, 'Do whatever is necessary to ensure that the gangs are smashed up', Sir Robert had backed Wickstead, unequivocally. Now he had gone, and so too had Ernie Bond, the previous year. The times, they were indeed a-changin'.

Wickstead went to work as security advisor to what was then News Group Newspapers; the *Sun* later serialized his memoirs taken from his book, *Gangbuster – Tales of the Old Grey Fox*. It was a sad little paperback which could have been good, but wasn't. Apart from a lack of photographs, there was also a deficiency of stories. The Ilford Bank robbery, the encounter with Charles Taylor and most damning of all, the Maynard and Dudley case, received no mention whatsoever.

He became a Freeman of the City of London but – apart from steadfastly following the fortunes of West Ham United – had little interest in anything other than police work. Strangely, he never became a member of the popular Ex-CID Officers' Association and seldom attended police functions or reunions. He kept only spasmodically in touch with a very few of his contemporaries, although the exception, according to Stan Clegg, was that 'he didn't forget his days on 'G' Division, and several of us had many lunches together'.

One of Britain's most active (and most charitable) criminals said of Wickstead, 'He didn't take money and, if you're a policeman, you have to deal with scumbags every day. You have to go down to their level to achieve any results, so I understand he did what he did.'

Apart from being known for not taking bribes, Wickstead was something of an anomaly amongst senior officers. Firstly, he was certainly not a rich man. In fact, he could not even be said to have been even comfortably well-off. For all of his career he had lived in rented council accommodation, which included his semi-detached, four-bedroom house in Wellfields, Loughton. Although in 2018 it was valued at approximately £730,000, it was a council-owned dump when he moved there in 1972, and it was only later, courtesy of the Thatcher Government's Right to Buy scheme under the provisions of the Housing Act, 1980, that he was able to buy it.

And secondly, practically throughout his career, he was not a Freemason. One of his contemporaries told me, 'I admired him so much, to get to the top of his profession without the assistance of Freemasonry, when just about every other senior officer was "on the square".' Wickstead did eventually become a Freemason, but it was right at the end of his police service.

His son told me, 'He wanted nothing to do with any of the police lodges because of the taint of corruption in respect of some of them. Instead, he joined a lodge in Loughton, through a friend who was a builder.'

Dave McEnhill recalled, 'In the days that he was there, he was a very strong man. He had the backing of people like Ernie Bond. If there was any opposition, he went straight for it. He had his enemies but he did his own thing. He was a man's man. He led from the front – always the first in the witness box.'

Many of Wickstead's contemporaries echoed McEnhill's sentiments. 'Bert wasn't the most popular amongst his peers, but the skills of Ian Forbes rubbed off on him when he [Wickstead] was a First-class at Dalston', Stan Clegg told me. 'As an investigator, he pursued every case with vigour until he got a result. He was fantastic in the witness box; he just waited for the moment defence counsel asked a stupid question and he was off, supported by the judge and that was 'game over'. Michael Hall's opinion was, 'I thought he was one of the world's best coppers.'

'I loved being on the Serious', Graham Howard (who had known Wickstead since the days of the Ilford Bank Robbery) told me. 'Bert could be difficult to get on with but if you worked for him, he was a good Guv'nor.'

When West Ham were playing at home against Newcastle, Peter Binstead, deputising for Wickstead's usual driver, drove him to the match.

'Afterwards', Binstead told me, 'Bert said to me, "What would you be doing if you weren't driving me?" I was working on the crime squad at Woodford at that time and I replied, "Out catching thieves, Guv". The following Monday, I was on his team working at Loughton.'

Wickstead's demeanour was at best bluff and at worst staggeringly rude, but make no mistake about it, he was a tremendous detective and a first-rate murder investigator. He knew the worth of keeping a strong, cohesive team around him. He recognized their capabilities by getting them officially commended for their work; this extended to him writing to Peter Condon's divisional commander to pass on his thanks for Condon's court protection duty in the Maynard and Dudley case. Former Flying Squad driver Mick Gray was a 'K' Division 'Q' Car driver who produced a creditable number of arrests when Wickstead was a detective chief inspector. He received a hand-written note from Wickstead congratulating him – and both Condon and Gray still treasure those written approbations.

'I look for three main qualities in my officers', Wickstead once said. 'Honesty, integrity and professional capability.'

The Serious Crime Squad typist told me that when a report had to be compiled, Wickstead would walk around her, chain-smoking and holding a sheaf of papers which was covered in his scrawl, dictating to her. When he was finished, he'd say, 'Right, give us it 'ere – I'll sign it'; and without reading the report, he would do so. Was this arrogance, a faith in his infallibility that he would have left nothing out, or complete confidence in the typist's ability? Perhaps it was a bit of all three; but having seen some of those reports, I can say they were undeniably excellent both in content and presentation.

*

In his private life, Wickstead had married Ella White in 1943 during his war service; a son, Graham (whom Wickstead idolized), was born in 1957. But when Wickstead, as a detective inspector, laid eyes on Jean Simonette, the CID typist at Stoke Newington, in the words of one of his contemporaries, 'He was smitten.'

Their son Andrew told me, 'On the first occasion he took her out for a drink he told her he was going to marry her.'

Wickstead's first wife left the family home and, taking Graham with her, went to live in Fleetwood, north of Blackpool. However, in those days, 'cohabiting with a woman, not your wife' was very much frowned upon by the Police Force; it was a disciplinary offence which could lead to the officer being sacked.

Wickstead offset this authoritarian action by swiftly reporting himself on a Form 728 in his inimitable, terse style:

Detective Chief Superintendent,

I have left my wife and am now living with the CID typist, Jean Simonette.

Submitted.

A.S. Wickstead
Detective Inspector 'G'

Epilogue

Those who drew up the rules of morality in the Metropolitan Police also set the amount Wickstead had to pay his separated wife, and he meticulously sent her maintenance money on a regular basis by means of recorded delivery. Wickstead had moved in with Jean, but it was a strain on their finances; Andrew told me, 'By the end of the week, they were living on sausages.'

Two sons – Andrew and Neil – were born in 1967 and 1970 respectively, but Wickstead's first wife adamantly refused him a divorce; it was not until 1 March 1972 that a degree absolute was granted, and Wickstead and Jean were married fifteen days later at a registry office.

It was certainly a busy, in fact a harrowing, period for Wickstead and his family. His marriage coincided with his investigation into the Tibbs gang whilst he was living right in the middle of their territory. Two weeks later, the arrests were carried out, one week after that the Dixon trial got underway, and within four months he was informing a judge at the Old Bailey that he had been obliged to move house, due to death threats being made against him and his family, and armed bodyguards were being employed to guard his wife and children.

Few marriages could have survived such a buffeting; however, the photograph taken outside St John's Church, Loughton, close to the time of Wickstead's retirement, when the couple's marriage vows were blessed, is one of the very few times that he was pictured smiling. He was utterly devoted to – and very protective of – his family.

Wickstead drank only sparingly (by the CID standards of the day he was considered practically teetotal) but he was always a heavy smoker; he died of emphysema on 19 March 2001, just before his seventy-eighth birthday.

The cremation took place at the Parndon Wood Crematorium, Harlow, Essex on 28 March 2001, and although it was well attended, the lack of senior officers from the Yard was noticeable. Jean died of cancer in August 2011 and their ashes are interred together with a memorial stone, displaying the Metropolitan Police crest, at St John's Church; six months later, their youngest son, Neil, died at the tragically early age of forty-two.

There are many amongst Wickstead's contemporaries who would think it fitting if, to commemorate his memory, a plaque fashioned in the shape of a red Book 40 might be mounted on the wall at the old married quarters, Limehouse police station.

I think the Old Grey Fox would have loved that.

APPENDIX

The Citation for Wickstead's Queen's Police Medal

That having joined the Metropolitan Police in 1948, Mr Wickstead was appointed the Criminal Investigation Department in 1954 and served on a number of Divisions.

He has undertaken a wide variety of investigations, including several murder enquiries. In 1969 he was promoted to detective chief superintendent and two years later, in view of his experience, ability and integrity, was placed in command of the Serious Crime Squad at New Scotland Yard where he has successfully investigated the activities of some of the most highly organised and violent criminals in London.

He has earned the trust and respect of the public in the most dangerous area of London life. His trust and courage and natural leadership has inspired his subordinates to achieve results which have raised the reputation and morale of the whole Metropolitan Force.

In recognition of his integrity, his tireless pursuit of dangerous criminals and his outstanding ability as an investigator, Mr Wickstead has been awarded the Queen's Police Medal for distinguished service.

Bibliography

Cox, Barry, Shirley, John and Short, Martin	*The Fall of Scotland Yard*	Penguin Books, 1977
Davidson, Earl	*Joey Pyle. Notorious: The Changing Face of Organized Crime*	Virgin Books, 2003
Donoghue, Albert and Short, Martin	*The Krays' Lieutenant*	Smith Gryphon Ltd., 1995
Fawcett, Micky	*Krayzy Days*	Pen Press, 2013
Fido, Martin	*The Krays: Unfinished Business*	Carlton Book, 1999
Fielder, Michael and Steele, Peter	*Alibi at Midnight*	Everest Books, 1974
Fordham, Peta	*The Robbers' Tale*	Hodder and Stoughton, 1965
Graham, Winston	*Great Cases of Scotland Yard, Volume II: The Wembley Job*	The Reader's Digest Association London, 1978
Guttridge, Peter	*The Great Train Robbery*	National Archives, 2008
Kelland, Gilbert	*Crime in London*	Harper Collins, 1993

Kirby, Dick	*The Guv'nors – Ten of Scotland Yard's Greatest Detectives*	Wharncliffe Books, 2010
Kirby, Dick	*Scotland Yard's Ghost Squad: The Secret Weapon against Post-War Crime*	Wharncliffe Books, 2011
Kirby, Dick	*The Brave Blue Line – 100 Years of Metropolitan Police Gallantry*	Wharncliffe Books, 2011
Kirby, Dick	*Whitechapel's Sherlock Holmes: The Casebook of Fred Wensley OBE, KPM, Victorian Crimebuster.*	Pen & Sword, 2014
Kirby, Dick	*The Wrong Man – The Shooting of Steven Waldorf and the Hunt for David Martin*	History Press, 2016
Kirby, Dick	*Laid Bare: The Nude Murders and the Hunt for 'Jack the Stripper'*	History Press, 2016
Kirby, Dick	*London's Gangs at War*	Pen & Sword, 2017
Kirby, Dick	*Operation Countryman: The Flawed Enquiry into London Police Corruption*	Pen & Sword, 2018
Kray, Reg	*Villains we Have Known*	Arrow Books, 1996

Bibliography

Ladd, James D.	*SBS: The Invisible Raiders*	Arms & Armour Press, 1983
Ladd, James D.	*Commandos and Rangers of World War II*	David & Charles Publishers, 1983
Levy, Norma	*I, Norma Levy*	Blond & Briggs, 1973
Morton, James	*Bent Coppers*	Little, Brown, 1993
Morton, James	*Supergrasses & Informers*	Warner Books, 1995
Morton, James	*Gangland, Volumes 1 & 2*	Time Warner, 2003
Morton, James	*East End Gangland*	Time Warner, 2003
Morton, James	*Gangland Soho*	Piatkus, 2010
Pizzichini, Lilian	*Dead Men's Wages*	Picador, 2003
Read, Leonard, with Morton, James	*Nipper*	Macdonald, 1991
Read, Piers Paul	*The Train Robbers*	W H Allen & Co, 1978
Smith, Jim	*Undaunted*	'Round Midnight' Editions, 2009
Stoodley, Roger	*My Incompetent Best*	Privately published, 2012

Tibbs, Jimmy with Zanon, Paul	*Jimmy Tibbs: Sparring with Life*	Sport Media, 2014
Wickstead, Bert	*Gangbuster: Tales of the Old Grey Fox*	Futura, 1985
Windmill, Lorna Almonds	*A British Achilles*	Pen & Sword, 2005
Woffinden, Bob	*Miscarriages of Justice*	Hodder and Stoughton, 1987
Woodland, David	*Crime and Corruption at the Yard*	Pen & Sword True Crime, 2015

Index

Miss 'A', 119–20
Aarvold, His Honour Judge Carl, OBE, TD, 3–4, 27
Abray, Roswitha 'Rocha', 96–7
Adams, William John, 4
Agious, Lawrence Charles, 132–8
Ahmed, Ramsey, 9–11
Ambrose, Elizabeth, 145
Ambrose, William David 'Billy', 145
Andrews, Freddie, xix–xx
Arnold, George, 150, 151
Ash, Leonard, 144–8

Bailey, Kathy – see Dudley, K.
Bailey, Michael, 54–64
Baker, Mr, 41
Baldwin, (Solicitor), Mr F. W, 75–6
Baron, Ray, 151, 156, 158
Barratt, John Peter, 2–5
Barrett, Donald Walter, 46
Bartolo, Emmanuel, 130–8
Bartolo, Janet, 130
Basu, AC Neil, QPM, BA (Hons), 169, 172–3, 177
Beaumont, (Magistrate), Mr Herbert, 22
Bee Gees pop group, 55–6, 62
Bergin, Ronald George, 112, 119, 123–4
Berry, Harry 'Kid', 53
Berry, Henry 'Checker', 53
Berry, Teddy, 53
Bidney, Harry, 22–6
Biggs, Ronald Arthur, 108
Binstead, DC Peter, 181
Birkeff, William Henry, 75
Bishop, Peter John, 16
Blaber, Robert, 37
'Black Frank' – see Spiteri, F.
Black, Ralph Lewis, 7–11
Blackhall, Dennis Raymond, 4
Bland, D/Supt John William, 112–15, 117, 118–19, 128–9, 141, 144–8
Bond, DAC Ernest Radcliffe, OBE, QPM, 89–98, 180, 181
Borg, Emmanuel, 137
Bowman, Charles, 44
Brennan, Mr, 58
Brett, Frederick Henry, 132–8
Brett, George, 70
Bromley, Harry, 162–3
Brooks, PC Alan, 54, 116
Brown, Bruce, 46
'Brown, Mary' – see Levy, N.
Brown, Rodney John, 1–5
Brown, DS Ronald, 11
Brown, DS Terrence Victor, GM, 4–5, 110, 137
Browne, Kim, 90, 91
Bruce, DC Anthony, 13
'Bullwhip Bert' – see Wickstead, A. S.
Burge, James, QC, 79
Busell, Mr, 18–19
Butler, DCS Thomas Marius Joseph, MBE, xix, 174
Butlin, Sir Billy, 88
Byrne, DCS Brendan, 121–2

Cadogan, Aubrey Desmond, 14
Calleja, DI Fred, 111, 132
Calvey, Micky, 52
Cameron, Professor James Malcolm 'Taffy', 151
Campbell, Duncan, 167
Capstick, DCS John 'Jack' Richard, xix
Carleton, Leon, 58–64
Carr, Home Secretary Lord Robert of Hadley, PC, 82
Carrol, PS 'Big Jim', 52
Carter, PC Charlie, 174
Carter, DS Michael, 154–7, 171–2

Caruana, George, 111
Cashmore, WDI Joyce, 96, 97
Cassell, His Honour Judge Sir Harold, QC, 134–5
Cater, Commander Frank, 83–4
Cauci, Tony, 136–7
Cawthorne, D/Supt Gordon, MBE, 18, 22
Cazalet, His Honour Judge Edward, DL, 94
Challenger, Brian, 59, 63
Challenor, DS Harold Gordon, MM, 104–5
Chant, Graham, 24–6
'Charlie Artful' – see Capstick, J.R.
Churchill, Winston Spencer, MP, 93
Citron, Gerald, 117, 138–40
Clark, John Arthur, 75, 78
Clark, John Ernest, 149
Clarke, Charles Edwin, 157–77
Clegg, DI Stanley, 5, 110–11, 180, 181
Collero, Emmanuel, 128
Collins, PC Pat, 79
Collinson, Donald Frederick, 75
Compton, Leonard, 9–11
Condon, PC Peter, 161, 182
Connolly, John, 75, 78
Cook, Charles, 83–4
Coomber, Ronald Thomas, 65–6
Cooper, SPS Jack, 70, 77
Cooper, Terrence Robert, 26, 27–8, 32–3
Corkery, Michael, QC, 61–4, 78–82, 123–4, 132–8, 159–62
Cornell, George, 24
Corner, DS John, 40–1, 56, 58
Cornwall, Michael Henry 'Micky', 151–77, 179–80
Coulthurst, Peter, 1–5
Cousins, Alexander Gordon, 73–4, 75
Cox, Albert – see McCandless, R.
Crighton, Albert Edward, 139
Curtis, Ronald Patrick, 68, 75, 76–7, 80
Cusack, Mr Justice, 30–2
Cussen, Mr E. J. P., 30–2

Dance, DDI Alfred, xx
Dann, John, 151
Dann, Kathy – see Dudley, K.
Dark, Ronald, 36–48
Davey, TDC Roger, 36
Davies, Mr Justice Edmund, 66
Davies, Commander Frank 'Jeepers', MBE, 39–40
Davies, John, 68, 83–4
Davies, Stanley William, 61
Davies, Trevor, 116–17, 119
Davis, Mr & Mrs – see Dark, R. & Hepburn, B. M.
Davis, Bernard, 89
Davis, DAC Reginald Arthur, BA (Hons), 83–4, 144–8
Day, Robin, 99
Dellbridge, DC Kenneth, 154, 157
De Mirleau, Le Comte Hubert, 33
Denby, (Magistrate), Mr W. E, 30
'Diamond Reg' – see Dudley, R. J.
Dickens, DAC Neil Barrington, QPM, 153
Dilley, Commander David Clarence, QPM, 126
Dior, Catherine, 17
Dior, Christian, 16
Dior, Françoise Suzanne Marie, 16–34
Diplock, Mr Justice William John Kenneth, QC, 99
Dixon Gang, 51–64, 65, 71–2, 73, 82, 101, 183
Dixon, Alan Derek, 51–64
Dixon, Brian Thomas, 52, 61–2
Dixon, George Kitchener, 51–64
Dixon, Lynne – see Flynn, L.
Donoghue, Albert, 53–4
Douglas, Charles Peter, 9–11
Douglas-Home, Sir Alexander Frederick (later Baron Home of the Hirsel, KT, PC), 89
Dove, Brian Benjamin, 61
Downes, Ronald, 78–82
Driscoll, June, 103–4
Drury, Commander Kenneth Ronald, 106–9, 117, 128–9, 141
Dudley, Katherine 'Kathy', 151–77
Dudley, Reginald John, 149–77

Index

Duggan, Colin Michael, 4–5
Dukes, Paul William, 23–5
Dunn, Patrick 'Coloured Pat', 116–17, 119
Durand, Victor, QC, 147
Dyer, Frank, 125, 130–8

Edlin, Anthony, 45–46
Edwards, Jeff, 71
Eist, DCI Alexander Anthony, BEM, 173–6
Ellul, Philip Louis, 136
Elwell, Charles, 94
Enever, John Keith, 83–4
Escott, PC John, 70, 81
Evans, John William, 26–7, 29, 30–2

Falzon, Mrs Albertine 'French Betty', 103–4
Farley, D/Supt. John 'The Ferret', QPM, xv, 8–11, 56, 78, 95–6, 100, 115, 129–30, 136
'Fat Bob' – *see* Maynard, R. J.
Fawcett, Frederick, 68
Fawcett, Micky, 53, 68, 72, 73, 76, 79, 80, 83–4
Feenech, Joseph, 137
Ferguson, Kathleen 'Dominique', 106–7, 127
'The Ferret' – *see* Farley, J.
Fitzgeorge, David, 120
Fleet, James Frederick, 83–4
Flynn, Lynne, 55–6
Flynn, Michael Patrick, 55–6, 57, 58, 61
Flynn, PS, 74
Forbes, DAC Ian 'Jock', QPM, xiv, 5, 39, 181
Foreman, Freddie 'Brown Bread Fred', 49
Fraser, Francis Davidson 'Mad Frankie', 24–5, 49
Fright, Elaine 'Frankie', 150
Fright, Ronald 'Ginger', 150–77

Gable, Dr Gerry, DUniv, MA (Crim), 22–32
Gaitskell, Baroness Anna Dora, 98
Galea, Derek, 136–7

Galea, Nazarene, 130–8
'Gangbusters' – nickname for SCS personnel Garfath, Peter 'Pookie', 102, 103–4, 109, 112–14, 117, 118–19, 120, 123–4, 141, 145
Gaynor, June Beryl – *see* Humphreys, J. B.
Geiger, Jack, 99
Gerrard, DCS Frederick, xx–xxi
Getty, J. Paul, 88
Gibbons, Robert, 97
Gibbs, Mr Justice, 169–73
Gillespie, D/Supt Liam, 39–40
Gladwin, George, 44
Gold, Lionel, 117
Goldberg, Jonathan, QC, 164–6
Goodere, James, 117
Goodsell, Peter, 88, 90–1, 98
Gordon, Alex, 24–5
Gower, DS Dougie, 95–6
Gray, PC Johnny, 59
Gray, PC Mick, 182
Green, Michael John Paul, 41–8
Greeno, DCS Edward 'Ted', MBE, xix
Griffith, Insp. John, 52

Hall, DC Michael, 112–13, 145, 181
Hall, Roy, 49
Halliday, DAC Bernard 'Doc', OBE, 57–8
Hamilton, Bernard – *see* Silver, B.
Hannigan, DS Harold, 107
Hanratty, James, 159
Hardcastle, Dr Robert Anthony, 169–73
'Harrington, Mrs' – *see* Levy, N.
Harris, Brenda, 95
Harvey, DAC Ronald, QPM, 153–77
Hassan, Ray, 68
Heath, Prime Minister Sir Edward, KG, MBE, PC, 92
Hemsworth, Raymond Francis, 26–7, 30–2
Henderson, DS Bob, 59
Hepburn, Barbara Mary, 39–44

Hickson, DC Graham, 175
Hill, John, 9–11
Hill, William Charles 'Billy', xix, 65
Hills, Michael, 157–8
Hing, James, 133–4
Hogg, Gloria, 152
Hogg, Quintin McGarel, (Baron Hailsham of St Marylebone), MP, KG, CH, PC, QC, FRS, 14
Holman, Mr Justice, 169–73
Howe, D/Commissioner Sir Ronald, KBE, CVO, MC, 180
Horn, Regina Jean, 88, 96–7
Howard, D/Supt Graham, 96, 181
Hoy, John Stephen, 9–11
Hudson, DAC Harold William, OBE, 56
Hughes, Hugh Llewellyn, 23–6
Hughes, (Magistrate), Mr W., 29–30
Humphreys, James William 'Jimmy', 102–24, 140–2
Humphreys, June Beryl 'Rusty', 102–24, 140–2
Hussey, Jimmy, 38
Hutchinson, Jeremy, QC, 80

Inguanez, Paul, 133
Iran, Shah of, 88
Irving, David John Cawdell, 23

Jacobs, Lambert 'Lammy', 62
Jacobs, Philly, 54–64
James, Lord Justice, 47
James, TDC 'Taff', 112
Janes, Joey, 106
'Jefferies, Mr' – see Jellicoe, G.
Jeffrey, James William, 45–6
Jeffrey, Lionel Thomas Herbert, 43
Jeffryes, Alan Henry, 9–11
Jellicoe, 2nd Earl George, Lord Privy Seal, Leader of the House of Lords, KBE, DSO, MC, FRS, 87, 92–5, 98
Jenkins, Ch. Supt Randall, 154
Johnson, Margaret, 2–5
Jordan, Françoise – see Dior, F. S. M.
Jordan, John Colin Campbell, 15–30

Kaufman, Harry, 22
Keeler, Christine Margaret, 90–1
Kelland, AC(C) Gilbert James, CBE, QPM, 118, 122–4, 139–40, 142, 144
Kenny, Oliver, 159, 164–6, 168
Kenyatta, Jomo, 16
Kersey, Diane, 69
Kersey, Leonard, 68–9, 72, 73, 75, 76, 79, 80–1
'Killer' – see McElligott, J.B.
King Jr., Dr Martin Luther, 176
King, Robert Alles, 46
King, Ronald – see Bergin, G.
'The Kipper' – see Dilley, D. C.
Kray brothers, xx, 49, 50, 51, 52, 54, 65, 79, 111
Kray, Charles David, 24, 49
Kray, Reginald, 49, 52, 53
Kray, Ronald, 24, 49, 52, 53, 54

'The Landlord' – see Bartolo, E.
Lake, Stephen John, 9–11
Lamb, Sir Albert 'Larry', 93
Lambton, Viscount Antony Claud Frederick, 87–100
Lambton, Lady Lucinda, 92, 98
Lane, Mr Justice Geoffrey, 30, 47, 132–8
Lawson, Mr Justice, 78–82
Lawson, John, 117
Lawton, Mr Justice, 30
Lazarus, Robert, 59, 63
La Comptesse de Caumont La Force – see Dior, F. S. M.
La Comptesse Françoise Dior-de Mirleau – see Dior, F S M
La Force, Anne-Marie Christiane de Caumont, 17
Le Comte de Caumont La Force – see Nompar, R–H. A. F.
Leck, Mr J.E., 76
Leigh, Ronald, 120, 121
Leese, Arnold Spencer, 17
Levy, Colin, 88–100
Levy, Norma, 87–100, 124
Lewis, DCS John, 101–2, 109, 115, 116, 118, 119, 127–9, 134, 136, 143

Index

Lieberman, David, 8–11
'Little Highburys' & 'Big Highburys', 7–11
Lloyd-Hughes, Commander Trevor, 172–3
Lock, Commander, John, QPM, 68
Logan, Michael Gerald, 69, 72, 75, 78–82
Love, James William, 39
'Lucas, Mr' – see Lambton, A. C. F.
Lupson, Peter, 78
Luxford, Phil, 150, 153, 175
Lyell, Mr Justice, 67

Macchione, Louis, 99
Machin, Michael Sidney, 68, 69–70, 74, 76, 78–82, 83
Machin, Edward 'Teddy', 65, 68, 114
Macmillan, Maurice Harold, Prime Minister, Earl of Stockton, OM, PC, FRS, 90
Mangion, Anthony, 130–8
Mansfield, Michael, QC, 166–7
Mantell, Lord Justice, 169–73
Mark, Commissioner Sir Robert, GBE, QPM, 101–2, 108, 180
Marks, 'Ginger', 64
Marriott, PS Alf, 170
Matthew, John, QC, 43–4, 47
Maude, His Honour Judge, 102–3
Maudsley, WDC Sue, 43–4
Maynard, Ernest, 150–77
Maynard, Robert John, 149–77
Maynard, Tina, 163
McArthur, ACC Gerald, MBE, QPM, 49–50, 56
McCandless, Robert, 38
McCarthy, Edward William, 41–8
McDonald, Frankie, 68, 76
McElligott, John Brian 'Killer', 1–5
McElligott, (Magistrate), Neil, 75–6
McEnhill, DC Dave, 79, 90, 91, 95, 99, 109, 181
McKay, Mrs Muriel, 114
McLean, (Magistrate), Mr Ian, 84, 117
McVicar, John Roger, 40, 44
Medina, Joseph, 132–3

Melinek, Dr A., 13
Melito, Frank, 131–8
Messina brothers, 102
Micallef, Anthony, 128
Micallef, Victor, 131–8
Mifsud, 'Big Frank' Saviour, 101–3, 112, 126–38
Mifsud, Joseph, 130–8
Miles, ACC Richard George, xv
Millen, DAC Ernest George William 'Hooter', CBE, xix
Miller, Alan, 117
Miller, John, 117
Mockford, PC Gerry, 154–5
Moody, DCS William 'Wicked Bill', 106, 115, 140–2
Moriarty, John, 152
Morton, Revd Andrew Queen, 167
Moseley, Ann, 150, 151
Moseley, 6th Baronet Sir Oswald, 17
Moseley, William Henry 'Billy', 149–77
Murdoch, William, 117, 119
Murphy, Patsy, 107–8
Myerson, Aubrey, QC, 139

Nash brothers, xx, 110
Naylor, Stanley Walter, 69–70, 74, 75, 76–7, 78–82
Niarchos, Stavros, 88
Nichols, Albert, 83–4
Nichols, Albert James, 66–86
Nichols, Terry, 69, 70, 72, 73, 75, 80
Nicholson, Johnny, 58, 61
Nield, Mr Justice, 119
Nompar, Robert-Henri Aynard François, 17
Norman, PS Terry, 154–5

O'Carroll, Peter, 9–11
O'Connor, Mr Justice, 61–4
'Old Grey Fox' – see Wickstead, A. S.
Ormrod, Lord Justice, 166–7

Packard, June Beryl – see Humphreys, J. B.
Pain, Ch. Constable Barry Newton, QPM, 146–8

Palmes, Peter, 3
Parker, Gordon, 26–7
Patience, Bob, 65–6
Paton, DS Clifford, 74
'Paul the Priest' – *see* Inguanez, P.
Payne, Leslie, 55
Pearman, Mrs Linda, 69, 80
Phillimore, Lord Justice, 25–6
Podola, Günter Fritz Erwin, 83
Pownall, His Honour Judge Henry Charles, 2–3
Price, Daniel Michael, 4
Price, Dr Harold, 151
Prill, Alfred – *see* Dark, R.
Prill, Mr & Mrs – *see* Dark, R. & Hepburn, B. M.
Pritchard, DCI David, xx
Probyn, Walter 'Angel Face', 137
Profumo, 5th Baron, John Dennis, CBE, 90–1
Pulley, PC Frank, BEM, 144–5
Purdy, DS Raymond William, 83
Pyle, Joey, 107–8

'Queen of Britain's Nazis' – *see* Dior, F. S. M.

Rainbird, Colin William, 24–6, 30
Rawden-Smith, (Magistrate), Rupert, 93–4
Ray, James Earl, 176
Raymond, Paul, 105
Read, Frank, 159
Read, ACC Leonard 'Nipper', QPM, xix, xx, 4–5, 50, 55, 56, 83
Rees, His Honour Judge Geraint, 78
Rees, Gwynneth, 52
Revington, (Magistrate), Dorothy, 43
Richards, Ivor, QC, 120
Richardson Torture Gang, 49–50, 51, 54, 61, 65
Richardson, Charlie, 49–50
Richardson, Eddie, 49–50
Richardson, Supt. Gerald, GC, 107
Roberts, George Frederick, 4
Robertson, (Magistrate), Nigel, 18
Robinson, DS Derek, 56
Robinson, Ch. Supt. Robert, 57

Rogers, His Honour Judge, 10
Rose, PS Michael, GM, 1–2, 4
Roskill, Lord Justice, 166–7
Rowlands, PC Allan, 174
Runham, DS Gerry, xv, 56–7, 60–1, 79
Russell, (Magistrate), Mr Evelyn, 16
Russell, Honora Mary – *see* Levy, N.

Saggs, Colin, 151
Saggs, Sharon, 151–2, 160, 166–7, 168
Saliba, Romeo, 131–8
Salmon, Cyril, QC, 119
Salmon, Michael Henry, 46
Sandison, DS Walter 'Sandy', 125
Sargeant, Revd W., 16
Sassoon, Vidal, CBE, 22
Saunders, Arthur John Frederick, 35–48
Scott, Commissioner Sir Harold Richard, GCVO, KCB, KBE, 50
Schwartz, Ronald, 61
Scrivener, DC Dave, 36
Sewell, Freddie, 107
Sewell, Ronald, 75, 76
Shaw, Mr Justice, 43–4
Shimell, Elizabeth, 60
Shimell, DCS William George, 60
Shindler, George, QC, 141
Short, John, 46, 47
Silver, Bernard, 101–7, 111, 112, 114, 117, 125–38
Simmonds, Barbara, 20–1, 22
Simmonds, DCS John, 19–21
Simpson, Commissioner, Sir Joseph, KBE, 51
Simpson, Robin, QC, 81
Sinner, Mr, 138
Skelhorn, DPP Sir Norman, KBE, QC, 93
Skinner, Kenneth Leonard, 8–11
Slack, John William, 9–11
Smalls, Derek Creighton 'Bertie', 45–7
Smart, Tina – *see* Rees, G.
Smithson, Tommy 'Scarface', 103, 110, 136–7
'The Snake' – *see* Dyer, F.

Index

Snooks, Phil, 54
Soekarno, President, 88
Soskice, Sir Frank (Baron Stow Hill) PC, QC, 14
Southwold, Miss Jean, QC, 123–4
Spampinato, Victor George Sebastian Alfred, 136
Sparks, Malcolm, 23–6, 28
Spencer, George Thomas, 150
Spiteri, Frank, 131
Springer, Joseph, 30–4
Springer, (Magistrate), Tobias, 120
Stanton, Mr, 147
Starritt, D/Commissioner Sir James, KCVO, 117–18
Stevens, DI Anthony, 41–2, 47, 55–6, 58, 63, 64, 74
Stevens, Vincent Saviour, 132–8
Stocker, Harold, 136–7
Stoodley, DCS Roger, 67, 73–4, 83, 95–6, 109–10, 113–14, 115
Storey, David Victor, 83–4
Stresznyak, Gabor 'Hungarian George', 166–7, 169
Stringer, Bernard, 58, 61
Stuart-Moore, Mr Justice Michael, 77–8
Sturge, (Magistrate), Harold, 2–3
Sullivan, Michael Patrick, 4
Sultana, Carmelo, 137
Swanwick, Mr Justice, 159–62

'The Target' – see Moriarty, J.
Taylor, Alfred, 114, 143–8, 180
Taylor, Brian, 63
Taylor, Charles see Taylor, A.
Taylor, John Henry, 9–11
Taylor, DAC Michael Bradley, QPM, xv
Thorne, David, 26–7, 29, 30–2
Tibbs, Claudette, 71
Tibbs, George 'Bogey', 66–86
Tibbs, George, 66–7
Tibbs, James 'Big Jim' (father), 65–86
Tibbs, James Edward Patrick 'Jimmy', 66–86
Tibbs, Jimmy (son of Tibbs, J. E. P.), 70–2

Tibbs, John, 66–86
Tibbs, Kathleen, 74, 76, 81
Tibbs, Robert Terence, 66–86
Tighe, DI Bernard, 57, 58, 64, 74, 90, 101, 109, 116, 119, 120–2, 127–9, 134, 136
Tolbart, DCI Ken, 57, 136
'Trainer' – see Taylor, A.
Trowbridge, Michael, 26–7
Tudor-Price, His Honour Sir David, 76–7, 93–4, 119–20, 146–7
Tuffen, John Thomas, 61
Turner, Bryan James, 46
Turner, PC Geoff, 128
Tyndall, John Hutchyns, 15–33

'Undertaker' – see Evans, J. W.
'Underworld's Public Enemy No. 1' – see Greeno, E.
'Untouchables' – nickname for SCS personnel, 82

Vassallo, Frank, 133
Veli, Ibrahim, 119
Virgo, Commander Wallace, QPM, 106, 110, 126

Waite, DS Bill 'Mr Memory', BEM, 51,
Waldorf, Steven, 149
Waldron, Commissioner Sir John Lovegrove, KCVO, 51
Walker, Albert, 44, 46
Wark, Kirsty, 235
Watkins, Mr Justice, 166–7
Welch, Bob, 38
West, Michael, QC, 173
Whaley, His Honour Judge Felix, QC, 167
Whitby, Charles, QC, 81
Whitehead, Cornelius, 49, 52
Wickett, Jenny, 39
Wickett, Lew, 39
Wickett, Phyl, 39
Wickstead, Commander Albert Sidney, QPM
Disposition, xv, xvi, 19–21, 32, 35–6, 57–8, 126

Attitude towards criminals, xvi–xvii
Antipathy towards Flying Squad, 37, 41, 56, 60
Threats made against, 63, 77–8, 82, 132, 183
Interview techniques, xvii, 40–1, 145
Obsessional secrecy, 60, 96, 126
Birth, xvii
Education, xvii
Army service, xvii–xviii, 51
Joins Metropolitan Police, xviii
Appointed DC, xix
Promotion to DS(2), xx
Promotion to DS(1), xx
Promotion to DI, 4
Promotion to DCI, 35
Promotion to D/Supt, 35
Promotion to DCS, 35
Promotion to Commander, 143, 154
Commendations, xix, xx, 4, 10–11, 27, 35, 63, 82, 135
'Killer' investigation, 1–5
Anti-Semitic investigation, 7–11
Synagogue Arsons investigation, 13–34
Barclays Bank Robbery investigation, 35–48, 180
Serious Crime Squad formed, 50–1
Dixon case, 50–64
Tibbs case, 65–86
Norma Levy case, 87–100
Maltese Syndicate & associated cases, 101–48
Legal & General case, 149–77, 180
Awarded QPM, 127, 185
Retirement, 87, 180
Memoirs, 180
Granted Freedom of City of London, 180
Freemasonry, 181

Marriages, xviii, 182–3
Death, 183
Wickstead, Andrew (son from 2nd marriage), 182–3
Wickstead, Ella, née White (1st wife), xvii, 182
Wickstead, Graham (son from 1st marriage), 182–3
Wickstead, Ian (half-brother), xvii
Wickstead, Jean, née Simonette (2nd wife), 182–3
Wickstead, Jesse, née Chalkhorn (step-mother), xvii
Wickstead, DS John 'Jack' (uncle), xviii
Wickstead, Neil (son from 2nd marriage), 182–3
Wickstead, Peter (brother), xvii
Wickstead, Sydney Arthur (father), xvii
Wickstead, Winifred Alexandra, née Port (mother), xvii
Widgery, Lord Chief Justice, 47
Wild, Anthony, 158–77
Wilkins, Joey, 94–5
Williams, D/Supt 'Taff', 57
Williams, D/Supt Edwin, 63–4, 83–4, 90, 91, 97–8, 110, 113–14, 129
Wilkinson, Ronald Charles, 9–11
Wiltshire, D/Supt Gerald, 57–8
Wilson, AC(B) John Spark 'Jock', CBE, 146
Wisbey, Tommy, 38
Wood, George, 65–6
Wood, John, 30
Wood, DC Raymond George, OBE, xv
Woodhouse, DS John, 42

'Miss X', 157

Yorke, Commander Roy, 40
Young, Michel John, 54–64